D1528223

LISZT

From the painting by Nicholas Barabas, Budapest

Frontis.

LISZT,

COMPOSER, AND HIS PIANO WORKS.

DESCRIPTIVE GUIDE AND CRITICAL ANALYSIS, WRITTEN IN A POPULAR AND CONCISE STYLE

By HERBERT WESTERBY
Mus.Bac. Lon., F.R.C.O., etc.

Numerous music and portrait illustrations

GREENWOOD PRESS, PUBLISHERS
WESTPORT, CONNECTICUT

Originally published in 1936
by William Reeves, Ltd., London

Reprinted from an original copy in the collections
of the Brooklyn Public Library

First Greenwood Reprinting 1970

Library of Congress Catalogue Card Number 72-109874

SBN 8371-4365-9

Printed in the United States of America

PREFACE.

"The greatest musician of the nineteenth century."
"The last great European with the gift of universality."
—DR. EAGLEFIELD HULL.

This work is intended primarily as a guide to the student of Liszt's Piano Works. The biographer of Liszt has a specially difficult task, as the sources of information are mostly obscure and diffuse.* There are difficulties, too, for those who wish to make a really representative collection of his piano works, as they are widely scattered among publishers of various nationalities.†

Both as a virtuoso and as a composer, Liszt did what had not been done before—he developed the resources of the piano to the utmost. He invented a *New Phase* of technique, one that was necessary to express what he had to say, and this modern technique was naturally much more difficult to those who had not been systematically prepared for it. Liszt is now, however, coming into his own, and the Academies turn out many students who can play his most advanced works.

The author's task has been:

Part I. To give a short biography.

Part II. To examine all the accessible piano works in print and classify them, also play and appraise their worth.

---

* See Bibliography.

† See chapter "The Seeker after Liszt."

To estimate Liszt's position as a composer.

A new feature is the critical analysis of each separate Piano Work in the hope that such may form a reliable guide to students.

Part III.—A. To prepare and grade various PREPARATORY COURSES through the many easy works of Liszt as the best way of acquiring Lisztian technique. To prepare REPERTOIRES of moderately difficult works.

To prepare a STANDARD COURSE graded from moderately difficult to difficult works.

To present a SHORT CUT to the virtuoso stage.

To give a graded list of VIRTUOSO WORKS.

To suggest programmes for "LISZT RECITALS."

B. To ascertain the whereabouts of his numerous piano publications, both in EARLY AND MODERN EDITIONS, and provide a short Bibliography as a help to the pianist who wishes to be up-to-date, in which matter I am indebted to Mr. Harold Scull and to publishers of Liszt's works for their kind assistance.

The author has compiled a series of technical studies for students to ensure their due preparation for the performance of Liszt's works.*

Finally, he sincerely trusts that the perusal of the present work may lead to a better estimation of Liszt's supremacy as a composer of piano music.

H. W.

---

* These studies, entitled "The Approach to Liszt," are published in two books (London: Reeves), and include representative selections from Liszt. They are unique as the first adequate work of the kind.

CONTENTS.

LIST OF ILLUSTRATIONS AND MUSIC EXAMPLES.

PLATES.

MUSIC EXAMPLES.

CHRONOLOGICAL TABLE.

PART I. YOUTH.

1811 Oct. 22. Born at Raiding, near Odenburg, Hungary.
1817 Aged six. First lessons in music.
1821 Aged nine. Plays Ries Concerto in F with orchestra.
1821-23 Studies piano with Czerny and composition with Salieri in Vienna.
1822 Dec. 1. Liszt's debut in Vienna.
1823 Apl. 13. Liszt's second concert in Vienna. Plays before Beethoven.
1823 Autumn. Plays in Munich, Stuttgart and Strassburg and arrives in Paris.
1824 First appearance in Paris, with orchestra. Goes to London. Plays before George IV.
1825 Tour through French Province. Second tour in England. Early compositions. Attempts Operetta and Etudes (12 Exercises).
1826-7 Another French tour, and third tour in England.
1827 Aged sixteen. Death of Liszt's father.

PART II. FATHERLESS IN PARIS.

1828 Played Beethoven's E flat Concerto in Paris.
1829 Tyrolienne Trans. ("La Fiancée"), Op. 1.
1830-2 Hears Paganini play (March 31). Becomes friend of Berlioz and Chopin.
1833 Transcribes Berlioz's "Symphonie Fantastique."
1834 Fantasie on "La Clochette" published.
1835 Three Apparitions, also Album d'un Voyageur (pub. 1842).

PART III. SWITZERLAND AND ITALY.

1835 Travels in Switzerland. Various compositions.
1837 Thalberg and Liszt. Public rivalry. Compositions. Puritani Transcription. Fantasia Quasi Sonata. Paganini Etudes, etc. Hexameron Variations.

1837 Autumn. To Milan and Italian Lakes.
1838-9 Concerts in Italy. Meets Ricordi. Compositions "Soirées Musicales." "Les Soirées Italiennes." Huguenot's Trans. "Petrarca" Sonnets.
1839 Bach Transcriptions. Liszt leaves Rome, June 1.

Part IV. VIRTUOSO YEARS.

1840 Concerts in Rhineland in aid of Beethoven's monument. Three visits to England. Hungarian Government present sword of honour. Three Caprices.
1841 Visits Weimar. Paraphrases. "Norma," "Prophète." "Roberto" and "Don Giovanni."
1843-4 Tours through Europe. "Heroic" March (later as "Hungaria").
1845 Beethoven monument inaugurated.
1838-46 Schubert Song Transcriptions. Seven Sets. Also Marches and Divertissement.
1846 Concert tours. Trans. of "William Tell" Overture.
1847 The "Chimes of Strasbourg" (chorus and orchestra).

Part V. AT WEIMAR.

1848 Settles at Weimar. Italian Album published.
1849 Three Concert Etudes published.
1849-50 Finishes several Symphonic Poems. First Wagner and Beethoven Song Transcriptions. Polish Song Transcription. Two Etudes de Concert. "Liebesträume." "Consolations."
1851 "Festklänge." Organ Fant. on "Ad nos." Harmonies Poétiques, 10 pieces. Mazurka Brillante.
1852 Swiss Album published. Two Polonaises. Book on Frederick Chopin.
1853 Sonata in B minor. "Lohengrin" Trans. Valse Impromptu.
1854 "Faust" Symphony completed. "Les Preludes." "Hungaria," "Orpheus," Ballades and Berceuse. Etudes Transcendantes. Ab. Irato.
1850-5 "Todtentanz."
1855 "Dante" Symphony. "Graner" Mass. Ps. 13.
1856-7 "Hunnenschlacht. Trans. Mendelssohn's "Wedding March."
1857 Organ Fugue on B.A.C.H.
1857-8 "Die Ideale."
1858-9 Choral Mass. Lenau Faust Episodes.

1859 Writes on Field's Nocturnes.
1860 "Il Trovatore" Fantasia. "Ernani."
1861 Left Weimar. Book on "The Gipsies and their Music."

PART VI. IN ROME, 1861-69.

1861-2 St. Elizabeth. Chapelle Sixtine. Twelve Part Songs for male voices.
1865 "Pathetic" Concerto for two pianos. ("Solo de Concert" of 1850.) Liszt becomes an Abbé. "L'Africaine" Trans.
1866 Finished "Christus." "Graner" Mass performed in Paris. Visits Paris and Amsterdam. Ps. 128 published. Liszt's mother dies in Paris, Feb. 6.
1867 Hungarian Coronation Mass. Liszt visits Pesth.
1868 Trans. Waltz from "Faust."
1869 Liszt settles in Weimar again.

PART VII. WEIMAR, BUDAPEST AND ROME.

1870 Beethoven Festival at Weimar.
1871 Ps. 116. Published Mass for male voices.
1873 "Christus" performed at Weimar.
1874 "St. Cecilia's Day." (Female ch. and org.)
1875 Transcriptions of Mendelssohn's Songs (7). Liszt President of Hungarian Academy at Pest. Visits Bayreuth, 1875 and 1876.
1876 First Bayreuth Festival.
1877 Trans. of Saint-Saen's "Danse Macabre."
1878-9 Mass for Organ.
1880 Par. of "Onegin" Polonaise and Dargomisky's "Tarentelle."
1883 Vol. III of the Années, and Hungarian Pictures. Twelve Church Hymns.
1886 Visits London, Antwerp, Paris, Weimar and Bayreuth. Death at Bayreuth, July 31. Age 75.

THE BRITISH BROADCASTING CORPORATION LISZT 1936 CELEBRATIONS.

This celebration of the fiftieth year of the death of Liszt was under the direction of Mr. Bernard van Dieren—who also contributed three articles to the "Radio Times." The first article, on "The Originality of Liszt," points out that Liszt "opened up a new world of sound" and "discovered æsthetic possibilities that had not been dreamt of before," and that Liszt's variations on operatic airs are "more coherent and more brilliant" than those of Beethoven. In his second article—on "The Songs of Liszt"—he says: "All have some original beauty, some fascinating features, some powerful appeal, to set them apart in a position of eminence in the company of the great songs of the great song composers."

The third article refers to some small pieces played in the third recital of the sixth series, which were composed in Liszt's last years, and were unknown until recently, pieces which reflect "seeming resignation" and "bitterness of soul," revealing a dramatic contrast with the works of his early triumphant virtuoso career.

THE BRITISH BROADCASTING CORPORATION CELEBRATIONS.

First Series. December 30, 1935.

(1) Transcendental Studies, Nos. 1 to 5.
(2) Transcendental Studies, Nos. 6 to 9.
(3) Transcendental Studies, Nos. 10 to 12, and the "Gnomenreigen."

(4) Paganini Studies, Nos. 1, 2 and 4, Gounod Waltz Transcription.
(5) Donizetti, Valse on "Lucia" and "Parisina" motives.
Pianist, Egon Petri.

SECOND SERIES. January 6, 1936.

(1) "Mephisto" Valse, No. 2, "Cantique d'Amour."
(2) "Consolations," Twelfth Rhapsody.
(3) Two "Ballades."
(4) Two "Legendes." "La Lugubre Gondola."
(5) "Praise of Tears," "The Wanderer" (Transcriptions from Schubert), "Mephisto" Valse, No. 1.
Pianist, Frank Mannheimer.

THIRD SERIES.

Twenty-seven Lieder.
Vocalists, Parry Jones and Henry Cummings.

FOURTH SERIES.

Twenty-seven Lieder, including the "Liebestraum," No. 2, and the three "Petrarca Sonnets."

FIFTH SERIES.

(1) Sonnet No. 47, Chopin Transcription, "The Maiden's Wish, Wagner Transcription, "The Spinning Chorus."
(2) The "Années," First (Swiss) Year, Nos. 1 to 5.
(3) Ditto, Nos. 6 to 9.
(4) "The Christmas Tree," Nos. 1 to 4.
(5) Ditto, Nos. 5, 6, 7, 9 and 10.
Pianist, Freda Kindler.

SIXTH SERIES.

(1) Four Small Pieces, Hungarian Rhapsody No. 8.
(2) Two "Elegies," three "Valses Oubliées."
(3) "Trübe Wolken," "Schlaflos," "Frage und Antwort Unstern," "Sinistre. Disastro," Heroic March in Hungarian Style.
(4) The "Années," Third Year, Nos. 1, 2 and 3.
(5) Ditto, Nos. 5, 6 and 7.
Pianist, Franz Osborn.

LISZT AND THE JOSEFFY COLLECTION IN THE U.S.A.

Following are some of the interesting particulars given in the Report (issued 1936) by the Librarian of Congress in the "Library of Congress, Division of Music, 1934-35."*

"*Joseffy collection.*—By the time this report is printed the musical world will already have begun to plan its commemoration of the fiftieth anniversary of the death of Franz Liszt (1811-86). There will no doubt be concerts and festivals devoted to his music, special exhibits portraying his career. Old biographical materials will be re-interpreted, new documents brought to light. In announcing the purchase of an important collection of Liszt manuscripts, until now unknown to his biographers, the Library is privileged to make an early and outstanding contribution to the semicentennial year."

"The purchase of the Joseffy collection puts the Library of Congress in third place as a repository of Liszt materials, its holdings being surpassed only by the Liszt Museum in Weimar and the Hungarian National Library in Budapest."

"The twenty-one Liszt manuscripts acquired through the Joseffy purchase are briefly enumerated below."

* U.S.A. Government Printing Office, Washington, 1936.

Original Compositions.

"Polnisch (Polonais)," 8 p. For piano, 2 hands. (Raabe 71 : 12.)*

"Zu den Munkacsy festlichkeiten in Budapest . . . Ungarische rhapsodie," 9 p. For piano, 2 hands. (Raabe 106: 16.)

"'Die heiligen drei könige'—marsch," 15 p. Transcription for piano, 4 hands. (Raabe 335 : 2.)

"Salve Polonia!" 12 leaves. For orchestra; score, partly in another hand. (Raabe 430.)

[Ungarischer marsch zur krönungsfeier in Ofen-Pest], 12 p. For orchestra; score. (Raabe 438.)

"Rhapsodies hongroises pour orchestra," Nos. 1-6. 6 vols. Transcriptions for orchestra by Franz Doppler; scores, in Doppler's hand, with Liszt's changes and corrections. (Raabe 441 : 1-6.)

Graner fest-messe; clavier-partitur (vierhändig) von M. Mosonyi. Pest, Rózsavölgyi & comp. [1865]. Liszt's copy, with his corrections for the second edition. (Raabe 484.)

"An den heiligen Franziskus (von Paula)," 7 p. For men's voices, harmonium, trombones, and kettledrums; score. (Raabe 494.)

[Das lied der begeisterung], 1 leaf. For men's voices. (Raabe 561.)

An unidentified composition, 3 leaves. For piano, 2 hands.

---

* References in parentheses are to Raabe's systematic-chronological catalogue.

Transcriptions.

Egressy, Béni, and Franz Erkel. Szózat und Ungarischer hymnus, 1 p. l., 10 p. Transcriptions for 2 pianos, 4 hands.

Széchényi, Emerich. Ungarischer marsch, 9 p. Transcription for piano, 2 hands. (Raabe 261.)

Wagner, Richard. Ballade aus der oper, "Der fliegende Holländer," 6 p. Transcription for piano, 2 hands. (Raabe 274.)

[Schubert, Franz.] [Die allmacht.], 14 p. Transcription for tenor solo, men's voices, and orchestra. (Raabe 652.)

Beethoven, Ludwig van. Clavier concerte, Nos. 4 and 5. 2 vols. Transcriptions for 2 pianos, 4 hands.

"The most interesting manuscripts in the lot are the scores of the six Hungarian rhapsodies arranged for orchestra by Liszt and Doppler."

"Liszt's manuscripts, like Beethoven's, are fascinating and revealing documents."

"They call to mind the man himself—a conscientious and a very human artist."

Joseffy had written to Liszt from New York in June, 1885, mentioning his performance of "the B minor Sonata, the 'Dante' sonata, and the Concert solo [the 'Concerto Pathétique']."

Liszt's unpublished reply is dated:

"ROME, *November* 5, 1885.

"FAMOUS FELLOW-ARTIST: During the same

week in the course of which your friendly letter reached me in Weimar, I received the manuscript of a capital orchestral arrangement of the 'Concerto pathétique.' It led me to add a few new touches to the work, chiefly to provide more opportunity for the soloist. . . .

"F. LISZT."

"Kindly present my grateful acknowledgments to Steinway."

PART I.

CHAPTER I.

EARLY DAYS (1811-21).

Liszt's parentage. First lessons. First public appearance. A subscription list.

"Génie oblige."

PARENTAGE.

Liszt's father was of Hungarian descent, his mother was Austrian and German speaking. On his father's side he was of noble lineage, though the previous generations had become impoverished. Both his grandfather and father (Adam) were stewards to the Hungarian Prince Esterhazy—with whom Haydn had been Kapellmeister. His father was musical and acquired a knowledge of orchestral instruments, and through that was familiar with the members of Haydn's orchestra; this led to acquaintanceship also with the renowned composers, Cherubini and Hummel.

Ferencz (or Franz) Liszt was born in 1811 (Oct. 22) at Raiding, a somewhat neglected village near Buda-Pesth (the capital), where his father was in charge of that part of the estate.

As a boy Franz was slender in build with expressive features and fair hair; his eyes were blue and deep in their sockets. He was a very obedient child, and the quiet country life intensified his early love of music and of the Church.

The wandering bands of gipsy musicians attracted him with their songs and dances, and with the pathetic *Lassan* and stirring *Friskas.*

His father, as steward, had a good deal of spare time, and devoted himself to the piano, and we can imagine that the young Franz drank in the strains of Beethoven with avidity.

The boy plagued his father to teach him the piano, and eventually the latter promised to give him lessons—Franz was asked what he would like to be, and he pointed to the picture of Beethoven.

First Lessons.

At the age of six his lessons began and he made rapid progress, showing an extraordinarily acute ear. He could name every note in a chord without seeing it, and after he had once played a piece could recognise bars taken from it. Franz could hardly be kept away from the keyboard and from scribbling notes, and this before he had learnt the alphabet. Only one thing troubled him, and that was his naturally small hands.

Unfortunately sickness attacked the boy, and malaria fever brought him to death's door. The crisis passed, however, and young Franz was once more happy, playing duets with his father, experimenting with chords and melodies in Fantasia style; but there remained, as an aftermath, extreme nervous sensitiveness.

From the village priest he gained the usual rudimentary education—there were no schools there. He did not learn Hungarian, as his mother spoke only German, which was the language of society in those parts of Hungary, as French was in Russia.

First Public Appearance.

Some three years elapsed, and young Franz was taken out among the neighbours who were frankly astonished by his accomplishments, his fluency, sight-reading, and especially his gift of extemporisation. His father, like the father of Mozart, began to vision a future for the boy, and, making excursions to neighbouring towns to visit musical friends, made the boy known to them. It so happened that a young man, Baron von Braun, who was blind, was to give a concert in Oldenburg, and Franz was asked to assist. At this, his first public performance, he was accompanied by the orchestra in Ries' Concerto in F, and in an extemporisation the young prodigy gave ample proof of his powers. This delicate lad was only nine years of age. His father, striking the iron while it was hot, now arranged for a concert on his own account.

We find next that the boy was taken over to Eisenstadt and introduced to Prince Esterhazy, to whom he played. The applause, the exalted audience and the rich Hungarian costume he wore, lingered in the boy's mind.

He was asked to give his autograph in Haydn's name book, and then the Prince offered his Palace at Pressburg for a concert. There the prodigy made so deep an impression that a subscription list was opened and six hundred guilders were collected to further the boy's education. With a grateful heart his father hurried back to Raiding and was so sanguine of his son's future success that he wished to resign his own poorly paid post and chance all; but his mother, who was more practical, asked what was to become of them. Franz answered their fears with a fervent:

"Mother, what God wills: God will not forsake us, when the six years are over."

It was resolved to risk all, and forthwith the father wrote to Hummel. Hummel, however, wanted a gold "Louis" for each lesson and so, despite the warnings of neighbours, it was decided to go to the Austrian capital, Vienna. A special mass at the village church was celebrated, and the tears of friends followed their departure.

Thus, at the age of ten, young Franz found himself in the great capital.

Without loss of time the adventurous pair waited on Czerny, the one-time pupil of Beethoven.

CHAPTER II.

THE PRODIGY IN VIENNA (1821-23).

Liszt as a pupil of Czerny. The prodigy's debut. Beethoven's kiss. En route for Paris.

"You may become a greater pianist than any of us."—CZERNY to young Liszt.

Czerny was the leading teacher of his day, and when the Liszts, father and son, waited on him, he was already overcrowded with pupils and refused their request.

While the father was discussing matters, however, young Franz found his way to the piano stool, and played to such effect that Czerny was won over, and the youngster accepted.

PUPIL OF CZERNY.

Unlike Hummel, Czerny, when it came to settlement, refused to receive payment, and continued this attitude during the year and a half's tuition. For the study of theory, Salieri, the one-time rival of Mozart—now over seventy—took him in hand.

Czerny soon found that Franz had got into his own ways; his dilettante father had, of course, not been able to tutor him in anything but a rough and ready style. Rapidity of execution and reading were there, but the requisitory gliding—real legato touch and other conditions were wanting, and so the boy was put to technical finger exercises and scales, the study of touch, with Clementi's "Gradus" and Sonatas added. Thinking he was beyond all this, Franz rebelled and complained to his father, who thereupon waited again on Czerny.

It seems that Czerny relaxed somewhat as regards his choice of pieces, Franz's impetuous free interludes were not suppressed so severely and his artistic bent was thus recognised.

Liszt himself was grateful afterwards that Czerny had guided him in the right way.

Salieri, again, on the other hand, insisted on correct harmonisations and the reading, analysis and playing from scores. His early exercises in composition included a premature "Tantum ergo," which disappeared, and a contribution to fifty variations on Diabelli's Waltz by various composers. Liszt's was No. 24; it appeared as an Etude in C flat—and this by a boy of eleven.

Liszt's sight-reading powers were phenomenal. Thirsting for the unknown, he one day asked a Vienna music seller for "something very difficult." Hummel's B flat Concerto was put before him, and played at sight correctly.

His general education does not seem to have been cared for, but his father's position seems to have opened the way to the exclusive society of Vienna, in which his natural vivacity and charming manner helped him to make good in that way.

Liszt's Debut

Was made on December 1,, 1822, at the age of eleven—though the programme announced him as:

"Franz Liszt, a boy of ten years, a native of Hungary."

It included an Overture of Clementi, Hummel's Concerto in A flat, and a "Free Fantasia" in extemporisation.

The press notice says:

"The performance of this boy borders on the incredible." The critic admired the unabated force with which he thundered out Hummel's composition, so difficult and fatiguing, especially in the last passage. His "Free Fantasia" was designated a Capriccio, as "several themes united by voluntary passages do not deserve that title," and yet it was fine to see him "knead them, so to speak, into one paste."

After this the "young Hercules" played here and there, and the boy began to talk of the city. At this time Beethoven himself was the head of this musical capital. He was an inaccessible mortal, deaf to the world, immersed in grandiose schemes, but his friend Schindler had been approached, and in one of the "written conversations" pleaded Liszt's cause, thus:

"Little Liszt has entreated me to ask you for a theme on which to play a fantasia for to-morrow's concert. One can't take the little chap very seriously, he plays very well, but it cannot be said that he extemporises. It will amuse Karl (Beethoven's sixteen-year-old nephew) to hear him play. It will encourage the boy. Promise me you will go."

Beethoven went, but would not provide the theme. A concert, however, was given on the 13th, and Beethoven again attended. Young Franz recognised him, and, spurred on, excelled himself in his improvisation; the crowd pressed round him, and Beethoven, mounting the platform, kissed him.

BEETHOVEN'S KISS

Set the seal on young Liszt. His nephew Karl, in the "written conversations" told how Czerny had praised young Liszt to the skies and compared him "with you and Mozart in your young days."

Liszt himself relates later on how his father, in the spring of 1823, said: "In six months we will go to Paris. There you will enter the Conservatorium and work under the protection and guidance of the most celebrated men." The autumn now saw them in the stage coach—*en route* for Paris—a long, wearisome journey with many stages. Pauses were made at the principal cities and concerts announced, just as with young Mozart at an earlier period—only Mozart started from an intermediate centre—Salzburg in the Tyrol.

At Munich, the art capital of Bavaria, the critics wrote:

"A new Mozart has appeared to us," this Munich announces to the musical world. Young Liszt played Hummel's Concerto in B flat—"We have heard Hummel and Moscheles, and do not hesitate to affirm that this child's executon is in no way inferior to theirs. Liszt extemporised on a theme of Molique used by Moscheles and that of 'God Save the King,' which he united and combined together in the most ingenious manner."

Another stage took them to Stuttgart, where the local critic speaks of "the great treat given by Franz Liszt, a young Hungarian twelve years old, a pupil of Czerny's in Vienna, in which he displayed all the qualities which mark a distinguished pianist." The critic remarked his knowledge of counterpoint, of fugue in the "Free Fantasia." Similar reports of his extemporisations appeared at the concert given at Strasburg, the ancient cathedral city on the Rhine, on December 3.

CHAPTER III.

FRANZ IN PARIS AND LONDON (1823-25).

The Paris Conservatoire. His appearance with orchestra. Young Liszt the fashion. He plays in London and before the King.

"His own life stands in his music. Taken early from his fatherland, thrown into the exciting atmosphere of a large city, wondered at even as a child and as a boy, he appears in his early compositions, now as longing for his German home, and now as frivolous and brimful of the frivolity of the French nature."—SCHUMANN's Critique on Liszt's Etudes.

In the middle of December (1823) father and son arrived in Paris, where, in spite of high recommendations, Cherubini refused to admit the boy to the Conservatorium, as foreigners were not admitted.

Liszt himself relates the scene.

"What a thunderbolt! I trembled in every limb. Nevertheless my father courageously persevered, and implored for me, and I, too, stammered out some words."

Cherubini's decision was adamantine and Adam had to yield.

Private arrangements, however, were made with Paër for composition, and then the letters and recommendations to aristocratic friends were presented. These found the way to the *salons*. The Duke of Orleans gave him special attention, and asking the boy to say what he would like, young Franz asked for a toy Punchinello, which on being granted led to their being overwhelmed with toys at home. The child was still uppermost.

At that time Rossini was the principal star of Paris, but Herz, Moscheles and De Beriot were also there, and to these was soon added the "Petit Litz," as he was called. Franz became a favourite of the *salons*, which, in general, took the place of the more public concerts. At length—on March 8, 1824, he made a PUBLIC APPEARANCE at the Italian Opera House with the orchestra. So excited were the orchestra with the prodigy that they forgot to come in at the return of the Ritornello—the audience showing their forgiveness by their laughter and applause. At the end he was called into the boxes and introduced to distinguished people. This was a feature of his other appearances. A critic reports: "He is a true artist, and what an artist he is! They say eleven years old, but to all appearance only seven." (Really twelve and a half.) "When he is applauded he appears astonished and rubs his hands—this childish trait exciting loud laughter." Another critic wrote: "His little arms can scarcely stretch to both ends of the keyboard, his little feet scarce reach the pedals."

In order that the public could see, the piano was turned with one end obliquely towards them, as is now the custom, and the Hummel Concerto was played from memory.

YOUNG LISZT THE FASHION.

Young Liszt became the fashion, and many stories went the round.

One day a young street sweeper begged a sou. Franz put his hand into his pocket and found only a five franc piece. In the dilemma he asked the youth if he could give change. "No," he said. "Well, go and change it," and off he went leaving his broom in charge of the young virtuoso. Meanwhile the passers-by were astonished to see a fashionably dressed boy holding a broom—but Franz held on to it undismayed.

Opera was then to the fore in Paris, as now, and young Liszt must perforce think of an opera—had not Mozart written operas? And so our youthful composer attacked the libretto of an opera entitled "Le Chateau de l'Amour."

HE PLAYS IN LONDON.

Fortunately, before long, however, Erard, the piano maker, who was going to London offered to take him over in May, and leaving his mother in Paris, both father and son set out for London. On arrival they lodged at 18 Great Marlborough Street. The first concert was given in New Argyle Rooms on June 21, 1824. Here Franz played before a distinguished audience, including Clementi, Cramer and others, and along with the orchestra under Sir

G. Smart. Liszt, as usual, begged for a theme, when at a pause, a lady in the audience called out "Zitti-Zitti" from Rossini's "Barber," upon which he immediately extemporised a Fugue. The "Harmonicon" of June, 1824, comments thus: "His extemporaneous performances are the most remarkable. He improvises with the fancy and method of a deliberating composer, and with the correctness of an experienced contrapuntist." He was later presented at the Court of George IV, and his playing earned the favour of the King. Here in London also he was learning English, as he did French in Paris. At Manchester Liszt was announced as having been engaged "at great expense" and as "the greatest performer of the present day." Master Liszt performed on an Erard-Grand, Hummel's A minor Concerto, and executed "an extempore Fantasia." At a second concert "a new Grand Overture"—probably that to his operetta, was played, and other variations by Herz.

A tour through the French provinces followed, and a second trip to England, with Manchester included.

Plays before the King.

He again played before the King, this time at Windsor Castle, and the King patronised his concert at Drury Lane Theatre.

The late Rev. R. Haweis, the musical *littérateur*, whom I had the pleasure of knowing, records Liszt's conversation in his latter days in Rome. He says:

"He went down to Windsor to see George IV, who was delighted with him, and Liszt speaking of him to me, said, 'I was very young at the time, but I remember the King very well—a fine, pompous-looking gentleman.' George IV later went to Drury Lane on purpose to hear the boy, and commanded an encore."

During the short stay he was greatly affected by the singing of the charity children at St. Paul's Cathedral, as were Haydn and Mendelssohn. A change came over him, and his youth began to manifest a new seriousness, self-consciousness, and turning towards deeper things.

Returning to Paris, his premature operetta was performed, amidst éclat. Both this and the Overture have disappeared—along with other early works. There were some other compositions which survived for a time, but are now out of print, viz.:

(1) Impromptu on Themes by Rossini and Spontini (Op. 3), 1824.

(2) Allegro di Bravoura (Op. 4), printed 1825.

(3) Etudes (Op. 1), printed 1826.

These are not original in thought, but show some launching out toward that more advanced style of technique which distinguished his later works.

No. 1 is in the lyrical pot-pourri style, No. 2 is in sonata style (Kistner), No. 3 contains the foundation of his unique "Etudes d'execution transcendante," which as such appeared in a considerably revised form later on.

CHAPTER IV.

HIS TROUBLES BEGIN (1826-31).

His father's death. He falls into a "decline." Socialist leanings. Paganini's influence. He transcribes Berlioz's Symphony.

"My piano is the repository of all that stirred my nature in the passionate days of my youth."—LISZT to Pictet (1836), Nohl, p. 158.

Returned from his French tour with his father, young Franz now settled down to a course of counterpoint and the study of composition in various polyphonic forms under Reicha, with some enthusiasm. Another French tour followed in 1826-7, and in May, 1827, a third journey was undertaken to England. Moscheles was present at his concert given on June 9, and in his diary says: "The Concerto in A minor contains *chaotic* beauties; as to his playing, it surpasses in power and mastery of difficulties everything I have ever heard."

HIS FATHER'S DEATH.

Liszt's spirit now was again tending toward the unknown, and one day he asked his father that he might "renounce the world." His father pointedly replied, "Thy vocation is music. To love a thing is not to say that thou art called to it. Thy duty is to Art and not to the Church." A doctor was consulted, and a course of sea bathing followed for both father and son. Adam Liszt had been in bad health for some time, and now an attack of gastric fever carried him off in August of that year. Poor Franz was left fatherless and alone at Boulogne, at the age of sixteen, and not only alone, but with a load of debt arising from his father's illness and funeral expenses. We can imagine the terrible blow, and the utter desolation and loneliness.

Heroically he disposed of his precious Erard Grand—paid the debts and started for Paris. Here the Erard family welcomed him, and he sent for his mother, who was in far distant Vienna. She had not seen her son for three years, and as soon as she could settle domestic affairs she set out for Paris.

In Paris with his mother to sustain, young Liszt determined to get together a teaching connection, and he was successful. Freedom had now to give place to routine, and no doubt the discipline was beneficial—one always learns in teaching others.

Liszt Falls into a Decline.

Among his pupils was the young Countess St. Cricq, with whom he became enamoured. Her father intervened, however, and in his great disappointment Franz again turned for consolation to religion, and passed much time in church. He fell into a decline, and his death was actually reported in the winter of 1828, and an obituary notice appeared.

Socialistic Leanings.

In July he recovered, and Lenz (the author) visiting him, found him pale and haggard and deeply absorbed, "lying on a sofa placed between three pianos." The count's snobbery had cut deep, and he began to listen to democratic and socialistic teachings—no longer now did he haunt the church door. Beethoven had been, and still was his lode star, but William Tell, the Swiss bulwark against the oppressor, became his hero and example. In this mood he wrote:

"I would sooner be anything in the world than a musician in the pay of great folk."

He was longing for independence, but circumstances drove him again to the *salons*; the Revolution came, and Liszt, with his hot Magyar blood, was hardly restrained from joining in the mêlée.

He sketched out a "Revolution Symphony," of which portions appeared later in his "Heroic March" and the "Heroide Funèbre." Then went the news around, "Liszt is no longer devout."

The St. Simonians with their idealistic, unpractical and social-philosophical ideas, together with their exaltation of both religion and art, attracted Liszt.

Fortunately the Abbé de Lamennais, whose teaching was "Art is in man what creative power is in

3

God," saved Liszt from drifting into utter negation in his revolt against society.

The character of Liszt was being moulded by his environment.

PAGANINI'S INFLUENCE.

In March, 1831, appeared that wizard of the violin, Paganini, and his incredible feats inspired Liszt with the feeling that there were new worlds to conquer, though Liszt had worked arduously to master all possible technical problems at the piano. He now derived fresh inspiration from Paganini's Twenty-four Caprices and wrote his Paganini Etudes, of which the "Campanella," with its tinkling little bell effects, is the most popular. Though Liszt wrote that Paganini's "unsurpassable and unattainable genius excludes all imitation," still Liszt's motto, "Génie oblige," urged him on to surpass the "unsurpassable."

It was the Paganini Caprices which inspired the brilliant "arpeggios and fioritura, the prodigious attack and élan that took audiences by storm, the meetings of extremes which abolished the spaces on the keyboard by making the hands ubiquitous" (Haweis).

The French orchestral genius, Berlioz, who though lacking in inspired melodic ideas, was, with his passion for the grandiose and *flair* for colour, the next great influence. Berlioz's romantic "Episode in the Life of an Artist," with its striking imagery and freedom of form and poetic bent, turned Liszt in the same direction—the result of which was seen later in his Symphonic Poems for the orchestra.

Meanwhile the fruit of Liszt's admiration was seen in his arrangement of Berlioz's "Symphonie Fantastique," one presented in rousing dramatic fashion. Dramatic *flair* is one of Liszt's strong points; in this he is akin to Weber and superior to Chopin.

Chapter V.

CHOPIN AND LISZT (1831-35).

"Let us, like Chopin, aim at leaving a celestial and immortal echo of what we have felt, loved and suffered, rather than labour to attract hearers, and sacrifice to them."—
Liszt ("Life of Chopin").

Mutual Influence.

Chopin now swum on to Liszt's horizon—at the end of 1831. Both artists, as striving in the same direction and with the same ideals through the medium of a highly developed technique, were destined to strongly influence each other.

Strongly contrasted in nature, Chopin was reserved, calm and polite—Liszt speaking to Rev. H. R. Haweis, said: "Chopin was an exclusive, self-centred personality. He lived inwardly—he was silent, reserved, never said much; people were deceived about him and he never undeceived them."

Liszt had the bigger soul, reaching out, as we have seen, in every direction—a generous, open-hearted man and a heaven-storming genius withal, and yet tender and sympathetic. Artistically they were allied, but the Franco-Pole interpreted the Polish spirit and Liszt that of Hungary. In one, the dignified Polonaise, in the other the pathetic *Lassan* and impetuous *Friska* were represented.

Liszt, in his "Life of Chopin" (Reeves), (1852), says: "In Chopin's *salon* were often found the most eminent minds in Paris."

"No doubt more than one of us can still recollect our first improvised evening with him. His apartment, which was invaded by surprise, was only lit up by some wax candles grouped round one of Pleyel's pianos. The corners of the room were left in obscurity, so that all idea of limit was lost, and there seemed to be no boundary save the darkness around."

It is curious that Chopin had the gift of imitation and mimicry, and when the two artists met, Liszt would, without sign of offence, look on while Chopin mimicked him. They remained friends: one evening Liszt played one of Chopin's Nocturnes and added some embellishments of his own—as he had a trick of doing then—Chopin was piqued, and Liszt said: "Play it yourself then." Just then a moth put out the lamp, and Chopin with the moon as a lamp extemporised for nearly an hour. His audience were in tears, and Liszt, deeply affected, apologised for his remonstrance about the embellishments, saying, "You are a true poet." "Oh, it is nothing," replied Chopin. "We have each our own style."*

Hiller in his "Recollections of Mendelssohn" (pp. 25-6) recounts the gay spirits of their party, includ-

---

* Karasowski, "Life of Chopin," 2 vols. (Reeves).

ing Mendelssohn, Chopin and Liszt, in a Parisian café (in 1832)—and how previously Mendelssohn had come to Hiller "with a beaming face and declared that he had just seen a miracle—a real miracle," for Liszt had played his hardly legible Concerto MS. "at sight in the most perfect manner, better than anybody else could play it—quite marvellously."

There is record also of a *matinée musicale* held at the Salle Pleyel in 1834, at which Liszt and Chopin played a "Grand Duo by Moscheles and another by Liszt for two pianos with great applause."

Liszt afterwards wrote of his friend: "Nothing equals his lightness and sweetness of touch," and that he could also "set in motion the heroic string—as in his Polonaises."

It is interesting to hear the experience of the late SIR CHARLES HALLÉ, the celebrated pianist and conductor, who knew both Chopin and Liszt about 1836. "Chopin," he says, "rarely played anything but his own works. Chopin carried you with him into a dreamland. Liszt was all sunshine and dazzling splendour. Such marvels of executive skill and power I could never have imagined." The "crystal-like clearness of his playing never failed for a moment in the most complicated passages." And again, "Such execution, such limitless—truly limitless—execution no one else can possess. He plays sometimes so as to make your hair stand on end."*

Chopin in Liszt's words was "an angel of fair

---

* Hallé, "Life and Letters" (Smith-Elder).

countenance with brown eyes, from which intellect beamed rather than burned. Chopin had a gentle, refined smile and dark blonde hair, soft as silk.

Liszt had stiff hair of a dark blonde hue thrown back without a parting, and reaching to his shoulders.

John Field the Model.

Chopin learnt from Liszt's bigger style, and his Etude Collection, Op. 10, is dedicated to him; Nos. 9 and 12 ("Revolution Etude"), and Nos. 11 and 12 of the Op. 28 are in Liszt's style—while in Liszt the lyric Chopinesque Nocturne style is to be seen in "En Reve" (Doblinger). (Example): "Au

"En Reve." Nocturne.

lac de Wallenstadt," "Eclogue," "Consolation," in D flat," "Liebesträume," No. 1, "Sonetto," 123, "Les Cloches de Genéve," "Liebesträume," No. 3;

and these, taken in this order, might themselves form an introduction to Liszt's works. We must not forget, however, that both Chopin and Liszt built upon John Field, the composer of lovely Nocturnes, and who was their direct predecessor. Liszt was enchanted with the Nocturnes of Field, and the first four of the above with the "Nonnenwerth Cell" might have been written by John Field himself.

We must not forget what Schumann—as critic—wrote:

> "Be Fields, write what you will,
> Be Poets, be men I beseech you."

RELLSTAB, a German critic, also wrote in 1834: "If one holds Field's charming Romances before a distorting concave mirror—so that every delicate expression becomes coarse, one gets Chopin's work."

LISZT AND LOUIS PHILIPPE.

An anecdote of Liszt belongs to this period. Since his socialistic tendencies had come to the front he had refused to play before Louis Philippe at the Tuileries—but one day when Erard was making an exhibition of pianos, the two met in the Erard *salon.* Said the King: "Do you remember that you played at my house when you were a boy and I was Duke of Orleans? Much has changed since then." "Yes," said Liszt, "but not for the better."

During the time of Liszt's convalescence he studied diligently. Speaking of Beethoven and the classics, and writing in February, 1832, to a friend, he said: "I study and meditate on them—I am all on fire. Besides this I practise four or five hours of exercises on thirds, sixths, octaves, arpeggios, repeated notes, cadenzas, etc."

LISZT'S CADENZAS.

The dramatic nature of Liszt comes out in his fiery and brilliant Cadenzas, and these, it may be said, need an apprenticeship, as through the one in his sixth "Soirée de Vienne," the first version of which is the easier. Learn to make them like a zephyr breathing on an Æolian harp—a sigh—an apparition.*

MACDOWELL, composer of brilliant and attractive Concertos, speaks of the "wonderful tracery of Orientalism" present in Liszt's and Chopin's works. With Liszt the embellishment itself made the starting point for almost a new art in tonal combination." He says: "Compare the easy mastery of the arabesque displayed in the simplest piano piece of today with the awkward and gargoyle-like figuration of Beethoven and his predecessors. We may justly attribute this to Liszt rather than to Chopin." (Gilman's "Macdowell.")

The "Symphonie Fantastique," a characteristically effective though not difficult transcription, was the first of a very large number of masterly paraphrases. There followed one of Schubert's songs, "The Rose"

---

* Liszt, by the by, wrote a brilliant cadenza, yet sound and classic in style, for Beethoven's Concerto in C minor, Op. 37 (Costellat).

(in 1834-35), succeeded in 1837 and 1838 by transcriptions of three and twelve songs, including the well-known "Erl-king" and "The Wanderer." The ethereal but dramatic three "Apparitions," of which the third was a Fantasia on a Schubert waltz, came next.

The Paris period came to an end in 1835, and Liszt made Geneva his home till the end of 1836.

CHAPTER VI.

LISZT IN SWITZERLAND (1835-37).

"Album d'un Voyageur." A virtuoso miniaturist. The Genevan transcriptions. Liszt and Thalberg.

"Of the artist it is specially true that he only pitches his tent for the hour—whatever he may do, wherever he may go, he always feels himself an exile."—LISZT to "George Sand" in 1837.

Liszt's stay in Geneva proved to be a great incentive to serious composition.

He was in distinguished literary company and the excursions to the Swiss mountains with "Georges Sand" and the Countess "Daniel Stern" bore fruit in the first compositions of his artistic maturity. Before this we had the virtuoso striving for recognition, but now at the age of twenty-four, we have artistic and soulful works, which, using his greatly extended technique, will endure and take their place along with those of his friend Chopin. They were not published until 1842, and then under the title of "Album d'un Voyageur," in three parts (now out of print). (1) "Impressions et Poésies" (six pieces);

(2) "Fleurs melodiques des Alpes" (nine pieces); (3) Paraphrases. Of these a selection appeared later as "Pélerinage en Suisse," with the three "Paraphrases" as "Trois Airs Suisses" ("Ranz des Vaches"; "Chant du Montagnard" and "Ranz des Chevres").*

The principal numbers of the Album were contained in Part I:

1. "Au Lac de Wallenstadt."
2. "Au Bord d'une Source" (Beside the Spring).
3. "The Bells of Geneva."
4. "The Chapel of William Tell."
5. "Vallée d'Obermann."

These numbers appeared later on in "Années de Pelerinage."†

The first three are lovely nature sketches and—if interpreted as they should be—will stand for all time.

It is estimated that about 375 of Liszt's works were original compositions; some were lost or destroyed, others fell out of print, but sufficient remain to give Liszt, now that we are able to estimate *and* perform his works, a very high place.

---

* In 1852. Meanwhile, in 1845, Liszt had met Huber, the Swiss composer, and he incorporated motives from Huber's "Alpine Horn Songs" in several numbers of the Album. ("Swiss Music Journal," August, 1934.)

† Others went out of print or were worked into other compositions. The original Album must not be confused with the "Album d'un Voyageur," published by Leduc (Paris), containing Hungarian pieces.

A Virtuoso Miniaturist.

Thoughtless and ignorant people apparently acquainted only with his Transcriptions, said he could not compose, and others who knew his original works judged them from the thematic development standpoint. He was not an adept at weaving a movement in the minute thematic way—that was not his *métier*. He apparently could not, or did not, try to write a Sonata or Fugue in the old way; neither could Chopin—but he could decorate and metamorphose a theme in a manner which is equally if not more, acceptable in a smaller work. In fact, Liszt is usually at his best as a miniaturist of the virtuoso school.

Genevan Transcription.

The transcriptions of the Genevan period are the Fantasia, Op. 5, "Niobe," "Fantasia Romantique," "Swiss Melodies," "Rondo Contrabandista" (on a Spanish theme by Manuel Garcia—out of print), Op. 7, "Puritani," Op. 8, "Serenata and Pastorelle" (Rossini), Op. 9, "La Juive," Op. 13, "Lucia di Lammermoor" (two parts).

These virtuoso works were the means of prolonging the life of certain one-time popular melodies. The "Niobe" and "Lucia" Fantasias were favourites with Clara Wieck, the virtuoso, who became the wife of Schumann. To this period belong also the Op. 6, "Valse di Bravura" (Ricordi), written in, but superior to, the style of his friend Chopin, and a violin and piano duo on "Le Marin de Lafont."

Liszt's Transcriptions have been termed REPRODUCTIONS. He himself compares a transcription to an orchestral work as a steel engraving to a painting, he says "colour is wanting, but it can get fine light and shade." In the process, he says, "we make broken chords like the harp—long drawn tones like the wind instruments, *staccati* and a thousand kinds of passages, which formerly it only appeared possible to bring forth from this or that instrument." In connection with this it might be remarked that piano-makers are singularly unenterprising if we compare what was done in the old days with the harpsichord. Few piano-makers have even adopted the "bass pedal," and the organ is far ahead as regards mechanical contrivances.

Liszt had such a grasp of orchestral effects—unlike Chopin's, that his friends urged him to devote himself to the orchestra.

The Symphonic Poems were yet to come, however, and in his early years he held fast to the piano.

Of the later operatic Fantasias which have survived there are the "Rigoletto," "Trovatore" and "Ernani" (Peters), the "Don Giovanni" and "Figaro" (B. and H.), the "Prophet" ("Les Patineurs") and "La Muette" ("Tarantelle"), (Lit.).

LISZT AND THALBERG.

From Geneva Liszt visited Paris twice. Thalberg the elegant virtuoso had appeared, and the fickle Parisians applauded him to the echo. Liszt, however, reappeared in Erard's rooms, and the gauntlet was thrown. The coteries declared for and against —Berlioz for Liszt and Fétis for Thalberg. In March (1837) Thalberg gave a *matinée*, and played a Fantasia on "God Save the King" and his "Moses" Fantasia. The following Sunday Liszt filled the Opera House and gave his "Niobe" Fantasia and Weber's "Concertstück." The "Gazette Musicale" reported that when the curtain rose "we saw this slender young man appear, so pale and so thin—alone with the piano on this immense stage. After the opening bar the victory was half won, the pianoforte vibrated under Liszt's fingers like the voice of Lablache."

The next move was a concert arranged by Princess Belgiojoso at which *both* artists appeared.

The verdict was summed up by a witty lady at the close: "Thalberg est le premier pianiste du monde," and another who made reply, "Et Liszt? -Liszt! Liszt, c'est le seul."

MENDELSSOHN, who belonged to the conservative, classic school, writing to his mother on March 3, 1840, infers that Liszt's works were inferior to those of Thalberg, but he admits Liszt's pre-eminence as a virtuoso. He says: "I have heard no performer whose musical feelings, like Liszt's, extended to the very tips of his fingers."

Heine thus comments on the Liszt and Thalberg musical duel, deprecating the praising of one at the expense of the other: "No more striking contrast could be imagined than the noble, soulful, intelligent, good-natured German or rather Austrian Thalberg, face to face with the wild, flashing, volcanic, heaven-storming Liszt."

It was the Princess Belgiojoso who got Liszt, Thalberg, Pixis, Herz, Czerny and Chopin to contribute to a most interesting and instructive six-composer Transcription, entitled "Hexameron" (Joubert) Liszt's share, a preponderating one, was the Introduction, theme from "Les Puritans" (second variation), Ritornellos for the fifth and sixth variations, and part of the Finale, all done in his own abounding dramatic style, and full of verve.

Theme for the Hexameron.

Liszt easily carries off the honours. Apart it is interesting to see how the different styles and sections dovetail one into the other. Chopin's section is in the style of the Field Nocturne upon which he built his own. Thalberg is somewhat restrained, Pixis lacks harmonic variety, Herz is smooth and fluent, and Czerny consistently brilliant. The work is worth revival.

The name of Pixis recalls the fact that Liszt gave

a Beethoven concert in which "without announcing it to the public, a Trio of Pixis was played, instead of Beethoven's." The bravos were more stormy and numerous than ever, but when Beethoven's Trio took the place originally intended for Pixis', they found it cold and wearisome and mediocre.

Liszt was at this time staying with the famous *littérateures*, the Countess d'Agoult and Madame "George Sand," the friend of Chopin. Said Liszt one time: "Madame Sand caught her butterfly and tamed it in her box by giving it grass and flowers—this was the love period. Then she stuck her pin through it when it struggled—this was its *congé*—and it always came from her."

Apparently the two lady *littérateures* did not get on too well together. Liszt, however, avowed that: "From an artistic point of view, the sojourns at Nohant were highly interesting, but—there I played only second fiddle."*

It appears that the exclusive Countess, who was Liszt's senior, asked for his protection. She (as "Daniel Stern") acted as a *littérateure* and travelling companion until 1840. Her family's verdict was that Liszt in every way had acted as a man of honour.

On the return to Paris, from Switzerland, the two *littérateures*, the Countess d'Agoult and George Sand, formed a *salon*. In Switzerland George Sand had

---

* "Liszt and the Countess." Fr. Schnapp, "Musical Record," May, 1933.

been dressed in a man's blouse and smoked cigars. Balzac in a visit to the Chateau Nohant in 1838, describes her as "having a double chin and wearing red trousers," and, in her masculine Bohemian existence, as retiring to rest at 6 a.m. and rising at midday. Heine praises her as the greatest French writer. She was short and stout, while the Countess was tall, blonde, gracious and elegant.

Was it the busybodies Liszt had in mind when he wrote later in his life of Chopin: "With what arrogant derision do men contrast a poet's noble thoughts with his ignoble acts, and the artist's exalted compositions with his guilty frivolity?"

Other products of his stay at this time were the Transcriptions which he made of Beethoven's Pastoral, Second and Fifth Symphonies, also some songs of Schubert's, including the "Erl King."

CHAPTER VII.

VISITS TO ITALY (1837-39).

The transcendental studies. The Rossini soirées. "Sposalizio." "Il Penseroso." Italian Album.

A visit to the Italian Lakes now followed, and as a result, the Italian Album was begun. The first item was "On Reading Dante," and here was also that master work, the "Etudes d'execution transcendantes," evolved out of the youthful exercises, written some ten years previously—the wild and tumultuous "Mazeppa," bold "Eroïca," gloomy "Vision," flickering "Will o' the Wisp," and dreamy "Harmonies du Soir"; these created a new Temple of Art.

The light but brilliant "Chromatic Gallop" and the "Huguenot Fantasia" also belong to this time. Liszt's visit to Milan got into the papers, and an announcement was made that Italy "lodged the first pianist in the world."

Italy is not greatly devoted to the purer forms of music, being mostly given up to opera. Concerts were given in December, 1837, and the following February and March. A "Studio" (Etude—Prelude) on the programme called forth from a gentleman of the pit the exclamation, "we don't come to be entertained with studies," and a request for a theme for extemporisation actually elicited "The Cathedral of Milan"; "The Railroad"; and the query, "Is it better to marry or remain a bachelor?" as suggestions for extemporisation.

THE ROSSINI SOIRÉES.

Liszt also played at Rossini's soirées, and his friendship resulted in his Transcriptions of twelve Italian songs, in the "Soirées Musicales," including the gay "Regata Veneziana," a good, easy introduction to the bravura style. He transcribed also Rossini's "William Tell" Overture, and, later on, two sacred themes—(1) "Stabat Mater," and (2) "Charité."

A cry for help now came from Hungary. Floods had desolated Pesth, and Liszt wrote in support, "I, too, belong to this old and powerful race." Concerts in aid of the distress fund were arranged in Vienna in the spring of 1838.

Schumann was there, and comments thus: "When he seats himself at the instrument, he strokes his hair behind his ear, his glance is staring, his eye hollow, the upper part of the body quiet, only the head moves." Tones were hurled with the force of thunderbolts.

Another critic reported that "The pining youth had become a Goliath."

Besides the classics, Weber and Chopin, Liszt played some fourteen of his Transcriptions and three original works—Etude No. 2, in A minor, "Chromatic Galop," and the "Hexameron."

Liszt by his playing of Scarlatti's "Cats' Fugue" was the first to revive the favour of the old masters —and the old Italian virtuoso's works were collected into an edition by Czerny. Here also in Vienna Liszt popularised the collection of twelve of the beautiful *lieder* of its own composer, Schubert, through his charming Transcription. To these he added Transcriptions of selected piano valses by Schubert, the collection being entitled "Soirées de Vienne"—(Valses Caprices), and of Schubert's duet, "Hungarian Divertissement," military and Hungarian Marches.

Liszt later transcribed other collections of Schubert's songs, viz.:

"Four Sacred Songs."

Six songs, including "The Trout."

"The Miller's Songs" (six).

"Swan Songs" (fourteen), and

"The Winter Journey" (ten songs).

Another visit to Italy followed, this time reaching to Rome, where he was influenced by the antique and art associations of the ancient world capital. Two smaller works appeared: "Sposalizio," suggested by Raphael's picture of that title, and "Il Penseroso," as inspired by the Michael Angelo statue. The subjects are interpreted not of course in the music, but according to the mood or emotion experienced. The espousal of Mary and Joseph appears in the "Sposalizio"; in the hallowed yet joyful emotion with which we hear it, while "Il Penseroso" reminds us of Milton's poem on the same subject:

"Sweet bird, that shunn'st the noise of folly,
Most musical, most melancholy,
Thee, chantress, oft the woods among
I woo to hear thy even-song."

ITALIAN ALBUM.

Later on to these two works were added transcriptions of a song by Salvator Rosa, and his own settings of "Three Sonnets" by Petrarca, along with the "Lecture du Dante," thus forming the "Italian Album," or the "Années," Book II. Other three pieces originating in Italy, and entitled "Venezia e Napolia," (1) "Gondoliera," (2) "Canzone," (3) "Tarentelle," are based upon popular Italian airs. These were published much later, but meanwhile there appeared the "Soirées Italiennes," consisting of six pieces on themes by Mercadente, and the "Nuits d'Eté," three pieces on airs by Donizetti.

"IL PENSEROSO."

CHAPTER VIII.

THE WANDERING VIRTUOSO (1839-49).

More journeys to England. Visits to Leipzig. Tour in Russia. Beethoven Festival at Bonn.

"The King of Pianists is looked upon and honoured by all players as the unsurpassable ideal of an artist."—PAUER'S "Pianist's Dictionary."

Liszt left Rome in June, 1839, and for the next ten years, up to 1849, he became the peripatetic virtuoso, travelling from one country to another and playing at concerts or giving recitals. The only other courses that lay open to him, were those of a capellmeister or a conductorship. The latter would have been preferable. Attached to a German court and interpreting the symphonies of the great masters was nearer his ideal, but a Court Capellmeistership with its meagre salary did not then seem sufficient in a monetary sense—and the virtuoso, as he wrote, "feels himself King of all those spirits which raise others to the regions of the beautiful, the ideal, and the divine. Perhaps it is only a dream, but it is one which ennobles the existence of the virtuoso." Liszt had written before, in 1837, to Madame "George Sand": "Happy, a hundred times happy, the wanderer! Happy he who does not have to traverse the beaten paths!" Nevertheless, as Liszt afterwards experienced, the path of the virtuoso is not always "roses all the way."

More Journeys to England.

During these eight years he made several journeys to England, and in May and June, 1840, and June, 1841.

His previous visits were made as a boy. He was now a man, and within twelve months made four visits to England, crossing the Channel and later extending his tour to Scotland and Ireland. We hear of him at Sidmouth, Bath, Cheltenham, Dublin, Cork, Belfast, Edinburgh, Glasgow and Liverpool.

In 1840 he was invited to play before Queen Victoria at Buckingham Palace, and three times at the Philharmonic Concerts in London. A contract for the provinces at 500 guineas a month was made, but unfortunately the tour was mismanaged, and Liszt broke his contract and declined his fees. He was, however, too magnanimous to apportion blame, and later came back again. It was on June 1, 1840, that his cab was capsized, and Liszt was "thrown out and picked up insensible." "Liszt was violently shaken and required bleeding"—so reported the "Times."

His sprained wrist did not, however, prevent him playing at a concert a few days later on behalf of Polish refugees.

It was shortly before, in 1839, that the projected

memorial to Beethoven at Bonn (hitherto meagrely supported) caused Liszt to offer to make up the deficiency in the amount required, hence the proceeds of his Rhine tour were principally devoted to this cause. It was in the intervals of these Rhine concerts that he made the three visits to London, where he invented the term *recital*—with conversational intervals. It was in London that snobbery infected the critics. One writer reported, however, that:

"The critics may not understand M. Liszt, but the musicians crowd to hear him."

The musical world of 1841 went into ecstasies during one of these visits after this manner: "Of the miracle genus is M. Liszt, the Polyphemus of the Piano, the Aurora Borealis of musical effulgence—the Niagara of thundering harmonies."

Richard Hoffmann writing in "Scribner's Magazine" relates how he heard Liszt in Manchester at this time (1840-41): "At that time he only played *bravura* piano compositions, such as the 'Hexameron' and Hungarian March of Schubert in C minor, arranged by himself. I recollect his curious appearance, his tall, lank figure buttoned up in a frock coat, very much embroidered with braid, and his long light hair brushed straight down from his collar."

Liszt's phenomenal technique and the Thalberg opposition accounted for much of the criticism experienced. From his English concerts Liszt contributed 10,000 francs to the Beethoven monument—and sailing to Hamburg, he gave the proceeds of his concert there, 17,300 francs—to the distressed Musicians' Fund. In 1840 the Hungarian Government, of which his cousin Edward was a member, conferred upon him a Sword of Honour on his visit to Budapest, and in 1842 he accepted the position of Deputy Kapellmeister of Weimar, though he did not take duty till 1844.

VISITS LEIPZIG.

Liszt made his first visit to Leipzig in March, 1840, where his performance at the Gewandhaus caused great applause—although the programme, consisting of the Transcription from the Beethoven "Pastoral" Symphony, the Pacini Variations, "Chromatic Galop" and the "Etude Prelude," "played with marvellous delicacy," did not appear to be what the audience wanted. Schumann writes of this:

"Liszt arrived much spoiled by the aristocrats, and complained so continually of the absence of toilettes, Countesses and Princesses, that I became vexed and told him we had our aristocracy also; 150 Bookshops, 50 Printing Presses and 30 Journals, and that he had better take care. He only laughed."

A newspaper war followed. Mendelssohn related:

"It occurred to me that the bad feelings might perhaps be allayed if the people were to see and hear him privately, and I suddenly determined to give him a Soirée in the Gewandhaus with orchestra, chorus, negus, cakes, the 'Meerestille,' 42nd Psalm, Bach's Triple Concerto, Chorus from 'St. Paul,'

"LUCIA." FANTASIA.

Liszt's Fantasia on 'Lucia,' and the 'Erl King,' 'The Devil and his Grandmother,' and everyone was so delighted and played and sang with such enthusiasm that they said they had never passed a more enjoyable evening, and my object was accomplished." Liszt's second concert was crowded. Weber's "Concertstück," "Huguenot" Fantasia and Schubert Transcriptions were given.

Schumann, writing to Clara Wieck in March, 1840, says: "I am with Liszt nearly all day. He said to me yesterday, 'I feel as if I had known you for twenty years'—and I feel just the same. We have begun to be very rude to each other, and I have reason to be so, as he is really too capricious and has been frightfully spoilt at Vienna," but he says further:

"We all love him boundlessly and he played like a god at his second concert. The clamourers and chatterers have been silenced." By the way, Stanford,* speaking of Liszt's all-compelling charm, says: "He has two smiles; the one, angelical, for artists, the other, diabolical, for the satellite countesses." At Liszt's third concert he played Schumann's "Carnival" and the "Hexameron" (see Chapter VI).

The culmination of this tour (in 1840) came with the visit to Budapest—his first visit to his native land since childhood. A deputation came to Vienna to invite him to Hungary. On arrival he was welcomed by a choir of sixty voices and a military band, and after a concert given in the theatre he was presented by Hungarian nobles, clad in magnificent costumes, with a Sword of Honour.

Liszt returned at the head of a torchlight procession preceded by a military band.

Later on other continental cities were visited, and in 1842 Weimar and Berlin and St. Petersburg, then home to Paris, where his mother and the Countess stayed. Liszt left Berlin in a coach drawn by six white horses, escorted by thirty carriages and a company of students in their uniforms.

TOUR IN RUSSIA.

In 1842 came the tour in Russia, by way of Warsaw; the first concert in St. Petersburg realising £2,000. In Moscow six concerts had to be arranged instead of one. Liszt made frequent visits to Russia during the next forty years. It is reported that

* "**Pages from an Unwritten Diary.**"

"during a soirée at the Court of St. Petersburg, where he was always well received, it happened that the Czar Nicholas, who did not care much for music, began talking with a lady, and caring little for Liszt's playing, talked very loud. All of a sudden Liszt stopped dead and went away from the piano. The Czar was puzzled, and approaching the master, said to him:

"Why have you stopped playing?"

"When the Emperor speaks one ought to be silent," was the answer.*

Other tours followed up to 1849, when his career as a professional virtuoso ended—the last concert at which he played for money being at Elizabethsgrad, in South Russia, at the end of 1847 (see Chapter XIII).

It was during a visit to Madrid that he learnt that a personal introduction to the Queen was not possible. "Then," said he, "I cannot play—Queen Isabella received him and the crowd hailed him with "Salve, artista virtuosa."

THE BEETHOVEN FESTIVAL AT BONN.

Meanwhile, in 1845, the Beethoven monument was inaugurated at Bonn. For the festivities the Court and a number of illustrious guests were assembled, including Queen Victoria and Prince Albert. Owing to the introduction of an Archduke of higher precedence to Prince Albert, the Queen was not in a

---

* Janka Wohl, "Recollections" (Ward and Downey).

good humour, and Liszt had scarcely seated himself at the piano before she complained of the heat, and an attendant opened a window. The draught was too great, and the window was shut. The bustle upset Liszt, and at the end of the introduction he rose, bowed, and went out for a smoke. Half-an-hour later King Frederick came up and said:

"You went away just now! What was the matter?"

"I was afraid of disturbing her Majesty, Queen Victoria, while giving orders."

The King laughed and begged of him to continue, which he did later in silence, Queen Victoria having left shortly after Liszt disappeared.

Recently Friedheim (in "The Etude," January, 1932), who had the honour of playing before Queen Victoria at Balmoral, recounts that her Majesty remarked, "You belong to Liszt's inner circle?"

"Well, I knew him long before you did, I remember him quite vividly when he first came to London."

Liszt was not in England between 1827—when Queen Victoria was only eight years old—and May, 1840, when he was invited to play at Buckingham Palace before the Queen and the Prince Consort.

The Queen was very merry when Liszt told her that he was not at all hurt at her not then remembering him.

After the Philharmonic concert of June, 1841, Liszt did not appear again in England until 1886, at the age of seventy-five.

Liszt was the moving spirit at the Bonn Festival.

He appeared as conductor, pianist and composer. As pianist he played the solo part in the "Emperor" Concerto with the orchestra. We may recall that Wagner acclaimed Liszt as an ideal interpreter of Beethoven's works. As conductor, the C minor Symphony was in his care; as composer, a Cantata by himself, in honour of Beethoven was given.*

As a modernist of those days Liszt did not escape criticism: Berlioz accounted for this by writing:

"Some people were angry with Liszt because he possessed phenomenal talent and was exceptionally successful, others because he was witty, others again because he was generous."

Liszt contributed 60,000 francs to the Festival from his own pocket, nearly ruining himself in paying the organisation expenses.

Fétis says that:

"The ingratitude and injustice he reaped from his noble devotion and generous efforts to do honour to the memory of one of Germany's greatest children made a deep impression on his mind. It's the way of the world."

SIR ALEXANDER MACKENZIE† very aptly remarks: "When Beethoven kissed a prodigy in Vienna he

---

* "Spohr" (p. 270) relates the proceedings, the launching of the "van Beethoven," fireworks, ball, etc., at one concert owing to the late arrival of Royalty Liszt had to begin his Cantata over again. Meyerbeer directed the Court concert, which was vocal (with Jenny Lind as soloist) except for some pieces by Liszt.—"Autobiography" (Reeves).

† "A Musician's Narrative."

could not guess that his own monument was to be erected at Bonn, chiefly, one might say solely, by that boy's exertion."

Liszt's virtuoso tours terminated with visits to France, Holland, Bohemia, Hungary, Russia and Turkey, the political Revolutions which then broke out determined him to settle down to his appointment at Weimar. The turning point of his career had been reached.

As Saint-Saëns puts it in his "Portraits et Souvenirs":

"Liszt vanished behind the pall of clouds which hid the Germany of that day"—an almost mediæval Germany of petty princes and battlemented castles. "There at the Court of Weimar Liszt busied himself with the higher forms of composition, and dreamt of a modern renaissance of the art of music."

CHAPTER IX.

MUSICAL DIRECTOR AT WEIMAR (1849-61).

Wagner and Liszt. Weimar a musical centre. The Romantic movement.

"Liszt is besieged by people." "Liszt is just like a monarch, and no one dares speak to him until he addresses one first." "All Weimar adores him."—AMY FAY'S "Music Study in Germany."

WAGNER AND LISZT.

This period of Liszt's history is intertwined with that of his friend Wagner, who eventually became Liszt's son-in-law. Wagner had met Liszt in Paris in the early part of his career, and later in Dresden, when Wagner's "Rienzi" was given—with which Liszt was greatly charmed. Wagner's career at this time was a precarious struggle, and as related in his own words:

"But just when the case seemed desperate, Liszt succeeded by his own energy in opening a hopeful refuge to my art. He ceased his wanderings, settled down in the small and modest Weimar, and took up the conductor's baton, after having been at home so long in the splendour of the greatest cities of Europe."

It was there at Weimar that Wagner says: "I saw

Liszt conducting a rehearsal of my 'Tannhäuser,' and I was astonished at recognising my second self in his achievement."

Liszt's twelve years' tenure of the conductorship was an exceedingly busy one. Weimar as a literary centre had associations with Goethe, Schiller and others, and the Grand Duke, as Liszt found, was willing to help him in making it an equally great musical centre.

In the very attractive Liszt number of the "Revue Musicale" (May, 1928) we find:

"Liszt à Weimar est un spectacle magnifique. La petite ville allemande, si célèbre par la longue royauté de Goethe, a reçu de Liszt une gloire musicale qui égale l'autre. Pendant près de dix ans,—Weimar est un abrégé de tout ce que la musique européenne allait être pour un demi-siècle"—and for Weimar to become an epitome of European music for the next fifty years was no small accomplishment in those days of small German Principalities.

Every Weimar season saw produced at least one modern opera. Liszt's own orchestral ventures included two symphonies, the "Dante" and "Faust"—also the thirteen Symphonic Poems, besides eight Marches and Overtures, seven Concertos and other works for piano and orchestra, not to speak of numerous arrangements.

The reader is referred to the record of Liszt's orchestral achievements in Part II, Chapters XXIII-XXV.

Unlike Chopin and other pianoforte composers,

Liszt showed himself to be a great master of orchestration.

WEIMAR A MUSICAL CENTRE.

Liszt's ambition as to Weimar itself was realised. From all parts composers, executants and amateurs flocked to Weimar to learn at his feet and to hear the accomplishments of a small but exalted body of singers and instrumentalists under Liszt's direction. Their culture of modern music earned for Weimar the title of

THE SCHOOL OF THE FUTURE,

and their ambitions were centred in the MUSIC OF THE FUTURE. The artistic results for Liszt were great, but the financial aspect was not assuring. Liszt had managed to provide for his mother and his children, who were domiciled together in Paris, but he says:

"I have to manage on my salary of 1,000 thalers and 300 thalers by way of a present for the court concerts (about £200). For many years since I became firmly resolved to live up to my artistic vocation, I have not been able to count on any additional money from the music publishers. My 'Symphonic Poems' do not bring me in a shilling, but, on the contrary, cost me a considerable sum."

His programmes were not limited to modern works, but the classics, and especially Beethoven, were his care; nevertheless in his championship of modern music all Germany was against him.

Liszt wrote to Wagner in 1849:

"Once for all count me among your most zealous and devoted admirers; away or at home you can depend on my help"—which Wagner certainly did. Wagner was not tactful and his attacks on various musical quarters made things difficult. Owing to his senseless participation in a political revolution Wagner had to flee, disguised, and with a forged passport he found his way to Liszt. It is said that Liszt could never say no to Wagner nor to a pretty woman. Liszt, however, got him away safely to Paris, accompanying him as far as Eisenach. No wonder Wagner recognised the disinterested and noble-hearted friendship of Liszt, who by his continual advocacy of Wagner's interests acted as a real friend in times of need. Praeger, in 1851, stayed with Wagner, and remarks: "How changed: fifty-eight years old, and yet but one year in the possession of what is called a home"—and it was in exile that Wagner composed his best works. Wagner, writing in his autobiography in 1852 (when Liszt paid him a visit at Zurich), says: "Now for the first time I enjoyed the delight of getting to know my friend (Liszt) better as a fellow composer. My delight over everything I heard by Liszt was as deep as it was sincere, and above all, extraordinarily stimulating." Thus the admiration was mutual, and Wagner designates Liszt as the friend who had "devoted himself so absolutely to my own works." At the banquet given at Bayreuth in 1882, Wagner said that when "every voice was against me, it was he who set me up, supported me, and proclaimed me as no one else ever did."

THE ROMANTIC MOVEMENT.

The cause of romanticism in music was ably supported by Liszt, not only by the bringing forward of new works, but by literary contributions. He had on his side Schumann and Berlioz, both literary critics, Chopin, Raff and others.

When advised by the Weimar Court Intendant to support the classics, Liszt retorted, "But why not also sometimes live with the living?" It was his advocacy and the opposition to a work by Cornelius which ultimately led to his departure from Weimar in 1861.

Mendelssohn (1809-47) and Rubinstein (1829-94) represented the backwash of classicism, notwithstanding which Liszt was a friend to young Rubinstein. Liszt in 1854 wrote of him: "He is a clever fellow, possessed of talent. I do not want to preach to him—he may sow his wild oats and fish deeper in the Mendelssohn waters, and even swim away if he likes."

During the course of one of Liszt's many tours it so happened that, in 1854, Liszt and his young friend Rubinstein were attending a musical festival at Rotterdam. Exploring one of the quays, they found that their carriage had disappeared, and they started to walk home together.

The elder Liszt (forty-three years of age), "tall, stately, dandified—with long golden hair thrown back on his shoulders; Rubinstein with his lion head and Beethovenish cast of features, was no less striking in appearance. The brawny, red-armed fisherwomen loitering with their creels of fish, were attracted and gathered about the artists, and became hilarious. Liszt, aristocratic to his finger-tips, was in despair. Finally, the two had to come to a dead stop, the women forming a ring and dancing around them, plucking them by the sleeves and coat-tails and laughing uproariously.* At length Rubinstein, in a passion, broke through, and the two escaped followed by the taunts of their tormentors."

---

* "Anton Rubinstein," by Al. MacArthur. London, 1889.

CHAPTER X.

LISZT'S CLASSES (1849-61).

Liszt at home in Weimar. Amy Fay's reminiscences. Hero worship.

"I am having the most heavenly time in Weimar studying with Liszt."—AMY FAY.

"His lessons began where those of ordinary teachers end. They were lessons in accentuation, phrasing, interpretation, in expression, in eloquence."

In the realm of piano work Liszt exercised great influence through the large number of pupils who came to him at Weimar. Those who were specially distinguished alone numbered over sixty, and they included Sophie Menter, D'Albert, Von Bülow, Burmeister, Friedheim, Jaell, Joseffy, Lamond, Wm. Mason, Macdowell, Raff, Rosenthal, Reisenauer, Saint-Saëns, Sauer, Sgambati, Scharwenka, Tausig and Count Zichy. It is pointed out in the "Etude" that twenty-nine of the sixty toured as pianists in the U.S.A. Think of the immense influence of this artistic army, and the fact that Liszt would not take fees from these pupils, and that he died comparatively poor.

DANNREUTHER remarks that: "None of his contemporaries or pupils were as spontaneous, individual and convincing in their playing, and none, except Tausig, so infallible with their fingers and wrists."

LISZT AT HOME IN WEIMAR.

His piano classes or auditions have been charmingly described by Amy Fay, in her "Music Study in Germany." "Liszt," she says, "is the most interesting and striking-looking man imaginable. He is tall and slight, with deep-set eyes, shaggy eyebrows and long iron-grey hair, which he wears in the middle. His hands are very narrow, with long and slender fingers. One moment his face will look dreamy, shadowy, tragic, the next he will be insinuating, amiable, sardonic, but always the same captivating grace of manner."

AMY FAY'S REMINISCENCES.

"We always lay our music on the table, and he takes them, looks them over and calls out what he will have played." He remarked this piece, and called out in German (Liszt usually preferred to speak French from his early residence in Paris) "Who plays this great and mighty Ballad of mine?" She was told to play it, and afterwards he said, "To-day you have covered yourself with glory."

"At home Liszt does not wear his long Abbé's coat, but a short one, in which he looks much more artistic. His figure is remarkably slight, but his head is most imposing. A splendid grand piano stands in one window, which is always wide open, and looks out on the park. You cannot conceive without hearing him how poetic he is, or the thousand nuances he can throw into the simplest thing. One pupil was playing the melody rather feebly. Liszt suddenly took the seat at the piano and said, 'Lorsque je joue, c'est toujours pour la gallerie.' His personal magnetism is immense. Who was it that I heard say once, that years ago, he saw Clara Schumann sitting in tears during one of Liszt's performances?"

Miss Fay says: "Under the inspiration of Liszt's playing everybody worked tooth and nail to achieve the impossible." That is how he turned out such a grand school of piano playing. Walter Bache relates (in 1882): "There are some duffers among the ladies," and that is quite possible when it is computed that over four hundred pupils passed through his hands.

Reisenauer once gave a clever presentation of Liszt's method.* Going into another room and listening, Reisenauer "returned, imitating the walk, facial expression and the peculiar guttural snort of Liszt in his later years. Then followed a kindly sermon upon the emotional possibilities of the composition. This was interrupted with snorts and went with kaleidoscopic rapidity from French to German and back again many, many times."

It says much for Liszt that when travelling with his pupils "their expenses, hotel bills and concert

---

* "Great Pianists," J. F. Cooke (Presser).

tickets were invariably paid by himself," and this on a slender income (Mackenzie's "Liszt" (Jack)).

BORODIN narrates his experience thus:

"I went in. A Dutch pianist was performing a piece by Tausig. Liszt was standing at the piano, surrounded by fifteen pupils. 'Ah, there you are,' exclaimed the old master, giving me his hand. He then introduced me to his pupils. 'They are all celebrated pianists, or if they are not yet will become such.' The young folk all began to laugh. Little Vera Timanoff was his favourite. After a compliment, "Liszt tapped her kindly on the cheek and kissed her on the forehead, while she kissed his hand; this is the custom between Liszt and his pupils."

HERO WORSHIP.

BETTINA WALKER, in her "Musical Experiences," sympathises with the hero worship, mentioning that Tausig had been seen to "kneel to him and kiss the hem of his coat."

The pupils had to be assembled before Liszt came, upon which "everyone stood up and all the younger people went towards him and kissed his hand."

Liszt could, however, be sarcastic if not pleased. He would say, "I don't care for this, let us go on to the next." "Shame, shame," he said to another, "begin once more," or "You have no business here, go to the Conservatoire," or again, "We don't wash dirty linen here," or "What sort of playing is that? Playing indeed."

The author of "Personal Recollections" (Donajowski) narrates the visit of a young transatlantic lady accompanied by her "Mor":

She proposed to play to him the "Bees' Wedding"—"The what?" said Liszt. "'The Bees' Wedding,'" repeated the girl in a shrill voice. "Oh —ah!" said Liszt, eventually comprehending her. "I think I would prefer the 'Spider's Divorce' or the 'Rat's Revenge.'"

He told Miss Walker that "No pianofortes lasted anything like as well as those of Broadwood."

Miss Janka Wohl (also a Hungarian) said that his favourite pupils were Sophie Menter, whom he called the first pianist of his time, and the only one "whom I was able to teach what cannot be learnt. She has a singing hand." The other was Count Zichy, who, having lost his right arm, taught himself to play with his left, he performed *tours de force* which drew from Liszt the exclamation: "Well, none of us could do anything like that."

Liszt retired to Rome in 1861 (Chapter XIII), but during his residence there he made periodic visits to Weimar as well as Budapesth. When in Weimar, as Sir George Henschel relates: "Liszt held a sort of court. The picturesque old town fairly swarmed with past, present and would-be pupils and disciples of the master—with velvet coats, huge neckties, and long flowing hair."

Lamond has also given an interesting account* of a late period in Liszt's life. In July, 1885, Lamond arrived "in the rather sleepy but beautiful city of Weimar" on his pilgrimage to Liszt. He was called upon by three young men in succession, each wearing long hair and a tie-pin with a photo of Liszt, viz., Friedheim, Conrad Ansorge and Karl Schroeder. Each departed without waiting for a reply. On his visit to Liszt he was struck by the appearance of Liszt, "his white hair hanging in long locks, his face covered with warts, he stood before us gazing at us with earnest eyes." Lamond was permitted to call four times a week and he played to him his whole repertoire. He further relates that:

"He never accepted a penny from his pupils. They got, for that matter, no ordinary lessons. What money could pay for a lesson from Liszt! Bülow was a worthy successor of Liszt in that he too never took a fee from his disciples in art. Both masters held that 'Noblesse oblige.' Liszt, more than any other great master of his age, was a true and genuine Christian, in the finest meaning of the word."

"At Weimar the keyboard was pounded, softly fingered, sometimes passably well, often atrociously, and rarely to one's delight. The master expected of his pupils technical perfection. Mastery of every technical point was taken for granted and was not mentioned at all. The less gifted pupils derived

---

* "Daily Telegraph," September 15, 1934, "From Glasgow to Weimar in the 1880's."

nothing from his lessons; he scarcely listened to them, let them play to an end, or, at the most, accompanied their performance with stinging remarks. Towards the gifted ones he was severe and inflexible as regards *tempo* and interpretation."

CHAPTER XI.

THE PRINCESS AND THE ABBÉ (1861-75).

Liszt becomes an Abbé in 1865. *The annulled marriage. Liszt at the Hungarian Coronation.*

"Liszt was a profoundly religious man and all the more inclined to religion when I knew him—through the influence of Princess von Wittgenstein."—ROSENTHAL.

It was in 1847 that Liszt became acquainted with the Princess Sayn-Wittgenstein, the daughter of a Polish nobleman, who, very young when married, was estranged from her husband, settled in Weimar, and acted as his secretary and adviser. She along with Liszt, wrote his literary works, the somewhat flowery life of Chopin, "The Gipsies and Their Music in Hungary" and "Concerning the Nocturnes of Field."* As his patron and helper she also saw Liszt's potentialities as a composer and encouraged him to devote himself to higher forms of composition. She saw to the disposal of his daughters, Cosima and Blondine. They were brought from Paris and placed in the care of von Bülow and his mother in Berlin. In 1857 Cosima married von Bülow

---

* Liszt's literary works were written in French; German he spoke with difficulty and Magyar but slightly.

and Blondine espoused the French statesman, Emile Olivier.

It appears that the Princess was anti-Semitic in her views. Far from beautiful, and, moving in a narrow groove, she however so ordered Liszt's life that he became more systematic and thus accomplished more.

Eventually Liszt left Weimar in 1861 and joined the Princess at Rome. The year previous the Princess had obtained a divorce from the Pope, and Liszt was to be married to the Princess on October 22—but in the last hour the Pope, through family influence of the Wittgensteins, forbade the ceremony. Liszt seems to have taken the reverse philosophically.

Becomes an Abbé in 1865.

Four years later the Prince died and the marriage idea was revised—but not seriously, indeed the Princess suggested Liszt should devote his talents to the Church—and the next year, 1865, he took minor orders and "became an Abbé." The friendship with the Princess continued and Liszt spent his time between Rome, Weimar and Budapest.

The following year, 1866, Liszt wearing an Abbé's coat, conducted his "Missa Solennis" in the church of St. Eustache, Paris.

Liszt had made his abode in the Vatican, and during that spring, in 1865, had performed in public twice. GREGOROVIUS writes: "Now he wears the cloaklet of the Abbé, lives in the Vatican and, as Schlözer tells me, is happy and healthy. This is the end of the genial virtuoso, the personality of a sovereign. I am glad that I heard Liszt play once more, he and his instrument seemed to be grown together—a piano centaur." During the years of his stay in Rome (1861-1868) a state of dissension existed between Italy and the Pope Pius IX, who, admiring Liszt, called betimes on the Abbé. One day, very depressed, Pius asked him to improvise "I played, therefore," says Liszt, "as the spirit moved me." The Pope suggested by way of return that music ought to be employed to lead hardened criminals to repentance.

WHY DID LISZT BECOME AN ABBÉ?

Various reasons have been given for the step taken by Liszt in 1865 when he adopted the tonsure and the four orders of Doorkeeper, Reader, Exorcist and Acolyte, besides becoming an honorary Canon. The opinion of the world might have been reflected in the account given by Madame Gautier in her "Wagner at Home,"* where she says "the appearance of Franz Liszt astonished me." "Why that long cassock? Was he a priest?" The interview took place in Munich with Franz Servais.

THE ANNULLED MARRIAGE.

"It was only four years ago that he took orders and became the Abbé Liszt."

"In what way and why?"

"No one knows. On his return from a journey to

* (Mills and Boon.)

LISZT

Rome, he was a priest. Perhaps he wished in this way to explain to the world, which had been in a state of excitement over his projects of marriage with the Princess Wittgenstein that they were definitely abandoned. I believe also that he was relieved at being able to take away from all the women who adored him, the hope of obtaining his hand."

On the other hand, in a letter to Prince Constantine, Liszt says: "I entered into the ecclesiastical state on receiving minor orders in the chapel of H.S.H. Mgr. Hohenlohe at the Vatican. Convinced as I was that this act would strengthen me on the right road, I accomplished it without effort, in all simplicity and uprightness of intention—I do not intend to become a monk in the severe sense of the word. For this I have no vocation. It is therefore not the frock but the cassock which I have donned."

Liszt, at this time, occupied a cloister with a Dominican Father at the Santa Mario del Rosario, from which an extensive view of Rome is to be had.

Writing at this time Schlözer in his "Letters from Rome,"* says:

"To-day, April 25, 1865, something happened that will cause the greatest sensation everywhere. Franz Liszt has received the tonsure—thus renouncing the world, and garbed in canonical vestments he will seek in religion the peace which his life has not afforded him hitherto. (The Princess Wittgenstein

* (In German.) Publisher, Deutscher Verlagt Anstalt. (See the "Etude," August, 1934.)

fearing that Liszt might marry and thus not become a devotee, put the whole Vatican into motion to have him appointed as a Canon of the Church."

The Princess was devoted to the Church and wrote voluminously on church matters. Her petition to the Vatican was evidently intended to shield Liszt from the attentions of the "crazy satellite countesses"—and she was successful. (See Part III, Memorabilia.)

One part of his life was also spent annually at Weimar where he had now been invested with the sinecure office of Grand Chamberlain; a beautiful residence within the domain had been built and furnished for him.

A National Hero.

Liszt at the Hungarian Coronation.

In 1867 Liszt visited Budapest for the coronation of the king. The Emperor of Austria was being crowned King of Hungary. An immense crowd was collected to see the procession cross the bridge over the Danube joining Buda to Pesth. Suddenly "the tall figure of a priest, in a long black cassock studded with decorations, was seen to descend the broad white road leading to the Danube, which had been kept clear for the royal procession." "The name of Liszt flew down the serried ranks from mouth to mouth, swift as a flash af lightning. Soon a hundred thousand men and women were frantically applauding him, wild with excitement of this whirlwind of voices."

Not long after—from 1870, Liszt paid annual visits to Pesth, and in 1871 the Hungarian Government ennobled him and gave him a pension.

In 1873 his jubilee was made a national event. Liszt was the national hero of Hungary. His jubilee stipend of £600 he, however, returned to the municipality of Budapest for the artists, and the Patent of Nobility was declined. In 1873 he was appointed director of the new Academy of Music of Budapest.

CHAPTER XII.

HUNGARY AND THE RHAPSODIES.

The gipsy orchestras. The Rhapsody. Gipsy epics. Remenyi.

"They must be played as Liszt played them, as the gipsies played the melodies and the ornaments he borrowed from them—after the fashion of gipsy improvisations."—FINCK.

It was totally wrong to estimate and classify Liszt as a follower of the German classic and romantic schools of composition. A new era arose with Chopin and Liszt, the former as the exponent of the soul of Poland, the latter of Hungary.* The Magyars of Hungary are descended from the Turanian as allied to the Persian race. Besides the Magyars there are the Gipsies, also of oriental origin—really a dual people, and a most musical one. Hungary possesses its own folk songs and dances or Czardas, and its own national instruments—the reed, *furulya and tarogato* (oboe). The Zimbalon (a form of dulcimer) is the special feature of gipsy orchestras.

The gipsy string bands play the Magyar melodies from memory with an extemporised and highly

---

* See the author's "History of Pianoforte Music," Pt. IV. Era of National Music.

elaborate accompaniment on the zimbalom. The zimbalom is played with two wooden sticks, with covered ends. With its six octaves, it is not unlike a small grand, and the tone "wiry" like a piano. Quick arpeggios, tremolos and extended leaps are the features of the playing. These are reproduced in the piano rhapsodies and account for their unique individuality, though they also need the characteristic gipsy interpretation.

The "Hallgatok" and "Rhapsody" consists of both songs and dance melodies. The characteristics of the "Rhapsody" are scale work, augmented intervals, abrupt rhythms, accented weak beats, bold changes of key as exhibited in the alternating "Lassan" or slow and pathetic air and the "Friska"—a wild and furious air.

There are various collections of national music, and though Liszt composed much in the romantic style, Hungarian influence is certainly generally present, especially in his florid movements.

Liszt compared himself to the gipsies saying: "Like them I was a stranger to the people of every country." "I became a wandering virtuoso as they are in our fatherland." His "Gipsy in Music"* is very full and informative:

Part I. The Wandering Races (the Jew and the Gipsy. Liszt animadverts on the Jew).

Part II. Gipsy Life in Relation to Art.

Part III. Gipsy Music and Musicians.

---

* Two volumes (Reeves).

Liszt aims at proving that the so-called Hungarian melodies are originally of gipsy origin, but the Magyar composers have also composed in the same style. See introduction by Edwin Evans.

It is said that Remenyi, the celebrated Hungarian violinist (whom the writer met several times in South Africa, and heard extemporise in private), and who was a frequent visitor to Liszt, suggested the airs treated by Liszt in his rhapsodies.* The rhapsodies vary in form, but generally consist of (1) an introduction; (2) "Lassan"—treated in sequence, imitation or variation form; (3) a figura or trio which connects (4) with the "Friska." We must remember the natural improvisation manner of the gipsy music. Few gipsies read, and they play by ear and extemporise their parts.

Of all the rhapsodies of Liszt, No. 3 is perhaps the simplest. It comprises the heavy bass theme in the andante, the quicker allegretto in the relative minor, together with the andante and the allegretto now in the tonic major. One obstacle to the popularisation of Liszt's works with the ordinary amateur has been their difficulty. It is, however, possible to make easy and graded selections (see Part III) and the third rhapsody forms a good introduction to the series. No. 2 is the most popular; and the finest is No. 12 with its four separate themes. Note the *Quasi Improvisatore* of No. 1. Improvisation is as before

* See Remenyi's statement in Chapter XXII under "Hungarian Music." Liszt devotes two pages in his "Gipsy in Music" to a eulogy of Remenyi, p. 369-70.

mentioned a feature of zimbalom work; also the merry galop in octaves in No. 4. No. 5 is elegant and resembles a nocturne. No. 6 opens in martial humour and has a cadenza on the black keys and like No. 4 it closes with a merry octave allegro. No. 7 is comparatively easy, with a dramatic march theme in the vivace. No. 8 has a dramatic theme in the bass and a lively final presto on the black keys—there are none on the zimbalom, of course—but good technique on the black keys of the piano is a very necessary feature of the modern pianoforte school. No. 9 appropriately possesses a very jolly finale in "the Carnival of Pesth." No. 10 has the elements of a caprice with *quasi zimbalo* effects and *glissandos*. No. 11 enters with a tremolando *quasi zimbalo* and finishes with a merry Prestissimo in F sharp. No. 12 has its "Zingarese" or gipsy allegro. No. 13 features a pathetic ornate andante. No. 14 enters with a funeral march but also possesses a gipsy allegro. No. 15 is the famous "Rakoczy March" with zimbalom cadenzas. Other rhapsodies ap-

Twelfth Rhapsody.

peared later, viz., Nos. 16 to 19 (Universal Edition only), these are in similar style generally, but they are not so florid and they lack much of the characteristic zimbalom style. These and other Hungarian works are treated in Chapters XXII and XXIII.

As a boy Liszt had revelled in the music of Beethoven and the gipsy tunes; he early published two sets of Hungarian melodies and was among the first to use the national airs. So enthusiastic was he that he lived for a time in the gipsy tents in order to study and take down their traditional tunes. Miss Janka Wohl, Liszt's Hungarian biographer, says: "The Hungarian rhapsodies show us Hungary in its lyrical and martial aspect." "The saying that 'Weeping, the Magyar rejoices' describes exactly the Magyar disposition." The melodies "from the national lyre unfold the whole gamut of sentiment, resignation, love's sorrows, the joy of shared misfortune, desire and self-denial, and the mourning of the patriot."

Gipsy Epics.

Liszt's purpose was to form a series of "Gipsy Epics," they are much more than transcriptions, and, as he intended, they manifest "the close affinity of subject matter and the similarity of feature and unity in development."

Remenyi, the typical Hungarian violinist wrote: "I always improvise my variations before the audience, never playing them twice alike—as the writer on one occasion personally heard. Liechtenstein, the

Hungarian musician, aptly says: "The imagination of the Hungarian gipsy changes the songs into dances and the dances into songs." "With oriental fire the Magyar holds his maiden and turns her like a whirlwind till his breath is gone,"—"but his song is more earnest and his centuries of trouble and desire for grandeur are reflected." "He only smiles through tears, and mourning he rejoices."

Remenyi relates in his "Biography," how when on tour with the youthful Brahms, they went to call on Liszt in Weimar in 1852. Young Remenyi was almost overwhelmed by Liszt's presence, but Liszt's "kind manner and fine conversation put him completely at ease." Liszt invited the two to stay with him at the Altenburg and played over Brahms's MS. at sight. An audition of the Liszt "pupils" or admirers followed, when young Brahms, "overcome with fatigue, calmly slept in a fauteuil" while Liszt was playing. This unfortunately was the beginning of an estrangement between Liszt—the leader of the romantics—and Brahms as the subsequent leader of the classics.

The author of "Personal Recollections" ("Strelezki"—or Burnand) recounts a meeting with Liszt who declared that "Brahms is a very great composer; he may be said to be a continuation of Schumann, but he lacks Schumann's spontaneity." He also said that "Brahms is the worst pianist I ever heard." Von Schlözer also relates an incident at Liszt's monastic retreat in Rome:

"Remenyi, a splendid violinist, entered. Liszt

had recently composed Lenau's Gipsy Song and Remenyi played on his violin. Liszt accompanied at the piano." "The work is very original and Remenyi's Hungarian blood grew so frenzied that he started to dance about while playing, as his fellow Magyars used to do in Puszta."

CHAPTER XIII.

ROME, BUDAPEST, PARIS, LONDON.

Life in Rome. Visits to Russia. Last visit to London. Death at Bayreuth.

FINIS.

"No mortal can vie with Liszt; he dwells upon a solitary height."—TAUSIG.

It is difficult to realise that Liszt, the petted hero of the courts of Europe, should eventually have settled down to his quiet life in Rome, which he left only to make occasional visits to Budapest, Weimar, etc.

LIFE AT ROME.

One day Liszt in conversation said: "There is nothing so sublime as true independence of character unsupported by pecuniary independence.

He had come to learn the fickleness of applauding crowds, and so he practically retired in order to devote himself to composition. Writing to Mme. Lipsius, who under the name of La Mara, later published his correspondence, he says: "Since the end of '47 I have not earned a farthing by piano-playing, teaching or conducting. All this rather cost me time and money. Since the year '47 I have only played twice in public in Rome—in 1863 and 1864—at the gracious command of Pope Pius IX; occasionally in Budapest later on, twice in Vienna, once in Presburg and Odenburg (my native town) as a child of the country. Nowhere else. May my poor pianoforte performing terminate."

His powers did not seem to rust, however, and when he did appear his playing was marvellous. In 1874—asked to go to a festival at Liverpool he replied that he played only for charity. He had been asked to "state terms" and this drew the retort that no one "had dreamed of offering me any remuneration in money." In 1877 he appeared at a Beethoven Festival held in Vienna. For the rest he was occupied with his life of devotion and he was the centre also of an artistic circle in which the Italian-English Sgambati and Von Rendell were prominent.

Italy, with its romantic history, the ruins of Rome, Italian gardens, the Villa D'Este, etc., appealed to him; these—and the Italian poets inspired the Italian album and the symphonic poems, "Dante," "Tasso," "Orpheus," "Prometheus" and "Les Preludes."

His religious aspirations were the mainspring of such works as the two St. Francois legends, the oratorio of St. Elizabeth and Christus, the Graner mass, Psalms 13, 116 and 128, and the Hungarian Coronation Mass. His songs, organ works, part-songs and transcriptions are too numerous to mention here and reference must be had to the published list of his compositions. (See also Chapter XXV.)

During those years his mornings were spent in composing and answering his numerous correspondents. His secretary says: "Letters came to him from all parts of the world." "Always and invariably the same idolatry— he must have been sick of it." The autographists became so numerous that he had to refuse them through a printed paragraph. Begging letters came in shoals, and he was annoyed when found "with a pile of bank notes and letters with addresses on them in his handwriting. 'You find me hard at work on a tough job,' said he, 'I am playing at Providence. It is a thankless part, but still I have to go through with it.' Miss Wohl suggested it would be simpler to send these amounts by postal orders. 'No, my dear child,' said he, 'one must gild the pill with an affectionate line or two.'"

Liszt's afternoons were usually spent in teaching, and his evenings in the society of his friends.

With all his engagements Liszt had always a friendly word of encouragement for the aspirant.

It was during one of his periodic visits to Weimar that young MACDOWELL (1861-1908), aged twenty, called on Liszt in the spring of 1882. Liszt "received him with kindly courtesy and had Eugen D'Albert, who was present, play the orchestral part of the Concerto which Macdowell had brought with him in manuscript, arranged for two pianos. Liszt listened attentively—and commended it in warm terms: 'You must bestir yourself,' he warned

D'Albert, 'if you do not wish to be outdone by our young American.'"*

It is of this period that Weingartner† gives his impressions of Liszt in his old age, i.e., in 1882, mentioning that Liszt's striking features were not impaired by the large warts. He also mentions that at his auditions or classes Liszt made use of a typical gesture of emphasis—an imperious, vehement, downward sweep of his right hand, with a click of the second and third fingers, accompanied by a short guttural sound. On one occasion a pretty girl who played badly, was gently guided to the door. The master bestowed a parting kiss on her forehead, and whispered "You must marry, my dear child."

Guided by his motto, "Génie oblige," Liszt esteemed his deeds of self-sacrifice as a duty. Walter Damrosch‡ (whose father was a friend of Liszt's) who was born in Breslau in 1862, was brought up in America. As a young man of twenty he paid a visit to Bayreuth in 1882, and was kindly received by Liszt. Damrosch spoke of staying only two days. The same evening he was accosted by Lassen with "What did you do to the master this morning?" Lassen had found him in tears, and Liszt had said, "I thought he would stay and study with me. The younger generation think nothing of me.

---

* Gilman's "Ed. Macdowell" (Lane). D'Albert was born in Glasgow in 1862, and was trained at the R.C.M. in London.

† "Musical Times," March, 1933.

‡ "My Musical Life," Damrosch (Allen and Unwin).

They have no respect for us older men." Early next morning Damrosch waited on Liszt and apologised. He says, "Suddenly I felt his arms about me, and a very gentle furtive kiss placed upon my forehead."

Liszt spent the year 1884 at Weimar and Pesth. He went to Bayreuth to be present at "Parsifal," where his daughter was mourning the death of her husband (Wagner), then returning to Hungary he visited his friend, Count Zichy. The peasants on the estate gave him an ovation. Hundreds of young girls showered flowers on him. He was amongst his own people, and so he gave them a free concert, at the end of which an old peasant addressed him: "Your name the Count has told us. What you are able to do you have shown us; but what you are we have learned ourselves. May God, the Protector of Hungary, bless you."

One feature of Liszt's life was the succession of visits to Russia over a period of forty years, and during which he was fêted and made much of. Liszt said he was very happy at St. Petersburg. In 1885 the Grand Duke Constantine wrote to him as "the eminent musical genius revered by all," asking him to be present at the musical fête proposed to be given in his honour.

Rev. H. R. Haweis, who met Liszt some six times in all, spoke to Liszt in 1881 about his coming to England. Liszt was averse to coming. Haweis said to him:* "So you will not come to England?"—"I

* Haweis, "My Musical Life," p. 670.

have travelled so much; I have gone about the world till I am tired. I change residences three times a year, Pesth, Weimar, Rome; the first time I was in England I was taken there by Count Esterhazy; you know he was a great friend of George IV. That was in 1824."

"You were at Antwerp last year; we all thought you might have come across."

"I was there," he replied, "I shall never go across again."

Liszt was not fond of the sea; he was, however, ultimately persuaded, and the last year of his life, 1885-6, was distinguished by visits to, and special honours in Paris and London, where he had early won distinction. The visits to Paris were both on going and returning from London. His "Gran Mass" was performed at the Church of St. Eustache in Paris, at his first visit.

Last Visit to London.

Liszt had not been to London for forty-five years, but he was there accorded a great reception. He was entertained privately at the house of Mr. Littleton, at Sydenham, when three hundred guests assembled to do him honour, and led by Walter Bache, his great upholder in this country, a programme was rendered from Liszt's works. His distinguished and venerable appearance won the sympathies of all. He arrived on Saturday, April 3, 1886, and on the Monday attended a rehearsal of his "St. Elizabeth." On the Wednesday he was present at the concert, and was awarded a tremendous ovation. Next day, Thursday, Liszt went by invitation to Windsor Castle, and had the honour of playing before her Majesty Queen Victoria. At the reception given at the Grosvenor Gallery, attended by three to four hundred notables, Liszt played a Hungarian Rhapsody, and in the evening (Friday) attended a smoking concert given in his honour, at which the Prince of Wales (later King Edward) made Liszt sit by his side.

Every day witnessed some special function, and eventually, after a triumphal fortnight,* Liszt returned to Paris by way of Antwerp, where another performance was a great success.

Death at Bayreuth.

From there the master went to Jena, Sondershausen and Weimar, which was reached by May 17, some weeks later. He played, for the last time, at the Castle of Colpach in Luxembourg. Travelling thence to Bayreuth, he was apparently suffering from a chill, and though he sat through a performance of "Tristan" on July 25, he grew worse, and passed away on Sunday, August 1, 1886, at the age of seventy-five. He was buried near the grave of his friend, Wagner.

Walter Bache managed to get to the funeral—the notice was short, and he writes: "None of Liszt's *old* pupils were there, no Bülow, Prückner, Rubin-

---

* Described in Chapter XXVI.

stein; only Klindworth, to whom Constance Bache had telegraphed." Bache concludes: "Now good-bye, my dear friend, to whom I owe the greatest privilege of my life—his life was one of
self-sacrifice and self-renunciation."

PART II.

CHAPTER XIV.

LISZT'S TECHNIQUE.

A revolution in piano playing. Piano orchestration. Various opinions.

> "Behold! on that pale brow
> Precocious genius hath its seal impressed."

> "The whole school of piano playing of the present day takes its style and direction from Liszt."—DICKINSON.

Liszt was the supreme virtuoso of the piano of all time, his fame stands out beyond that of all others before or since. Altogether apart from his masterly compositions the query naturally arises—did Liszt accomplish anything in the realm of piano technique of permanent value? This can be answered by WEITZMANN, who says: *

REVOLUTION IN PIANO PLAYING.

"His indescribably vigorous and powerful playing caused a *complete revolution* in pianoforte playing, pianoforte literature and pianoforte construction; he elevated virtuosity to a dizzy height, and

* "Æsthetics of Piano Playing."

has seemingly exhausted the means of expression of his instrument so far that a further enhancement would seem hardly imaginable."

The technique which had centred in Mozart, Clementi and Beethoven was extended through Hummel and Moscheles. The great virtuoso, John Field, of Dublin, emphasised the lyric aspect, i.e., the art of singing at the piano, and this phase was adopted by Thalberg, Chopin and Liszt as a foundation. The Etude form then began to predominate, and, as Kullak says:* "Now all becomes movement—technique develops in everything." The wrist and arm touch came to the fore, and with the more powerful English piano action the instrument became an orchestra under Dreyschock and Liszt. "Les Etudes de Chopin, malgré leur émouvante beauté, continuent logiquement, les études de Clementi, Czerny et Cramer. Liszt amène un bouleversement, il crée la technique d'articulation du coude et l'épaule, reclamant des bras une gymnastique réservée jusqu' alors au poignet et à la main"—in short, Liszt created greater *freedom* in piano technique. Liszt made unheard of demands on the executant, and his technique was necessary to fulfil these demands. At the same time their difficulty was not so great as appeared. As Saint-Saëns says: "Sa musique effrayante à première vue pour les timides, est-elle, en réalité, *moins difficile-qu'elle ne parait.*"†

* "History of Pianoforte Playing" (Lessman Ed., 1887).

† "La Revue Musicale," Liszt number.

PIANOFORTE. ORCHESTRAS.

Chopin and Henselt shunned the glare of the platform, but their compositions pointed the way, one which was crowned by Liszt, both in public and in his compositions—and mainly at first through his Transcriptions, which at that time only he himself could play. Liszt was then induced to write less difficult arrangements, and Weitzmann enumerates of these the following:

BEETHOVEN, Fifth, Sixth, Seventh and Ninth Symphonies, Funeral March ("Eroïca" Symphony), Septet. BERLIOZ, "Harold" Symphony. WEBER'S "Freischütz," "Oberon" and "Jubilee" Overtures. ROSSINI'S "William Tell" Overture. BERLIOZ'S Overtures to "King Lear" and the "Francs-Juges." WAGNER'S "Tannhäuser" Overture, and NICOLAI'S Fest Overture. Under Liszt's hands, "the pianoforte was transformed to a thrilling organ, now to a soothing Æolian harp; the ear was charmed with demoniac harmonies and dulcet flute tones, while weird melodies were adorned with marvellous arabesques." Schumann, in 1840, said: "The instrument glows and flames under its master—no longer playing of a certain kind—but the manifestation of a dauntless imperial character." How then was all this accomplished? Different positions of the hand and different actions of the fingers had been used during periods of the development of the piano. Weitzmann says:

"Liszt did not hold his hand horizontally, but

with the wrist higher than the front part, so that a coin laid on the back would slide down to the keyboard."

Such a position undoubtedly gives more power and brilliance in chord and octave work. The depth of fall of the finger is reduced, however, and power comes from the *elbow*, and it is a question whether the more modern development of touch, as under Leschetitzky and Breithaupt, with a loose, supple wrist sloping the *reverse* way, giving scope for weight and rotatory touches and a deeper fall of the finger with more varied dynamics, does not give the best foundation. At the same time the crossing and interlocking of hands is favoured by a high seat; these technical features and the special development of the left hand are necessary for Liszt's works.

Breithaupt's Opinion.

Breithaupt writes: "What chiefly distinguished Liszt's technique was the absolute freedom of his arms—a thorough command and use of the freely rolling forearm. He played by weight—by a swinging and a hurling of weight from a loosened shoulder that had nothing in common with what is known as finger manipulation."

Chopin "lacks the broad sweep that gives Liszt's technique its peculiar freedom and adaptability to the instrument," and Liszt: "Everything he writes sounds well."

Of course, it is understood that Liszt adapted his touch to requirements, and we must not confuse individuality, interpretation and hypnotic influence, with any method of technique. It is significant that while in Liszt's time there were few executants equal to the technical work in Liszt's virtuoso pieces, nowadays the Conservatoriums turn them out by the score.

The REV. H. R. HAWEIS heard him play twice in Rome, and speaks of the "perfect effortless independence of his fingers," and "the first finger and thumb drawn together to emphasise a note, or the fingers doubled up, then lifted in a peculiar manner, with a gentle sweep in the middle of a phrase."

TECHNIQUE V. INDIVIDUALITY.

As an instance of technique v. individuality, let me quote from the "Musical Opinion" of December, 1930, when MR. OSMOND ANDERTON heard Liszt play at the Royal Academy, on his last visit to London.

"We had most of us felt some reserve beforehand, but no sooner did he appear than the whole gathering rose in a sort of frenzy of enthusiasm. Such was his peculiar hypnotic influence. He was persuaded to play; nothing big, merely an extemporisation upon a song; but no piano has ever sounded the same to me, before or since."

WEINGARTNER remarks his "dream-like touch—with arms and body so still that one got the impression of the piano being magnetised rather than played."

SIR ALEXANDER MACKENZIE, who was present,

avers that "even in his fiercest virtuoso days, Liszt never thumped." Liszt had remarked, "They do not *play*, they *thrash* the piano nowadays."

SIR CHARLES STANFORD, in his "Unwritten Diary" says: "It is the age of the *hit* instead of *pressure.* I shall always prefer beauty of tone to strength of muscle. And beauty of tone was precisely what I found to be the predominant quality both in Liszt and Rubinstein. Liszt always played for musicians with an immovable body and a quiet, repressed dignity, reserving his acrobatic performances for audiences whom in his heart he despised."

Regarding Liszt's downward, sloping position of the fingers, this may have been owing to his height, and as Busoni, his pupil, remarks: "Technique systems are best when they are individual." Hand, arm and fingers vary with each individual, and the ideal way is to ascertain the basic principles of execution as they are affected by one's own deficiencies. It is a noteworthy fact that Liszt did not discuss technique. "That you must work out for yourself," was his observation according to AMY FAY, though as DR. MASON relates, he would also say, "Don't play it that way, play it like this." Special effects he was always inventing. Asked how he got a certain effect in his "Flying Dutchman" Fantasia, "Liszt played the beginning of the arpeggio in a grand rolling manner," and then all the rest of it *pp* and so lightly that "the notes seemed to be just *strewn* in—a most striking and beautiful effect."

The special feature of Liszt's work is the Cadenza

which is always introduced for an artistic purpose. As a zephyr breathing gently, it may provide beautiful contrasts, or in a brilliant, sparkling way heighten a climax.

SAINT-SAËNS, the composer and virtuoso pupil of Liszt, wrote: "Power, delicacy and charm along with a rightly accented rhythm were his, in addition to an unusual warmth of feeling, impeccable precision and that gift of suggestion which creates great orators, the leaders and guides of the masses."

KLINDWORTH, the editor, says he did the most astonishing things with his left thumb, and with his long fingers could play tenths as easily as eighths. Apart from technique, what gave Liszt his great preeminence was his *spiritualisation*; and just as one must play the Rhapsodies in the gipsy improvisatory fashion, so, too, in general, in the interpretation of Liszt's works must one realise in their interpretation

The Spirit of Liszt.

CHAPTER XV.

LISZT AND ART.

Influence of art and poetry. Effectiveness first. His individuality.

"Beauty of sound is above all rule, as beauty of form is above æsthetics."—SCHUMANN.

"Liszt stands at the fountain-head of all the new developments of the second half of the nineteenth century."—DR. EAGLEFIELD HULL.

INFLUENCE OF ART AND POETRY.

Liszt, in his creative sphere, was strongly influenced by every branch of art, especially painting as a complement of music. The painting, "The Battle of the Huns," by Kaulbach, suggested the title for his symphonic poem of that name, while pictures representing St. Elizabeth on the Wartburg at Eisenach suggested his oratorio, "St. Elizabeth."

The poetry of Dante inspired his "Dante Symphony," and the "Legends of St. Francis" his "Sermon to the Birds" and "St. Francis Walking on the Waters."

It is curious that the painter, Doré, who heard the "Dante" Symphony, should have been in his turn inspired by Liszt's music, to depict the latter scene, as well as one of his "Inferno" scenes—also that the "Sermon to the Birds" has been depicted by an English painter, Smallfield. Liszt's artistic oneness is truly shown in a letter to Berlioz:

"Art first appears to my astonished eyes in all its glory and unveils her universality." "Raphael and Michael Angelo help me to understand Mozart and Beethoven."

It was Raphael's picture which, as mentioned, inspired the "Sposalizio" and Michael Angelo's statue his "Il Penseroso" (Années II).

Another work influenced by art is the "Todtentanz" or "Danse Macabre," for piano and orchestra.* This was suggested by a Florentine fresco, "The Triumph of Death," in the Campo Santo at Pisa. It consists of variations on the old plain-chant, "Dies Iræ."

Liszt, like all the great composers, has the defects of his qualities. We need only instance BACH'S choral works in instrumental style, BEETHOVEN, who was weak in his *lieder*, MOZART, the writer of fashionable but somewhat trifling educational sonatas, and others. Liszt's works encountered much criticism in his day. He was judged by past standards instead of new. Schumann, the romantic, could admire the Mendelssohn who clung to classic ideals, but the latter looked coldly on his more advanced contemporary.

---

* Not to be confused with the Liszt transcription (Durand) of the "Danse Macabre" by Saint-Saëns.

EFFECTIVENESS FIRST.

Liszt was quite correct in putting effectiveness first and in treating the form and thematic detail as of secondary importance, and, for the rest, we certainly expect his national traits to come to the front —they constitute the spice of life in music.

Just as we are attracted by the Norwegian rhythms and beautiful new harmonies of Grieg, so do Hungarian rhythms, unsual scale (or augmented) intervals, the aplomb, or the dramatic *flair*, of Liszt appeal to us. Play Liszt's "Liebestraume," No. 3, and similar works of Beethoven, such as the Adagio of the Moonlight Sonata, Mozart, Schubert and Mendelssohn before a representative and average audience who do not know the works or the composers, and Liszt, I am sure, will get most acclaim. Liszt's works have both individuality and magnetism, qualities which count in the long run. One critic, writing of Liszt's Symphonic Poems, says they are "not like the Sonata and the Symphony, condemned beforehand to follow a certain course, to fill a predetermined mould." Unfortunately for this statement, there is nothing freer in actual form than Fugue or Sonata form.

Beethoven, for instance, was always trying new ways in his Sonatas, and his various experiments and presentations of sonata form have given to his Sonatas a permanent place in the affections of all. Liszt trod new paths also, and now his greatness is becoming more and more apparent to unprejudiced hearers.

Calvocoressi, the critic, has well said, "Liszt was the first to apply the principle of *thematic unity* which composers of to-day have now universally adopted.

Liszt, for his part, tried to give new works a hearing at Weimar. He quotes from his experience when he says: "The questions of money, of clique, and of small professional jealousies, lie in wait for rising talent, like so many wild beasts." He tried to counter what he had to endure himself both in earlier and later times, and now that conflicting parties and passions have waned we are enabled to see him as he really is.

There is a significant story told. Liszt thought very highly of Thalberg as an artist. On one occasion a somewhat tactless friend asked of Liszt whom he esteemed to be the greatest pianist. Liszt answered:

"Thalberg, of course."

"And where do you place yourself?"

Liszt (grandioso): "*Hors concours*!"*

On the other hand, Liszt, astute as he was on some things, was not averse to playing to the gallery.

PERSONALITY.

Clara Novello, in her Diary, mentions that Liszt "was almost driven to eccentricities by the frenzies of women over him; some of whom absolutely pursued him, nay, ran him down. At Vienna, as elsewhere, when he broke the strings of the piano during

---

* Stanford, "Unwritten Diary."

concerts, the women rushed on the platform to seize them and have bracelets made of them."

No doubt his concert manager had a hand in this kind of thing—they usually do.

It is related that Liszt as "the Master," as he was called, sat for his portrait to Schäffer, the painter, in Paris. Liszt, in the French manner, theatrically posed himself. Schäffer indicated, however, his distaste, and Liszt cried out:

"Forgive me, master, but you cannot know how it spoils one to have been an infant prodigy."

Perhaps Schumann, both as a composer and a critic, had the best means of estimating Liszt's position in the musical world, and he writes:

"He appears to us good and lovable, as is every *sublime personality*—gifted and variable like every true artist.

Liszt's Versatility.

Wagner was also an astute personality, but he could recognise unselfishness and true nobility of character in Liszt.

In one of his letters he wrote:

"I am now convinced myself that you are the greatest musician of all times."

This verdict on Liszt was given by Wagner after a study of Liszt's Symphonic Poems. It is the way of the world not to be able to assess the true position of a composer until long after his death. Bach and Beethoven were striking examples of this, and to these we must add the name of Liszt. To sum up:

Liszt was known (1) as a virtuoso, (2) as a writer of piano transcriptions, (3) as a composer of piano solo works, (4) of orchestral works, (5) of choral works, (6) as a *littérateur* and author.

All great composers have their limitations, whether vocal, as in the case of Beethoven, or orchestral, as with Chopin, but, except in chamber music and opera, Liszt is to be numbered with the great.

HIS INDIVIDUALITY.

In the realm of the piano many pianists are so absorbed in the requirement of the necessary technical mastery that they are apt to overlook the *poetic* worth of his works. There are, of course, as with every composer, compositions immature and below their usual standard; but, if we select his representative works and, looking for characteristic features, do not forget also the emotional charm and tender expression, we shall be satisfied. His style is not that of Bach or Beethoven—his individuality is, however, striking and compelling. Interpretation is the keynote and, just as Chopin said, "I should like to rob him of his way of rendering my own Etudes," and, as Schumann declared regarding Liszt's interpretation of his own "Novellettes," Fantasia and Sonata, "the details were quite different from what I had conceived them—*but always inspired by Genius.*"

It has been well said that "Notes are but the symbols of music."

The average interpreter of these symbols gives merely a mechanical translation, but when the executant makes these symbols throb with life, we have the *artist.*

Best of all, when the interpreter puts in something beyond these, we hail him as a genius.

It is the spirit underlying the notes which signifies. It is intuition, or psychic insight, which displays *genius.* (See also Chapter XXI—Transcription.)

A Pioneer.

We must remember that Liszt was a pioneer. Classicism was going to seed in Germany, and as he told the Russian, Borodin:

"You know Germany, it is full of composers."

Liszt looked to the new Russian school to aid the romantic movement, and said, "With you there exists a vitalising stream," and later, "You Russians are indispensable to us." As we know now, it is the Russian school which has carried forward the development of Liszt's style to a summit.

As an innovator, Liszt was alive to modern ideas, the *leitmotif* (as developed by Wagner) was made use of to full extent, along with the principle of theme metamorphosis or transformation. He secured unity by new means. As a literary man he was also able to defend and publish his view. True to romanticism, his works were inspired directly by pictorial art or literature, to which in aim they were allied—they tended toward a programme. Every composer embodies in himself something of the past which is thus presented in a new light; in this Liszt was certainly supreme, and in that lay his originality.

He was not naturally introspective, but his muse is of the exalted, epic order, with ever sustained interest, and building up of the necessary artistic climax. His harmonies, especially, seek new paths, and he makes use of unwonted intervals derived from national sources. In himself he was a National, and yet he was a Universal; his music appeals to all. In striving for self-expression he always had in view the lofty incentive

Génie oblige.

Chapter XVI.

THE BRAVURA STYLE, ETC.

Liszt's easy pieces. Operatic Fantasias. Wagner Transcriptions. Mendelssohn "Wedding March."

"It is essential that you should train your mind more than your fingers."—Moscheles.

"I would give up all the plaudits of the crowd, if I could only create an imperishable work of art."—Liszt (von Schlözer).

Liszt wrote voluminously. Ramann's Biography in the complete German edition gives a long general list of works, from which Mr. Hervey in his Biography (1911) estimates the number at 1,200-1,300, including about 700 original compositions—Corder (1911) makes the latter 400. Like the works of all great composers, the works of Liszt vary in style and merit.

The bravura style of Liszt, and the exceptional difficulty of some of his works, have spread abroad erroneous ideas as a whole.

Liszt's Easy Pieces.

"Some day," writes Von Bülow, "I shall make a list of all of Liszt's pieces for piano which most amateurs will find much easier to master than the chaff of Thalberg, or the wheat of Henselt and Chopin." Whether Bülow did this is not known, but now the writer presents graded lists of Easy Pieces in Part III, Chapter XXVII.

Von Bülow was right in another way when he said, "There are no easy pieces; all are difficult"—that is, if you play them in the right way. Touch makes the pianist, and as Rubinstein, Liszt's pupil, said to his pupils, "Listen to good singing and endeavour to sing on the piano," and then we can master "easy pieces."

Rubinstein in playing "seemed to caress the sounds from the instrument where others struck them" (McArthur). Fuller Maitland, on Liszt in "Grove," speaks of "the peculiar quiet brilliance of his rapid passages," and says that "it is quite a mistake to suppose that the habit of thumping, which so many of his pupils and followers thought fit to adopt, came from himself."

TECHNICAL FEATURES.

It may be asked: What were the "technical requirements" of Liszt's compositions? Perhaps I cannot do better than quote from Oscar Bie.* There were unheard of *leaps* and *disjunctions* which seemed impossible, "deep tremolos of fifths like a dozen kettle-drums, which rushed forth in wild chords," a rhythmical polyphony, "chords set sharply over one

* "History of Pianoforte Playing" (Dent).

another throughout seven octaves." "Resolution of tied notes on octaves with intervening harmonies," "the extended use of tenths," "the interweaving of high and low notes for light and shade." "Tremolos, glissandos and interlacing of the hands with orchestral chording effect; and, to accomplish all this, an extended and original fingering was necessary."

These striking new effects and new disposition of the hands require special preparation. Beringer says in his "Technical Studies," as founded on those of Tausig, the distinguished pupil of Liszt:

"Chopin's advent knocked the first nail into the coffin of Clementi and Cramer system and fingering."

What Chopin introduced Liszt completed—and it is essential for any adequate preparation for Liszt that an all-round fluency on the black keys be first attained, by using the identical fingering of the central key of C on such keys as A flat, D flat, F sharp.* If an approach to Liszt be made through Chopin, then the distinctive features of the Pole are graphically illustrated by Heller's Op. 154, Twenty-one Special Studies (Ashdown).

Given the technical mastery of the black keys, is it possible for the ordinary student to successfully attempt all that is worth playing of Liszt's works? The answer is, Liszt's works in themselves provide all that is necessary if properly graded.

---

* An admirable short cut is available in O'Neill's "Exercises for the Weaker Fingers" (Novello), as practised in these keys.

TRANSCRIPTIONS.

One function of the piano is to bring within the scope of two hands, orchestral, chamber, choral and operatic music; all fall to be represented in this way and more or less faithfully. SIR EDWARD ELGAR has said:

"The piano dominates things in the present day, and no two things could be more dissimilar than the piano and orchestra. Moreover, harmonic effects differ in the one and the other because in the orchestra 'colour' could be emphasised. It might sound execrable on the piano, but very beautiful indeed on the orchestral instruments for which it was designed." It will be seen that it may be very difficult to give anything like a faithful representation of an orchestral or operatic work on the piano. The transcriber must indeed create anew to some extent, and in this art Liszt was supreme.

Liszt tried his prentice hand on the operatic Fantasias which had the advantage of presenting melodies which were then popular. BERLIOZ refers to Liszt's orchestral representations on the piano in a letter appearing in the former's "Musical Wandering through Germany."

"Proudly you can exclaim, like Louis XIV, 'I am the orchestra! I am the chorus! At my grand piano I sing, dream, rejoice, and it excels in rapidity the nimblest bows.' Like the orchestra it has its whispering flutes and pealing horns."

THE OPERATIC FANTASIAS.

"Whoever wants to know what Liszt has really done for the piano should study his old operatic Fantasias, they represent the classicism of the piano."—BRAHMS (Interview with Friedheim).

"Artiste puissant, sublime dans des grandes choises, toujours supérieur dans les petites."—("GEORGES SAND.")

There are some thirty-six operatic Fantasias in all. Liszt began his career in the realm of the operatic Fantasia. It was the best medium for his phenomenal technique of that time. He had thus to stoop to conquer—especially in Italy, which was devoted almost solely to opera. The Fantasias were probably at first improvised, and were so successful that publishers besieged him for the actual composition.

They resemble in some measure the opera overture since they are supposed to represent the leading themes artificially joined together. Liszt, however, went further, he gives a good deal of his own, and more than that, for—like the accomplished extemporiser who takes a theme for his task—he makes a composition of his own, with the original theme appearing here and there like a silver thread running through a cloth of gold. Berlioz, whose themes were used, pointed out how Liszt improved on the original, as in the ingenious combination of the composer's own ideas. The late PROF. NIECKS said in 1916:

"Liszt's Fantasias are marvellously effective,

dazzlingly brilliant, excitingly musical and intellectual. Flashes of *esprit* in the guise of novel and surprising harmonies, modulations and combinations of all sorts, are scattered over every one of them."

SAINT-SAËNS ON THE FANTASIA.

SAINT-SAËNS, in his "Portraits et Souvenirs," says, too: "There is a good deal of pedantry and prejudice, be it said in passing, in the disdain often affected towards works such as the Fantasia on 'Don Juan' or the 'Caprice' on the Waltz from 'Faust.'"

It should be remembered that Liszt also made admirable presentations of opera overtures, such as "Tannhäuser," "William Tell," Weber's "Oberon" and "Jubilee" Overtures.

Not content with that, he did what has been termed a great achievement, the transcribing, or forming of, practical piano scores (Partitions de Piano) of Hummel's Septet, Berlioz's and Beethoven's Symphonies. Let us remember Liszt's eminently unselfish character—he put others first, and, as Mr. Antcliffe* has said, "In the transmutation of simple, almost crude musical ideas, with novel expressions, he has been approached by few and excelled probably by Beethoven alone."

The early operatic Fantasias were Liszt's "battle horses," his means of displaying his great technique and of interesting his hearers also in good and popular themes. In so doing he raised the level of the

* "Art, Religion and Clothes."

operatic Fantasia of that day from the cheap variation form to one artistically moulded in every detail. He intensified the emotions expressed. Ramann says:

"Liszt's intensifications, each considered as one *crescendo*, do not extend to a certain number of bars or a passage, but rather to an *amplification of ideas* —which in Liszt's Fantasias often increase to an indescribably magnificent stream of tones—displaying the greatest brilliancy and variety of technique without lessening their emotional value."

His early "Pacini 'Niobe' Divertissement" (1837), a work of nineteen pages, is constructed on the "Palpiti Cavatina" (Hofmeister) with wonderful variety and contrast. It is straightforward, practical and not too difficult.

The "Pacini ('Niobe')" and "Lucia" Fantasias were favourite concert solos of Clara Wieck, afterwards Madame Schumann.

Other earlier and favourite works were the "Juive" and the "Puritani" Fantasias.

Opera Fantasias differ according to whether they are (1) constructed on one theme with developments or variations, or (2) contain two or more themes for treatment. The title may differ, appearing as Fantasias, Recreations, Illustrations, Amusements, Rhapsodies, etc. The highly developed Paraphrase and Fantasia should be distinguished from the Transcriptions. The Wagner Transcriptions interpret the one theme which they represent, and they are filled out, to a certain extent, to represent the orchestral score, and therefore they are scarcely to be termed Fantasias. The Rhapsodies and most of the others are built upon more than one theme.

OPERA FANTASIES.

Op. 7, "Reminiscences des Puritains" (Bellini), 1835-6. Dedicated to the Princess Belgioso (Ricordi —also Joubert). This was one of Liszt's early "battle horses." It is brilliant, varied and effective without being really difficult—also "facilité" alternatives are given. It comprises an "Introduction"—with dramatic Tremolando and a Cadenza—"Larghetto" a vibrant "March," duly ornamented, and the "Polonaise," closing with a *presto* climax. It has twenty-seven pages, but can be abbreviated for performance.

The "Polonaise"—with Introduction (nine pages) was also done separately (Schott)—a straightforward and only moderately difficult portion—likewise "Bravura Variations" on the March—which are out of print.

"Reminiscences de la Juive" (Halévy), (Schles.), 32 pages (Op. 9). Like the above, it is an early work (1836). Cuts are suggested, but it is too diffuse and the themes are not distinguished, though temporarily interesting through brilliancy of technique. (Out of print.)

The "Portici" (Auber) Tarantelle Fantasia (Hoff-

THEME OF "THE PROPHET," "LES PATINEURS." FANTASIA.

meister, Lit. and Peters) consists of an Introduction, Tarentelle,* with Episodes and Cadenzas leading to the March in E major. Comprising 23 pages, it needs a cut from the G major section to the Più Presto Scherzo of 6½ pages. This is an effective and attractive work, as is also "The Prophet" (Meyerbeer), "Illustration," No. 29, "Les Patineurs" (Augener) having 29 pages. A cut of 5½ pages from the Scherzo of the seventh page can be made. The scene is laid in Holland at a carnival on the ice. The *glissandos* represent the skaters. ("Portici" and "Prophet" Fantasias also Litolff.) No wonder Fantasias like these were very attractive

* "One of the most effective of his virtuoso pieces," (Sacheverell Sitwell). This should not be confused with the Tarantelle in the Italian Album.

where selected popular themes are used along with brilliant Lisztian technique.

"The "Prophet" Illustration No. 1, in E flat (29 pages), (B. and H.) This is based on the Prayer, the Chorale ("Ad Nos") and the Coronation March. The effect in this until the *tempo rubato*, Op. 20, is reached, is that of a pot-pourri, it lacks unity. The Coronation March, however, from page 20 makes a very effective solo, brilliant and practical.

The "Prophet" Illustration No. 3, G minor (27 pp.), (B. and H.), contains a charming Pastorale up to page 12, and the merry Orgie from page 22, with the three previous bars, makes a bright and attractive piece of about 17 pages, and one worth knowing.

"Huguenots" (Meyerbeer) Reminiscences. "Fantasie Dramatique" (Ricordi), Op. 11. This is one of Liszt's early works. It is 29 pages long, and presents a great variety of effective technical passages backed by intense dramatic atmosphere. A cut from the Cadenza on page 11 to the Finale would render it an attractive and not over-difficult concert piece.

"La Sonnambula" (Bellini). Fantasie on the motives. (Ricordi), 24 pages. Partly owing to the thematic material, this work sounds old-fashioned, and the technical treatment is more ordinary than usual.

Outstanding operatic Fantasies are the Meyerbeer ("Robert le Diable"), Verdi's "Rigoletto" and

"Troubadour" ("Il Trovatore") and Mozart's "Don Juan." (Editions, Peters, Univ. (Vol. 12) and Ricordi.)

The "Rigoletto" and "Troubadour" (1860)* Paraphrases or Fantasias are well known brilliant works, practical, and not too difficult for the average modern well-trained pianist. Both contain velocity arpeggios and chromatic scales. Octave work is taken for granted in more difficult pieces.

The "Don Giovanni" (1841), (Augener) Fantasia is one of the virtuoso works—some 43 pages long. Cuts are suggested in the Augener (M. Pauer) edition, but others are necessary in addition to sustain the interest—these I suggest to be from pages 12 and 13 (of the evolved Allegretto, which weakens it)—from middle page 15 to page 17 (Adagio)—from Cadenza, pages 19 to 22 (second variation)—page 26 *(sotto voce)* to page 33 *(sciolto)*, then omit 35 to 37 and 40 to 43 Andante. The material lacks variety for so greatly extended treatment, notwithstanding which it is a master work. Busoni edited five separate editions of this.

The "Lucia" Fantasia (1840) is published by Hofmeister in the Henselt edition, with interpretation or involved passages given in full of a sustained character. The theme bears well the elaborate ornamentation of shakes and arpeggios superimposed, and makes a brilliant work without excessive difficulty.

The "Norma" (Bellini) Fantasia (Peters), Vol. 8

---

* Peters, Universal (Vol. 12), also Ricordi Editions.

(1841), is long (22 pages), and not all the themes are of interest. It also needs cuts from the Recitative to the Arpeggiando and from the Tempestuoso to the Meno Allegro, but it is brilliant and the performer's powers are extended.*

"Ernani" Fantasia (1860), Verdi. Peters (Ricordi). This is one of the best. It is set out in massive and brilliant but cantabile style—somewhat difficult, but still practical.

"Figaro" Fantasia (Mozart). (B. and H., Busoni.) This is a splendid drill piece for Liszt's highest work —quite a repertoire as technique—but again its 30 pages require cuts for a concert solo. One might, for instance, go from the piu stretto on page 16 to the second line on page 27, thus reducing it to about 20 pages.

It is one of the best and most effective of Liszt's works.

"Don Carlos" (Verdi). Finale (Ricordi). This comprises the Coro di Festa and the Marcia Funebre. The first portion of 5 pages makes a separate piece, the Funeral March follows in the minor mode for 3 pages—the festive chorus again appearing in more brilliant guise. This makes a brilliant, attractive and valuable educational work of 14 pages and of moderate difficulty.

---

* Mr. Sacheverell Sitwell, in his admirable Liszt Biography, just to hand, says, p. 179: "All the Bellini transcriptions are admirable, but his Fantasia upon 'Norma' is a really beautiful work, which has been unduly forgotten. It is a perfect example of Liszt's method."

"Aïda" (Verdi). Sacred Dance and Finale (Ricordi). Apart from the Eastern atmosphere this solo is of no great interest. 25 pages.

"L'Africaine" (Illustration No. 1), (Meyerbeer), (Bote and Bock, also Ricordi). This is based on the "Sailor's Prayer." Though beginning unpromisingly, it works out effectively and has variety of technique. An attractive work.

"L'Africaine" (Illustration No. 2—"Indian March"), Ricordi. This work of 25 pages is too diffuse. By omitting pages 3 to 11 (resuming at "Les Jongleurs") and from the "Marziale" on page 18 to the *ff* on the last page, it is possible to make an effective solo.

"Robert le Diable"—Valse Infernale (Ricordi). This is one of the most effective of the Transcriptions, and may be compared to the Gounod Valse from "Faust." In length 22 pages, the composer suggests a cut from pages 17 to 19, but to the *prestissimo* on page 22 is better as not delaying the climax.

Besides the foregoing there are the early Donizetti "Lucrezia Borgia" Reminiscences (1841), also the Verdi "Simon Boccanegra" Fantasia (1860), and Mosonyi's "Zep Ilonka" Transcription.

Of other separate operatic Transcriptions in use there are the charming, vivacious and effective waltz from Gounod's "Faust" (Ricordi), Vol. 127 (Univ. Ed.). It is not too difficult, and the Cadenza can be omitted. "Les Adieux" from Gounod's "Romeo and Juliette" is of the ordinary transcription type.

It gives Gounod's music in moderately easy form, but it is not effective as a solo (Bote and Bock).

"Les Sabèennes," Gounod's "Reine de Saba" (Schott) is a tuneful transcription of moderate difficulty. The "Capriccio Alla Turca," Beethoven (Heugel) is based on the Turkish March from the "Ruins of Athens," and may be included here. The main theme, starting with immense aplomb, lends itself to Liszt's treatment, but not the subordinate matter, and it needs a cut from page 6 to page 13 (moderato). As thus reduced from 21 pages it makes an effective and practical solo.

THE WAGNER TRANSCRIPTIONS.

This collection is popular, (1) because of the interest of the original themes, and (2) the general practicability of the settings, being within the reach of the average advanced student.

Taking the Litolff collection of the Transcriptions in progressive order, one might give them as follows:

"LOHENGRIN."

"Lohengrin's Reproach." Mod. difficult, attractive and effective. Repeated chords with inner melody.

"Elsa's Dream." Mod. difficult. A favourite item—broken chords.

"Elsa's Procession." Mod. difficult. Popular. L.H. tremolando work.

"Bridal Music." Popular. The Bravura portion

not really difficult, making a very good wrist and arp. study.

"TANNHÄUSER."

"O Star of Eve." Mod. difficult. Popular. R.H. arpeggios with alternative.

"Pilgrims' Chorus." Middle part is difficult but not very effective.

"Tannhäuser" March. Favourite work. Practical and effective, suitable as introduction to difficult work on the black keys.

"PARSIFAL."

"Solemn March." Mod. difficult. Founded on a ground bass; the middle section based on the "Dresden Amen"; uses rotary wrist work.

"FLYING DUTCHMAN."

"Ballads." Mod. dif. Introduces L.H. chromatic work. Brilliant octaves and tremolando.

"Spinning Chorus." Diff. Interesting. Practical and not too difficult. Alternate and interlocking hands.

"MEISTERSINGER."

"Am Stillen Herd." Ditto, but using more octave work.

"RHEINGOLD."

"Walhalla." Section with chords and octaves, on black keys.

"TRISTAN."

"Isolda's Death." Favourite. Dramatic interpretation, difficult.

"RIENZI."

"Santo Spirito." Florid bravura work, very effective.

TRANSCRIPTIONS.

The Mendelssohn "Wedding March" and "Dance of Elves" (Augener), from his "Midsummer Night's Dream," is one of the most popular solos, but its 22 pages make a somewhat long solo. The Cadenza before the Presto and the Quasi Presto to the Stretta could be omitted. It is not over-difficult.

A useful, moderately difficult Paraphrase is that of the "Salve Maria" ("Jerusalem") from Verdi's "Lombardi" (Heugel), (1860), using mostly tremolando and arpeggio work. It has 7 pages, and is not difficult—given energy.

CHAPTER XVII.

THE ETUDES.

The Paganini Etudes. Transcendental Etudes. Concert Etudes, etc.

"Brilliancy of execution is valuable only when it serves higher purposes."—SCHUMANN.

"Less perhaps than anyone (except Paganini) did Liszt consider technique as an end in itself. The difficulties created by him were never evolved with the object of making the piece hard to play," but "because he had *something new to say.*"—BRUGNOLI.

The Etudes of Liszt, as representing his technique, if only from that point alone, must take an outstanding position in his pianoforte works. It has been aptly said that Liszt was the "dashing cavalier" of the piano, correcting the well-worn platitudes of the Hummel-Czerny-Mendelssohn school. Liszt was not merely a technician, however, he had soul and soaring genius. Technically he explored the utmost capacity of the piano—we hear the bassoon and trombone on the lowest register, and the rippling harp or piccolo on the highest. He accomplished the orchestration of the piano—but apart from that the IDEAS he thus put forward will live. Busoni claims that the Etudes "should be put at the head of his piano compositions" because they were the earliest of his works, the fruit of his virtuoso aspirations, and because they "reflect as do no others Liszt's personality." These fifty-eight piano pieces would serve to place Liszt in the group of the greatest piano composers since Beethoven, "and present him in manifold lights and poses." Dannreuther in his able Introduction to the "Transcendental Studies" says (Augener Ed.): "No pianist can afford to ignore Liszt's Etudes."

THE PAGANINI ETUDES.

These Etudes were inspired by the visit of Paganini to Paris in 1831; they were built upon Paganini's violin Caprices.

First issued in 1841, they were revised and again published in 1851.

There are two main editions: that of Brugnoli (Ricordi), which also includes the "Grand Fantasie de Bravoure" on the Campanella Theme (Etude No. 3)—and that published by Lemoine. Both possess facilitated or alternative versions or notes.

The Etudes form, together with suitable technical preparation, a very good introduction to Liszt's distinctive technique.

No. 1, "Preludio," opens with velocity scale work. Its main value, however, is as a left hand solo. There are also some R.H. extensions. No. 2 is valuable for interlocking chords, scales and octaves: it is effective and varied in interest.

The Ricordi Ed. gives two versions, the first of which differs somewhat from the original Caprice; the second version is nearer, and is more practical. Generally speaking, where there is a later version it appears in a more practical guise and, though sometimes more difficult, is also more effective. The first version of the No. 2 is given in Lemoine's Ed., the second in the Ricordi and Litolff Ed.

No. 3, "La Campanella," in A flat minor, appearing in its later form in G sharp minor, is a popular concert solo and capital study for skips with "little bell" effects: the whole is a good study for loose wrist chords and octaves.

The earlier version (as in Lemoine, and first in Ricordi Ed.) differs a good deal. The later version is more uniform—has more skips and is more effective—doubtless as the result of greater experience.

No. 4 is a study in the crossing of hands, and staccato chords in the key of E. Of the three versions in the Ricordi Edition the third is the easiest, the first next, and the second last, and they should be studied in that order. Litolff gives only the easy No. 3. Lemoine both versions one and two.

No. 5, also in E, in chords with imitation flute and horn effects, also appears in two versions in Ricordi. In the second one—alternate hands are more used and a scale in octaves becomes a glissando—again modern effects. The older version (only) is in Lemoine, and the newer (only in Litolff. No. 6 consists of a Theme and eleven Variations—a useful and concise introduction to the various phases of Lisztian technique.

Nos. 2, 5 and 8 are for quick, alternative hands. No. 1, L.H. independence. No. 3 opposes legato and staccato. Nos. 4 and 6, wrist eighths and thirds. No. 7, velocity. No. 9, pizzicato. No. 10, shakes. No. 11, arpeggio.

Of the two versions given in Ricordi the second is much more practical. The latter one is given in Litolff—the earlier in Lemoine. The Ricordi Ed. (105) contains also the "Grande Fantasie de Bravura," Op. 2, on the Campanella theme. (There is also a Cranz Ed. of 37 pages.) In this form it appears in A minor, and Ramann says:

"With this composition Liszt opens the series of his great and splendid virtuoso and concert pieces."

After a lyrical introduction and a short cadenza-like allegro, the Paganini theme is taken, and with its variations covers 31 pages.

The variety of technique makes the work somewhat scrappy, and the impression is that the theme is merely a framework for patchwork bravura. It is interesting to note how Liszt later on gradually economises his technique and becomes more effective with what is more natural and suited to his instrument. Huneker says: "What a superb contribution to piano literature is Liszt's"—"Have they not all tremendously developed the technical resources of the instrument, and to play them one must have fingers of steel, a brain on fire, a heart bubbling with chivalric force."

THE "TRANSCENDENTAL" ETUDES.

A master work for advanced pianists—these Etudes had their origin in a set of twelve Exercises written by Liszt in his sixteenth year (1827), under the title of "Etudes en douze Exercises," and published in 1839. It was suppressed, however, and considerably re-written. The set appeared thus in 1852, being dedicated to Czerny, as his former teacher. The change in form of No. 1 was so great that it might, in Dannreuther's opinion, "be taken to represent the history of the pianoforte during the last half century, from the Viennese 'square' to the concert grand, from Czerny's Etudes to Liszt's 'Danse Macabre.'" In its more mature form we have:

No. 1, Preludio. A concise velocity study in prelude form, and not difficult.

(2) Etude II. A study for alternate hands, somewhat uncomfortable and better done elsewhere.

(3) "Paysage" (Landscape). This is more practical. Legato thirds and crossing of hands. Agreeable and useful. As an Etude Van Dieren thus makes reference to it: "Such a lovely thing as 'Paysage.'" It requires delicacy and expression.

(4) "Mazeppa." This is the first real Liszt, tumultuous and telling, but requiring endurance and impetuosity—once the technique is acquired. It consists of passages for quick alternating hands, with octaves and chordal passages. The symphonic poem

"Mazeppa," for orchestra, is based on this work, and this, again, has been transcribed for two pianos. The title was taken from Victor Hugo's poem, a theme treated also by Byron. At this time Liszt wrote: "I have a tremendous fit of Byron on." In this poem the Polish page Mazeppa was bound to a wild horse and turned loose. The horse, taking fright, furiously makes for the Ukraine, where, exhausted, it drops dead, and Mazeppa is released. At the close of the Etude occurs the quotation (Peters Ed.) "Il tombe enfin—et se relève Roi" (Victor Hugo).

(5) "Feux Follets" ("Will o' the Wisp"). A capital Etude for velocity with delicacy, and one much more difficult to read than to play owing to its chromatic style and the great number of accidentals.

(6) "Vision." A fine arpeggio Etude, but requiring perseverance. Not too difficult. The first $7\frac{1}{2}$ bars is for left hand solo.

(7) "Eroïca." This begins with a broad, well-marked theme, and in a big style. The climax is on the page of arpeggio octaves.

(8) "Wilde Jagd" ("Wild Chase"). The name describes the work. Massed chords in conflicting rhythm. 12 pages.

(9) "Ricordanza" ("Memories"). A very interesting, impassioned work. Melody, with cadenzas and delicate arpeggio work. 12 pages. (Issued separately, Aug.)

"RICORDANZA" (MEMORIES). ETUDE "TRANSCEND," NO. 9.

(10) F minor Study. Agitated, passionate passages of interlocking chords and conflicting rhythm. 12 pages.

(11) "Harmonies du Soir" (D flat). "Evening Harmonies" ("Abend Klänge"). A Nocturne. Very attractive and practical work, consisting mainly of arpeggiando chords. (Issued separately. Aug. Ed.)

(12) "Chasse Neige" (B flat minor). A tremolando study with sudden skips.

The studies are not of equal value or interest. For purposes of concentrated study I should be inclined to select Nos. 3, 7, 11, 5, 6, 9 and 4 as the best—taken in progressive order.

EDITIONS. The best editions include the Augener, 2 vols., edited by Dannreuther; Peters, Vol. III (Sauer); Tonmeister Ed., Ricordi Ed. (Brugnoli), and Heugel's Ed. Française (Banks and Son, York). The Litolff selection has Nos. 7, 5, 4 and 9.

Schumann spoke of these Transcendental Etudes as "Studies of storm and dread, for at the most ten or twelve players in the world," but *now* our Conservatoires and private teachers turn out pupils in numbers every season who, thanks to modern teaching on systematic lines (as on the Tausig-Beringer method of mastery of the black keys), are able to master their formidable difficulties.

Three Concert Studies ("Caprices Poétiques"). These were published in 1849.

No. 1, in A flat ("a capriccio"), ("Il Lamento"). This is a beautiful work after the style of the "Liebestraum" No. 3, but more difficult. It might follow No. 7 or 11 of the Transcendental Studies. There are extended arpeggios, zephyr cadenzas and alternate passages which are not easy, but yield to practice.

No. 2, in F ("a capriccio"), ("La Leggierezza"). This also, is very attractive, but more difficult than No. 1. It is somewhat Chopinesque and requires great delicacy. The chromatic style makes it more difficult to read than to play.

No. 3, in D flat. This suggests a lovely serenade with an extended harp accompaniment in an impassioned manner, and yet finely spun. Editions Augener (Dannreuther), Tonmeister (Rosenthal), Française (Moskovski), Leduc Ed. In the French editions No. 1 is named "Il Lamento," No. 2 is "La Leggierezza," and No. 3 "Un Sospiro" ("A Sigh"). The French title used is three "Caprices Poétiques." In the Ricordi Ed., E.R. 73 (Brugnoli) they are included in the "Six Concert Studies." Ed., Peters Ed., Vol. 4.

"Two Etudes de Concert." These, of later date, are perhaps the most popular of the Etudes.

No. 1, "Waldesrauschen," or "Dans les Bois" (D flat). As conveying a picture of the rustle of the woods, it appeals to the imagination. Beginning in a whisper, it eventually reaches a stormy *fff*. Technically it is splendid practice and not too difficult.

No. 2, "Gnomenreigen" ("Ronde des Lutins"). As a fairy piece—suggesting the influence of Mendelssohn, the prince of fairy revels—it is not easy to depict with the necessary grace and fantastic light-footed step, still the lay-out is practical and not very difficult. Editions Litolff (2594); Augener (4994). Ed. Française. Ricordi (Six Concert Studies). Peters, Vol. 4.

"Ab Irato." An early version of this, dated 1842, was named "Morceau de Salon." It was expanded and revised, and reappeared in 1852, with the above suggestive title ("In a Rage"). In the Augener Ed. (Dannreuther) both versions are given. As an octave and chord study, taken *presto*, with its attractive second "salon" portion using an arpeggio bass, this work is both useful and effective. Every advanced pianist should know it. Also in Ricordi Ed. (Six Studies, E.R. 73).

CHAPTER XVIII.

THE CONSOLATIONS, SONATA, APPARITIONS, VALSES, POLONAISES, LEGENDS, BALLADES, ETC.

"In sweet music is such art,
Killing care and grief of heart."—SHAKESPEARE.

In company with religion, music, "sweet consoler," exists to soothe the sorrows of mankind; as a universal balm it exerts great influence also in the healing of disease due to nervous derangements. The "Consolations" (1850) are among the most popular of Liszt's piano works.

No. 1, in E, is an introductory meditation, and gives the keynote to the collection.

No. 2, in E. This is a lovely "Song without words" of moderate difficulty. Note the unexpected modulations. In the middle section the melody is between the two hands.

No. 3, in D flat. This nocturne is, like some of Chopin's, modelled on those of John Field. A quiet, pensive melancholy pervades it, and while the little characteristic cadenza and *ppp* ending proclaims it Liszt's, the work, as a whole, might easily be taken for a Nocturne by John Field, whose works Liszt admired so much and wrote about.*

No. 4, in D flat. A soft, devotional piece in the style of an organ voluntary. Note how the bass pedals boom out the theme quietly in the last section.

No. 5, in E. This is another charming song without words in the style of Field. It is hopeful and confident in feeling.

No. 6, in E. Begins with an eerie atmosphere of despair, followed by a passionate baritone solo, with sweeping arpeggiando accompaniment. It closes with a song of triumph and a final sigh of thanks. An expressive and effective work—educationally valuable for rotatory work.

Prof. Niecks refers to the "Consolations" as the work of a true poet and a man of feeling.

"If Liszt had composed nothing else, we should be justified in calling him a great composer."

The length of a composition does not weigh in the balance. The great artist is apparent in the simple miniature. "The real value of a composition lies in its genuineness and originality."

"Grande Valse di Bravura," Op. 8 (Ricordi), 13 pages. This at once challenges comparison with the "Grande Valse" in E flat, by Chopin, Op. 18—the nearest approach, and Chopin's first valse. Liszt's

* "J. Field et ses Nocturnes," par Franz Liszt, 1859.

work was published in 1824, at the age of thirteen, Chopin's in 1834, at the age of twenty-five. His previous output was mostly Mazurkas, with three Nocturnes and the twelve Studies. Chopin's valse is simple, melodious and somewhat old-fashioned by comparison. Liszt's is much superior in variety and effect of technique and development of idea. It has a dashing Finale with a Presto Furioso in duple time. As a bravura piece it is not really difficult.

"Allegro di Bravura," Op. 4 (Kistner). This is the earliest extant work of Liszt's, written and published in 1825—i.e., his fourteenth year.

Preceded by an impressive Adagio in E flat minor, the Allegro emerges in the major, thus:

Allegro di Bravura, Op. 4.

It is in fluent and melodious style, and might easily be taken for a work by Dussek. More or less in sonata form, with an arpeggio second subject in the dominant key, it makes a good educational piece in broken chords and arpeggios.

THE APPARITIONS, ETC.

"APPARITION," NO. 2.

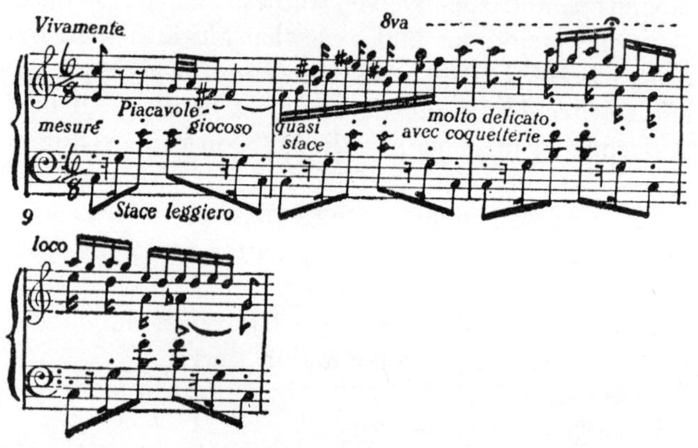

"Apparitions," Book I (Hofmeister). This is an attempt to produce atmosphere—a purely impressionistic picture—with a ghostly twilight, and successful only if considered as such. 6 pages. Key, F.

No. 2, in A. This is a gem, and one of the earlier works. Delicately interpreted as an ethereal fairy scene, it is very effective. A beautiful Nocturne modelled on Field.

No. 3 was one of the Schubert Valse Transcriptions.

"En Reve" (Wetzler—now Doblinger). A Nocturne in B in the style of Field, melodious and delicate. It is played throughout *una corda*. Mod. difficult only.

"Chromatic Gallop." One of Liszt's earlier "battle horses," played at a furious rate. Very effective, but light, not really difficult. Selections Lit. Alb. 2643. Universum. Leduc and Albums.

"Mazurka Brillante" (Litolff 2643). Effective and varied in style. Useful educational piece.

"Berceuse" in D flat (1854). Lit. 2643. One can only compare this with the "Berceuse" of Chopin, and if the latter is a lullaby for ordinary mortals, then Liszt's is for fairies. One of Liszt's best works —yet rarely played.

Editions also Peters, Vol. 6. Compare this with the charming "Berceuse" in F sharp in the "Christmas Tree" collection.

"Valse Impromptu" (Litolff Ed.). A piquant Chopinesque Valse with characteristic syncopated effects, cadenzas and varied technique. Mod diff. Other Eds., Augener, Peters and also Bosworth and Steingräber Albums.

"Impromptu" in F sharp (Lit.). A charming work and a true impromptu. Impassioned and delicate, with a fragment of melody here and there in an atmosphere of impressionism. It recalls the "Liebestraum," and ends with a sigh.

"Valse Melancolique" (Universum Ed. 2998). This is in similar mood, a meditation in valse rhythm. A charming work if rendered with due expression. It is best rendered in an improvisatory and rubato style. It is one of the three Caprice Valses, and is only mod. dif.

"Spanish Rhapsody" (Lit. 2590). One of the

best of Liszt's Rhapsodies, it is of a robust type, brilliant, yet always intelligible, and founded on the Spanish themes "Folies D'Espagne" and a "Jota Aragonese." Another theme, at the *sempre presto* in $\frac{6}{8}$ time appears later in the bass at the *martellato*, and also the first theme metamorphosed on the last page. There are 23 pages, not too many and not too difficult.

THE POLONAISES.

"Two Polonaises" (Lit. 2596). No. 1, in C minor, is written in an introspective, pessimistic mood. Muttering tones in the bass are answered in the treble. It sounds almost like an altercation, but a soothing *amorosamente* section in E flat follows with relief, the work becomes attractive, and finishes with power.

No. 2, in E, is one of Liszt's best works, a favourite, and quite equal, if not superior (in the hands of a virtuoso) to any of Chopin's Polonaises. The group of the first theme is equalled by the nobility of the second, in A minor. The delightful Lisztian Arabeske which follows establishes its individuality and charm. Editions, Augener, Universum, Simrock (Busoni added Cadenza).

"TWO LEGENDS" (Litolff, 2626), (1866).

(1) "St. Francis' Sermon to the Birds." Here we have an instance of programme music, bird music, the twittering and song of birds abound, accompanied

LISZT

by a slender theme. A Hymn of Praise in D flat ascends at the *Maestoso*, and then a melody appears in the bass. These are woven with bird song, and the discourse ends in a whisper.

(2) "St. Francis de Paule Walking on the Waves." This also is programme music. A stately theme with accompanying billows of sound in the bass voice with increased emotion, and then—the theme itself is transferred to the bass regions, and the tumult gains until we reach the triumphant *Maestoso* expressed in massed chords—an expressive coda concludes the work.

Calvocoressi describes the Legends as "deux superbes tableaux musicaux."

Saint-Saëns, in a sympathetic sketch, gives a personal reminiscence of his meeting Liszt in the home of Gustave Doré, gazing upon that pallid face and those eyes that fascinated all listeners, whilst beneath his apparently indifferent hands in a wonderful variety of nuances, there moaned and wailed, murmured and roared the waves of the "Legend de St. François de Paule marchant sur les flots." "Never again will there be seen or heard anything to equal it."

THE BALLADS.

"Two Ballads" (Litolff 2598). In this, No. 1, in D flat, a sweeping *con amore* melody, richly endowed almost from the first, is prominent, it is relieved by a second march-like theme (in A), which is

BALLADE, No. 1.

repeated in grand style in F. The D flat theme reappears in bravura form, and the second makes a close in D flat. Quite a brilliant, yet expressive and melodious work.

It is a pity that neither Chopin nor Liszt indicated the source of inspiration for their Ballads. It might be possible to fit some old traditional story, even now, and for the "Ballade," No. 2 (in B minor) of Liszt, one is tempted to do this. It opens with a moaning, waving chromatic bass, and a lamenting theme in B minor, followed by a pleading Allegretto in F sharp; this section is repeated; the theme a semitone lower the allegretto a semitone higher. A martial and tempestuous part succeeds, the pleading is now in D. The original lament and allegretto now appear in massed chords. A final *ff* grandioso gives the climax, but the Coda ends *pianissimo.* This powerful work can only be compared with his "Mazeppa." It has a world of meaning. Campbell's poem, "Lord Ullin's daughter," seems to interpret it, the "dark and stormy water—the pleading with the boatman, the tempest, and the pleading 'come back, come back,' he cried in grief." The joy of escape from pursuit, the catastrophe, and the final lament seem to meet us in its pages. Bülow wrote: "Liszt's Ballades and Polonaises have proved most strikingly that it was possible after Chopin to write Ballades and Polonaises." For my part, I think it must be conceded that Liszt greatly excelled Chopin in dramatic power, his melody is also more subtle, and his wonderful, compelling technique excels that of Chopin.

Bülow says: "The Liszt Ballade in B minor is equal in *poetic content* to Chopin's Ballades." As a dramatic composition I think it is superior, as is also Liszt's Second Polonaise in E to those of Chopin. Huneker thinks the Polonaise in C minor more poetic of the two, but states (in 1911) that the E major is a "perennial favourite" and that the "Two Polonaises capture the heroic and sorrowing spirit of Samara."

"Scherzo and March." The Scherzo (17 pages) lacks inspiration, is sardonic and pessimistic, while the "Marziale" (14 pages), possessing limited tune, does not rise above mediocrity. Edition (Peters, Vol. 12).

"Fantasia and Fugue on B.A.C.H." (B flat, A, C,

B), (Litolff, 2850, and Peters, Vol. 12). This fine work is very chromatic and somewhat pessimistic in tone. As written in a big style it is an effective work, but one that, however, sounds better still in the version for the organ, where its magnitude is impressive. Calvocoressi says: "Not less fine from the musical point of view than a Fugue in Bach, it is vibrant with life, free and spontaneous."

THE SONATA.

SONATA.

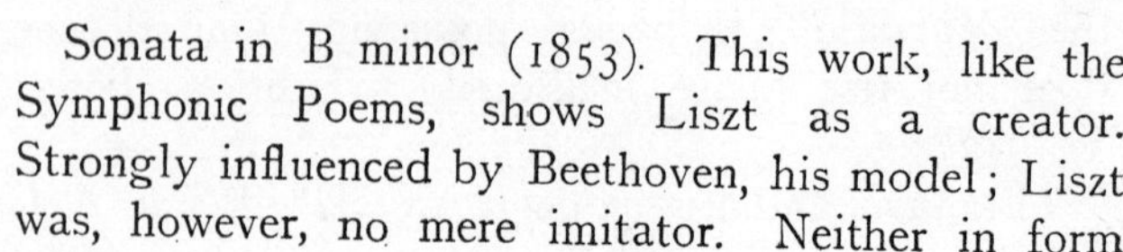

Sonata in B minor (1853). This work, like the Symphonic Poems, shows Liszt as a creator. Strongly influenced by Beethoven, his model; Liszt was, however, no mere imitator. Neither in form nor contents was he content to be a follower on; he believed in getting out of the rut.

The Sonata is in one movement. Beethoven had occasionally connected movements and evolved them out of one theme. Liszt here makes the theme of the Introduction the source of his inspiration for the principal part of this work. It had been proclaimed that the sonata form was exhausted—dead. Mr. Shedlock in his work, "The Pianoforte Sonata," asked: "Is Liszt's Sonata a Phœnix rising from its ashes?"

Liszt adhered to his plan of one movement metamorphosis—usually making one subject serve, and by rhythmical and other changes of the same, securing artistic unity. In the peroration all the accessory melodies appear as a summary of the whole. The Concertos and Symphonic Poems are much on the same plan. The musical Tories of the period protested, or, as Clarence Lucas* amusingly puts it, "Ah! those miserable dwellers in the caves of Theory raised their encircling dust in controversy. These toilers in antiquarian research shook their heads in sorrow and exclaimed: 'Ichabod! Ichabod! His glory has departed.'"

In this work depicting the struggle of one filled with the noblest aspirations, battling against relentless destiny and ending in a spirit of sad yet peaceful resignation, and notwithstanding his use of "metamorphosis" instead of thematic development, we

* "Musical Form" (Reeves).

have "a work of extraordinary unity and astonishing originality.*

Wagner's opinion was: "The sonata is beyond all conception, beautifully great, lovely, deep and noble —sublime."

THE "ARBRE DE NOEL."

"Christmas Tree." This is a collection of twelve pieces of only moderate difficulty (Heugel). (1) "An Old Noel," (2) "O Holy Night." Neither is of interest apart from Christmas, No. 3, the "Shepherds at the Manger." Here we have the old chorale, "In Dulci Jubilo" ("Good Christian Men Rejoice") in D flat, with a swinging bass throughout—an attractive piece educationally useful. No. 4, "March of the Magi," is "Adeste Fideles" extended and developed in the latter half. No. 5, "Scherzoso," a pleasing wrist study. (6) "Carillon"—programme music—the effect of chimes—six pages. An attractive study but requiring cuts. (7) "Berceuse," expressive work in F sharp—educationally useful. (8) "Old Noel," carol. (9) "Evening Bells," in A flat, attractive and useful, but requiring cuts. (10) "In the Olden Days," A flat, melodious and expressive; useful and effective. (11) "Hungarian," F minor, piquant and characteristic—good introduction to the rhapsodies. (12) "Polish," in D flat, nine pages, this polonaise is an effective mazurka—but it requires cuts.

---

* Dr. Eaglefield Hull, "Music" (Dent).

This is a desirable collection and separate numbers can be had. Calvocoressi praises them as "delicieux petits tableaux d'inspiration fraiche et recueillie à la fois."

"Une Soir dans les Montagnes" (Heugel). One of the original three Swiss pieces, it is an artistic presentation of a storm piece, such as is heard at organ recitals in Switzerland and elsewhere.

The Swiss village church bell is heard in the distance and the shepherd's horn and a fragment of Swiss melody. "L'Orage"—the storm enters and is effectively worked up. At its close the last rumbles among the mountains gone, the church bell is again heard and a peaceful close ensues.

The pastorale is easy and the storm not difficult. For another Swiss piece, see "Le Mal du Pays" (Swiss album).

"Romantic Fantasia on Two Swiss Melodies." In Hoffmeisters Edition, Op. 5, No. 2; Breitkopf and Härtel Edition, Op. 5, p. 1, 1836. This is founded on fragments of two melodies. An introduction yields to the well known "Ranz des vaches." An allegretto, pastorale and adagio follows, and then "Das Heimweh" ("Longing for Home"). These are developed, and a vivace takes up the "Ranz" and expatiates on it in massed chords, octaves, shakes, in a brilliant manner. The last four pages (out of twenty-one) are mostly in a graceful and light style. As an early work from his aspiring virtuoso days, this is both practical and effective.

"Two Album Leaves" (Steingräber). Two charming pieces. No. 1, in A flat, is in the style of a *valse*, airy, graceful and melodious. It requires delicacy and is not difficult. It is named "Valse Elegante" in Ashdown's Album. No. 2, in A minor, is an impassioned "Cantilena" ("Die Zelle von Nonnenwerth")—see Chapter XXI—in the style of the No. 3 "Liebestraum." A cadenza (with interlocking chords) and left hand arpeggios figure in it, but it is not difficult. Hoffmeister's Edition presents two versions. "Two Elegies" (Kahnt). These two poetical works, telling of sorrow restrained, are elusive and somewhat chromatic in style and doubtless sound better in the orchestral arrangement. They can be had also for violin or 'cello and piano. The first was written in memory of his friend, Marie de Moukhanov, who had been ill for a long time. Her last letter to Liszt had said: "To live in your memory is to give peace." The second elegy is dedicated to Lina Ramann, his biographer. A third elegy (the "Funeral Gondola"), appeared afterwards in the third book of the "Années." This was intended as a dirge for a gondolier on the Grand Canal.

"Künstler Festzug" (Kahnt). This piece of eighteen pages is an extended, energetic composition, but it claims greater interest in its orchestral form.

"Three Valses Oubliées," 1879-86 (Bote and Bock). No. 1, in F sharp, is in impromptu style, elusive in its way and with an acid flavour suggesting bitter-sweet memories. This has been named "Valse Elegiaque." It requires delicate expression, but is not difficult. See also Lemoine's "Pantheon," Vol. 9, and Bosworth's Liszt Album, seven pages.

No. 2, in A flat, has a similar atmosphere, a restless, discursiveness pervades throughout its nineteen pages. Omit pages 4, 5, 10, 11, 16, 17, 18 and 19, except last line, and we have an attractive piece and only moderately difficult.

No. 3, in D flat (eighteen pages) is in a like mood. It follows on introductory figures up to page 11 when the theme appears. Nos. 2 and 3 end on a single note—not the tonic. Besides the above there are or were the "Bulow March" (1884), also arranged for four hands, Via Crucis, 1865; the "Hymne du Pape" (1865), which appears arranged for the organ in the Peters collection, a fourth "Mephisto Valse," 1885, a "Romance Outliėe," 1881.

"Heroic March" in Hungarian style (Busoni Edition, Schles, fourteen pages). In D minor. A stirring work decked out in varied Lisztian technique—not unduly difficult and educationally valuable.

CHAPTER XIX.

THE "ANNÉES DE PÉLERINAGE."

The Swiss Album. "Italie." Italian supplement. The third year.

"What is the musician's calling? Is it not to send light into the deep recesses of the human heart?"—SCHUMANN.

There are three books, or years, of this collection, with a supplement in addition—Ricordi and Schott —are complete editions.

The work is associated with Liszt's stay in Geneva, his pilgrimage or wanderings in Switzerland and Italy.

The first year, i.e., the Swiss Album comprises pieces interpreting emotions and memories of Liszt's impressions of Switzerland. These, in order, are:

(1) "William Tell's Chapel"; (2) "The Lake of Wallenstadt"; (3) "Pastorale"; (4) "Au bord d'une Source" ("Beside the Spring"); (5) "Orage" ("The Storm"); (6) "Vallée d'Obermann"; (7) "Eglogue"; (8) "Mal du Pays"; (9) "The Chimes of Geneva."

Nos. 1 and 4 were inspired by Schiller. Nos. 2, 5, 7 and 9 by Byron. Nos. 6 and 8 by Senancour.

LIFE AT GENEVA.

Guy de Pourtales gives a sympathetic account of the life at Geneva, thus: *

"And peace, love, the small, tranquil circumstances amid which he was living, stirred him to composing once more. He sought to catch on the piano the impressions of a walk along the lake, an excursion into the Alps, the poetic colouring of which had been suggested to him by Obermann's orchestration" (sic.). Marie read Shakespeare or Byron to him while he improvised. In this way were formed one by one the first poems of the "Années de Pélerinage" which opened with the Cloches de G—. As an epigram, they chose a text from "Childe Harold":

> "I live not in myself, but I become
> Portion of that around me."

"While he was writing, the bells of the neighbouring Cathedral of Saint Pierre flooded the rooms with their sweet chimes." Here he jotted down the "Lac de Wallenstadt," "Au bord d'une source," "The Vallée d'Obermann," "Fleurs Mélodiques des Alpes" and "Psaume"—leaves for his first lyrical and pictorial album, i.e., "Album d'un Voyageur," of 1835. Afterwards they were rewritten (except "Psaume") for the Swiss Album of 1852, but only three numbers from the "Fleurs Mélodiques" were included. The "Three Swiss Airs" appeared separately.

---

* "The Man of Love," p. 56 (Butterworth).

THE SWISS ALBUM.

(1) "Wm. Tell's Chapel," in C. This begins in organ style. A patriotic hymn is succeeded by an agitated and dramatic section leading to thoughts of the national conflict; the return of the hymn (with all stops out) and a meditation, brings finally a triumphant close. Not difficult.

(2) "The Lake of Wallenstadt" is a true idyll. Rippling waves and moonlight complete this nocturnal picture—a nocturne inspired by Field. Moderately easy.

(3) "Pastorale" in E. This is in the true old Italian style—in 12-8 time—calm and peaceful. A simple sketch.

(4) "Au bord d'une Source" ("Beside the Spring"). Perhaps the most popular number. A simple meandering streamlet goes rippling on its way, while the zephyr breezes and the distant village church bell are borne across the tide. This is not difficult, but requires delicacy and expression.

(5) "Orage" ("The Storm"). It is ushered in by rushing of chromatic octaves. Bass octave passages supply the thunder in the *furioso* and double thirds are added. The ad lib. cadenza in swift arpeggios reaches to the *martellato* where the theme is resumed and hurries to the final crash.

The work is not so difficult as it looks, but requires perseverance.

Liszt's Storms. Regarding the "Storm," Liszt was one day showing his pupil, Miss Amy Fay, one of his effects. "He began," she says, "by playing a double roll of octaves in chromatics in the bass region. It was very grand, and made the room reverberate." "Magnificent," she said, "and he asked: 'Did you ever hear me do a storm?' 'No,'—then: 'Ah, you ought to hear me do a storm. Storms are my forte.'"

In his preface to the first edition of the album, Liszt speaks of having visited "many spots consecrated by history and poetry," and that he had "tried to express in music a few of the strongest of my sensations, of my most vivid perceptions." Liszt was profoundly inspired by nature and these romantic and impressionist pieces have a place all their own.

(6) "Vallée d'Obermann." This is named after the romance of that title by Senancour, the pessimistic though philosophical French author.

The work opens in a meditative mood. It is full of noble sentiment and dramatic expression. From a *pp* opening it advances wave on wave until at the *expressivo*, a pleading, tender melody is heard, followed by the *piu lento*, now transposed. A beautiful etherealised *piu mosso pp* section, with the theme metamorphosised leads through hopeful and rising passion to the recitative, which now issues in the stormy *appassionato* and the *presto tempestuoso*. The linked third movement—the Lento in E—is lyrical, calm and *dolce*, and yet conceals florid unrest, which again finds vent in the *fff molto agitato*. It ends with a passionate feminine cadence. Through its nineteen pages it is moderately difficult only to the recitative—but in the tempestuous octave and chord portion, greater command of technique and some virtuosity are required.

A dramatic poem—one may call it the "Tristan" of piano music.

(7) "Églogue." An eglogue is a pastorale poem, breathing peace and repose. The atmosphere in this work is similar to that in No. 4—a rippling movement requiring delicacy of interpretation. It is of moderate difficulty.

(8) "Le Mal du Pays" ("Homesickness"). This pictorial sketch is founded on the "Ranz des Vaches" —or call for the cattle, sounded on the Alpine horn. Beginning in E minor it is developed through E major and other keys in a plaintive manner. Moderately difficult. In the Ricordi Edition there is a long quotation from Senancour on the "De l'expression romantique et du Ranz des vaches."

(9) "The Chimes of Geneva." This is really a nocturne with the chimes as a basis. It is in the style of John Field, the nocturne composer, whom Liszt admired so much. A middle rubato section is followed by a passionate animato *(ff)* with arpeggio accompaniment. It ends as calmly as it begins and is only moderately difficult.

THE SCHOTT EDITION OF THE ALBUM (complete) has notes by Klindworth. The LITOLFF EDITION has: Book I, Nos. 1, 2, 4, 5 and 9; Book II, "Sposalizio" and three sonnets and the Italian supplement; Book III has "Les jeux de L'eau." The Ricordi complete edition, in which the Italian supplement is separate, is edited by Tagliapietra, composer and professor at the Lyceum of Music at Venice.

The second set or Album is entitled

THE ITALIAN ALBUM.

"ITALIE" (1848).

It comprises seven pieces, which had been previously published separately: (1) "Sposalizio" and (2) "Il Penseroso," inspired, as mentioned by Raphael and Michael Angelo respectively. (3) "Canzonetta du Salvator Rosa"—a transcription of an old Italian song. (4) The "Three Petrarca Sonnets"—originally songs by Liszt and rearranged; and (5) "The Reading of Dante," the latter an emotional work progressing from gloom to triumph registering impressions of his favourite poet.

"Sposalizio" ("The Wedding"). This enters with chimes, the opening andante ending with the chimes in the left hand part growing louder and louder. The succeeding hymn, "Andante quieto," suggests the consecration, and then in the allegretto the wedding bells continue to ring in combination with the theme of the wedding hymn. This favourite is of moderate difficulty only.

"Il Penseroso." A picture, noble and dignified, inspired by Michael Angelo's statue. No definite melody seems to arise and the music is occupied in creating an atmosphere of meditation. This may be almost classified as a *psychic* work. It is short and moderately difficult.

The original title pages of "Sposalizio" and "Il Penseroso" showed respectively Raphael's picture of the espousals of Joseph and Mary, and Michael Angelo's statue to the pensive man, the Duke de Nemours.

"Canzonetta del Salvator Rosa." This song transcription has bold, rhythmical melody and its marchlike presentation should make it a capital educational piece of moderate difficulty. The Schott Edition gives also the words of the song. "Salvator Rosa was not only an artist and a popular poet," but he "gave to his poetry fitting melodies." As a popular song of the people Liszt made a piano solo of it. The words begin:

"Vado bon spesso cangiando loco
Ma non so mai cangiar desio."

THE PETRARCA SONNETS.

Petrarch, the Italian poet, was the source of the composer's inspiration in these sonnets. "The sonnets to Laura, the incomparable, beautiful apotheosis of love, so delighted Liszt that it led him to render them in music" (Ramann).

Sonnet No. 47. This is a syncopated, meditative work. A hovering twixt heaven and earth, with an Italian close.

Sonnet No. 104,* seems to breathe passionate aspiration. A beautiful work, ranking in depth of

* Transcribed by Busoni for orchestra.

feeling with the "Liebesträume." Florid but effective with a peaceful ending.

"SONETTO PETRARCA," 123.

Sonnet No. 123. A poetical work in the style of a nocturne with an impassioned middle section leading to a sweet and calm ending.

These sonnets, which are of moderate difficulty, have an individual place in piano literature. Refined and noble in sentiment, vivid and romantic, they are a work in themselves. In the Ricordi Edition, the words of the sonnets are given (in Italian) as a key to the emotions interpreted. Helpful annotations are also added by the editor.

"I said Dante's poem was a song; it is Tieck who calls it a mystic, unfathomable song and such is literally the character of it" (Carlyle, "On Heroes and Hero Worship").

"Après une Lecture de Dante." This work had its inspiration during the stay at Bellagio on Lake Como. Says Ramann: "The two travellers (Liszt and the Countess) passed a great deal of their time on the lake, the picturesque, sloping shores ever tempting them to new excursions. During the heat of the day they took refuge under the shade of the plantains that surrounded the Villa Melzi, and read the 'Divina Commedia' at the feet of Cornelli's statue, 'Dante led by Beatrice.'"

It is entitled "Fantasie quasi Sonata." First impressions are declamation, nobility, tragedy and gloom during the Presto lamentoso, succeeded at the "precipitato" (in F sharp) by strains of love and hope in the Andante, which again are later hid in a Chopinesque Arabesque at the "improvisando." A dramatic orgy of development now sets in, leading to the Allegro in D, the climactic—with massed battalions of chords; followed in stretto by the increasing excitement of the allegro Vivace and Presto. A difficult work—this needs an artist to rise to the height of Liszt's inspiration and the due interpretation of one of the finest works in the literature of the piano.

THE ITALIAN SUPPLEMENT. VENICE AND NAPLES.

This set, consisting of three Transcriptions or Paraphrases, and comprising the "Gondoliera," "Canzone" and "Tarentella," originated in Italy, and was published in 1838. In the Schott Edition the pieces are appended to the "Third Year," and in the Ricordi Edition as a "Supplement" to Vol. II —"The Italian." The "Gondoliera" in F sharp is based on a gay gondola song, "La Biondina in Gondoletta," which is embellished with pretty shake and arpeggio accompaniments on the black keys. A nightingale warbles above while the left hand chants the air. It makes a capital educational piece for cultivation of delicacy on the black keys—and is not too difficult.

The "Canzone" (4 pages), in E flat minor, is a dramatic arrangement of a gondola song from Rossini's "Otello," with a tremolando accompaniment. The melody is put down into the bass regions. Liszt frequently makes striking use of the extreme bass and treble registers. It is of moderate difficulty. In the "Tarentella" we have a very effective concert piece in bravura style without excessive difficulty, valuable as an educational work for the variety of technique it employs. Intervening folk-song episodes enhance the interest of the "Tarentella." A "Canzone Napolitana" (Neapolitan song) is thus introduced, and Liszt in his happiest mood proceeds to spin brilliant variations on it with intervening cadenzas.

Separate editions of the Italian Supplement are in the Augener, Schott Album, and Heugel Editions. It is also included in Peters, Vol. VI, and the Années (3603)—the Peters Edition includes but one item from the third Année. There are separate numbers published in the Universum Edition.

THE THIRD YEAR.

"Works of art are the manifold expression of the Divine Being."—LAMENNAIS.

The Third Album comprises pieces issued separately, and written many years later than the others in the seclusion of the Villa d'Este, Tivoli, near Rome. It was published in 1890, after the Abbé's death.

Liszt had become an Abbé, and we have in this album pieces of a religious turn or with sacred associations.

No. 1, "Angelus, Prière aux Anges Gardiens." An Angelus with bell effects, and a Hymn or Prayer, simple and restful, but not exactly pianistic, nor very effective until the harmonium enters on the fifth page.

To the Rev. H. R. Haweis, visiting the Abbé at Villa d'Este, Liszt observed: "As we are talking of bells I should like to play you an 'Angelus' which I have just written. You know they ring the Angelus in Italy carelessly; the bells swing irregularly and leave off, and the cadences are often broken up thus," and he began a little swaying passage in the treble—like bells tossing in the air. It ceased—and silence fell—the bells went on, and "then rose from the bass, the song of the Angelus." Notice how the Angelus answers to this description.

(2) "Aux Cyprès de la Villa d'Este." A Threnody or Lament; as the title suggests, gloom permeates this work. Not until the fifth page does the

cloud lift, and then after an agitated section the lament ends firmly in hope.

(3) This has the same title as No. 2, and opens in similar mood, but on the second page it strikes a welcome octave theme leading to the attractive arpeggiando theme, and these presentations alternate. On the whole it is effective, though in a somewhat difficult style.

THE CYPRESSES OF VILLA D'ESTE. The Cypresses of the Villa d'Este have become famous.

The Signor Commendatore as the Abbé was called, occupied apartments in the Villa, which was situated on the hanging terraces from which could be discerned a view of the campagna with St. Peter's in the distance.

The fountains, cascades and cypresses gave an atmosphere of joyous quietude, while in the Cardinal's gardens children would gather to kiss his hands. Liszt loved children, and would throw handfuls of small coins to them.

(4) "The Fountains ('Jeux d'Eaux') at Villa d'Este." A brilliant and attractive impressionistic piece suggestive of cascades of glittering water and perpetual motion. There are 13 pages of arpeggio and tremolando effects, and the key is F sharp—until the modulation to D, when Liszt attaches the 14th verse of the 4th chapter of St. John, beginning "But whosoever drinketh of the water that I shall give him," so that this number has also sacred associations. The work is somewhat difficult—including an awkward left hand solo.

HAWEIS writes: "Down the slope of a precipitous mountain stretched the Villa d'Este gardens; tall cypress-trees marked the lines of walk and terrace; groves of olive, between which peeped glittering cascades and lower parterres. Presently we came to a central space, led into by four tall cypress groves. Here, up from a round sheet of water in front of us, leapt up four jets to an immense height."

LISZT, in a letter to Dr. Nohl (March 20, '78) thanking him for a drawing of the cypresses, says: "I attempted (last October) to put down on music paper the conversation which I frequently hold with these same cypresses: ah, how dry and unsatisfactory on the piano, and even in the orchestra—Beethoven and Wagner excepted—sounds the woe and sighing of almighty Nature!" (Letters, Vol. II.)

MR. DENIS POWNALL says about the "Jeux d'Eaux": "This work is priceless, probably the finest, certainly the most coherent and controlled of all Liszt's piano pieces after the Sonata."(—("Musical Opinion," Jan., 1934.)

It is interesting to note that later on in 1886, the last year of Liszt's life, Liszt was visited at the Villa d'Este by the poet Longfellow and a painter friend, Mr. Healey. The door was opened by Liszt himself holding a lighted candle. Longfellow was so struck with the picturesque appearance of Liszt as he stood in the old doorway in his long black soutane, holding a lighted candle, that he asked permission to have Healy paint a picture of him. The picture went to Longfellow's house at Cambridge (Mass.), U.S.A., and has been photographed by permission.

Two sombre pieces follow:

(5) "Sunt Lacrymæ Rerum"—in the Hungarian style, employing characteristic augmented intervals, and though "tearful" it is an effective item. Liszt was in his element.

(6) "Marche Funèbre," in memory of Maximilian I of Mexico. This opens with drum effects and pursues its way amid gloom, until the triumphant close in his favourite key of F sharp is reached.

(7) "Sursum Corda." The title suggests a message of hope as a conclusion. It maintains a broad resonant melody almost throughout, and concludes *grandioso*. The whole tone scale in octaves is used just before the Finale.

With the exception of No. 4, the various items are not difficult.

CHAPTER XX.

"HARMONIES POETIQUES ET RELIGIEUSES." THE "BÉNÉDICTION DE DIEU," "CANTIQUE," "INVOCATION," ETC.

The key to this outstanding series lies in the Preface quoted from Lamartine:

"There are hearts broken by grief, repulsed by the world, which take refuge in the world of their thoughts."

The collection consists of ten works. Four of these were published in 1834 and the whole in 1851. It originated in a period of trial and depression. The loss of his father in 1827, when he was barely sixteen, his struggle to make a living for his mother and himself, his repulse in his first love, whose mother's death also affected him, and his resolve to enter the Church—thwarted by his own mother—all left a deep impression on him.

The collection in its complete form (Edition Ricordi) comprises: (1) "Invocation," (2) "Ave Maria," (3) "Bénédiction de Dieu dans la Solitude," (4) "Pensée des Morts," (5) "Paternoster," (6) "Hymn de l'enfant á son Reveil," (7) "Funèrailles," (8) "Miserere," (9) "Andante Lagrimoso," (10) "Cantique d'Amour."

They are partly transcriptions of his own songs or characterisations of poems. Liszt was very fond of the "Cantique" and the "Bénédiction de Dieu."

No. 4, an Elegy, is an early work, 1834—others in similar vein are the "Paternoster," "Miserere" and "Andante Lagrimoso."

The "Funèrailles"—also elegiac—belongs to the 1849-51 period.

THE "BÉNÉDICTION DE DIEU."

The best known pieces are Nos. 3 and 10. No. 3, "Bénédiction de Dieu dans la solitude." This work presents a hymn-like theme in the key of F; over and below the theme is woven a succession of chords moving in quavers. The Andante in D and B flat furnishes contrasts, while the arpeggiando recapitulated rises to a *fff* climax, followed again by a simple, expressive and calm Andante as a Finale. The atmosphere is that of dignity and resignation, and yet the whole is full of movement. Strong and attractive as it is, it has been entitled a glowing

Hymn of Gratitude to the Deity.

Pourtales recounts a visit to Lamartine (who inspired the work), and who, with Mme. de Lamartine (an Englishwoman), received them at his threshold surprised and delighted. "A night of stars rose over this Burgandian peace. After dinner, the Councillor-General read by the open window his "Bénédiction de Dieu dans la Solitude" in an exquisite voice that seemed to break every moment. Liszt was stirred to his depths and felt rising within him the majestic Andante of serenity. "Then the artist sat down at the piano and played his 'Harmonies du Soir,' dedicated to this lord of music and melancholy."

"CANTIQUE D'AMOUR."

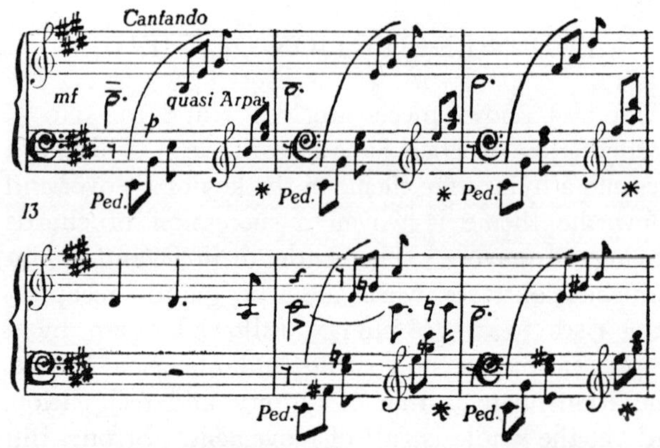

No. 10, "Cantique d'Amour." A Canticle or Hymn of Love. This is no mere sentimental ditty, and there is no mistaking the air of nobility, that great soul which distinguished Liszt himself. It reminds one of the Apostle's injunction to his brethren of the Church, "Love one another." The work is typical of Liszt's orchestration of a simple broad melody in the grand, impassioned manner. Harp effects come first, then crisp chords for reeds. A vibrato section in massed chords and sweeping arpeggios brings it to a close. An effective but not difficult work.

Liszt, writing in 1865, from Rome, says: "I played the 'Cantique,' and as there was no end to the applause I added my Transcription of Rossini's 'Charité.' Everybody in Rome with any claim to culture was present, and the Hall was more than full."

The collection as a whole consists of religious pieces written between 1846 and 1850, and may be said to express the religious aspirations of the composer at this time. The opening No. 1, "Invocation," paraphrases Lamartine's work.

> Elevez-vous, voix de mon âme
> Avec l'aurore, avec la nuit,

and an exhortation to seek God in Nature—as also poetically put forward in the words of the "Bénédicite" ("O all ye works of the Lord bless ye the Lord")—a tremendous theme which requires a great organ to do it justice. A broad theme over a moving, eddying bass, interprets the

> "Mingle with winds, storms, thunder and noise of the waves,"

while a *pp sotto voce* episode gives us the "shadowy silence of the night." A "cadenza *ad lib*" intervenes before the Recapitulation. A powerful work of moderate difficulty.

No. 7, "Funèrailles"—a still more powerful, nay, a magnificent work. Written in memory of three of

Liszt's friends killed in the Hungarian revolutionary disturbances of 1849, it goes straight to the heart. We hear first the muffled drums *en marche*, succeeded by the deep bass theme of savage resentment, for was not Liszt a revolutionary in spirit (as was Wagner)? A suave "Lagrimoso," reminding one of Chopin, follows as an episode. At the *piu moto* we get in the bass a reminiscent sketch of cavalry charges, diminished by the blare of the military theme overhead, and in the recapitulation a masterly review of all the elements. If one compares this with the Funeral March (and the B flat minor Sonata) of Chopin, we see how much more intense is the feeling and the mastery of the emotions with Liszt.

A recent criticism of a Horowitz recital says: "The feature of the recital was the Liszt 'Funèrailles.' It brought tears to the eyes and a lump to the throat. The grandeur and spiritual quality with which it was imbued was superb."

The other religious items of the collection are in different mood.

No. 2, "Ave Maria" in B flat. Liszt made several settings of this Prayer. A well-known one in E. (Rozsalvolgyi and Universum Ed.), and air, "Ave Maria Stella," also a setting of the "Ave Maria" of Arcadelt. The one in B flat begins with bell effects and resembles the style of an organ voluntary based on each line with interludes. It is refined and sincere in character.

The other numbers are (4) "Pensée des Morts,"

(5) "Pater Noster," (6) "Hymn de l'Enfant," (8) "Miserere," and (9) "Andante."

No. 6, the "Hymn de l'Enfant á son Reveil" ("Child's Morning Hymn") is in A flat, $\frac{6}{8}$ time. Its sincerity of expression and style remind one of No. 1 of the "Liebestraume." It should be taken cheerfully, and is effective within its scope of quite moderate difficulty.

SACRED ASSOCIATIONS.

No. 4, "Pensée des Morts." This work—an early one published in the 1834 collection—was suggested to Liszt by his friend, the Abbé de Lamennais.

It is an impassioned Elegy in memory of his dead father, the mother of his former love, Caroline, and of his severe illness when he was given up for dead (and an obituary notice appeared). All these left on him an indelible impression.

Pourtales, in his poetic sketch of Liszt, says: "As for Franz, he finished his 'Pensée des Morts,' which he had begun at La Chênaie (with the Abbé). The magic of Caroline ran through it, and he yielded himself to an alternating memory of his voluptuous delight and his childhood."

In later years Liszt said to his friend, Miss Janka Wohl, "One ought not to weep for the dead, but rejoice with the living"—but the "Pensée des Morts" weeps "billows of grief," and this for 5 pages, at first simply and then the theme gradually unfolds with increasing agitation and massiveness until the climax is reached in the rhythmical chant, "De profundis clamavi ad Te Domine" ("Out of the depths have I cried to thee, O Lord"), Ps. 129. By masterly metamorphosis is gained the "Adagio," a beautiful "Consolation" of $4\frac{1}{2}$ pages, in G.

No. 8, "Miserere." This is set in chant form, "after Palestrina," giving the opening words of the 51st Psalm (in Latin). The chant is repeated, first with tremolando accompaniment, and then with arpeggio harp-like embellishment.

No. 9, "Tombez, larmes silencieuses" ("Fall, silent tears"). This also is an Elegy, as the "Andante Lagrimoso" implies—a beautiful cantabile movement full of impassioned sympathy. The presentation is well varied, and it is effective.

No. 5, "Pater Noster," is a simple plainsong setting of the Prayer repeated with varied movement and harmonies.

"Art for the sake of Art is a platitude,
Its aim is the perfection of beings."

—LAMENNAIS.

Chapter XXI.

THE TRANSCRIPTIONS AND SONGS.

Re-created works. Rossini transcriptions. Schubert song transcriptions. Liszt's own Polish song transcriptions, etc.

"I build my song of high, pure notes,
Note over note, height over height,
Till I strike the arch of the infinite."—Browning.

"What could be more deep and poetic than Liszt's transcriptions of Schubert's and Wagner's songs? They are altogether exquisite."—Amy Fay.

Re-created Works.

A good piano transcription of an orchestral work is, to some extent, on the standing of the original. Orchestral colouring and other special effects, which cannot be reproduced on the piano, may have a large part in the effectiveness of the orchestral work, and these may be impossible in the pianoforte arrangement. Again, it is not usually possible to reproduce all the notes of a score of a large orchestra, and the pianist has to make shift with his ten fingers and a plentiful use of the sustaining pedal. An artistic and effective transcription may really have to be a re-creation, or reproduction of the work—and it is here that Liszt excelled—and where his genius outshone. On the occasion of his visit to London in 1840, Liszt played three of Moscheles' studies at one of the Philharmonic Concerts. Moscheles records:

"Faultless in the way of execution, by his talent he has completely metamorphosed these pieces; they have become more his studies than mine."

This was interpretation rather than transcription, but it shows where Liszt's talent lay. Regarding Liszt's treatment of orchestral works, we can repeat Professor Niecks' opinion: "Marvellous in the reproduction of orchestral effects are the transcriptions of Symphonies and Overtures."

The composer-pianist, SAINT-SAËNS, in support also says with regard to the "Don Juan" Fantasia or the "Caprice" on the Waltz from "Faust":

"There is here more talent and veritable inspiration than in many productions of serious mien and pretentiousness such as one sees every day."

He also says: "Overtures are Fantasias on opera motives. Liszt's Fantasias *differ from* ordinary potpourris and pieces where the airs serve only for ornament."

Liszt's transcriptions may be divided into two classes, (1) a plain *re-statement* with, or without Cadenzas, as in the Beethoven "Adelaide" Transcription. (2) A *Paraphrase* resembling an *Extemporisation* in which the original theme forms a basis for development by thematic metamorphosis, variation, etc. As is well known in a sermon or extemporisation, the original theme or text forms a very small part of the whole.

The *early* Paganini Transcriptions or Caprices, inspired as they were by that extraordinary virtuoso, urged Liszt to find new technical means of expressing them on the keyboard. Liszt's Paganini Etudes were re-written, and not finally published till 1851, and we can discern where Liszt is striving to make the utmost of the technical possibilties of the piano. Not content with this (as in the five Paganini Etudes) he puts alternately "*imitando il Flauto*" and "*imitando il Corno*" (imitating the flute and the horn), and also in the sixth Caprice "*quasi pizz.*," in order to suggest, in addition, orchestral effects.

The questions that naturally arise, first, in trying over a transcription are:

(1) Is it a good representation of the work? If a song or instrumental solo—does it give both solo part and accompaniment effectively differentiated. Then:

(2) As a song or solo when transferred to the piano may be quite *ineffective* in itself, can the whole be so readjusted as to present a work which is really satisfactory and effective both from a technical and emotional aspect?

Naturally Liszt's efforts were not equally satisfactory—they vary as depending on inspiration and on the adaptability of the original theme.

To those who know the original, the transcription should be of value as a souvenir or recollection, but its chief rôle ought to be that of arousing great interest in those who are ignorant of it.

THE ROSSINI SONG TRANSCRIPTIONS.

These charming works were the result of Liszt's travels in Italy from 1835 to 1840. Italy is the land of opera, and instrumental music did not, and does not, appeal greatly there. As Liszt wrote from Milan in 1837: "The Italians generally regard instrumental music as subordinate, not to be compared with vocal. Very few great pianists have come to Italy, Field is the last to my knowledge. Privately, things were different, and Liszt frequently played at the *salons* and at Rossini's soirées, and his own "Soirées Musicales," published about 1838, are the result, in which the élan and sparkle of Rossini's melodies—and of Rossini at his best—are intensified and artistically developed. Liszt had the dramatic *flair*, and their gaiety appealed to him. The "Soirées Musicales" are of moderate difficulty, in free Lisztian style, and not overloaded with technical figures.

THE "SOIRÉES MUSICALES."

(1) "La Promessa" is a popular air treated in the style of a Chopin Impromptu. In the final section the left hand has the melody.

(2) "La Regata Veneziana." A light and gay air brilliantly treated in easy bravura style.

"L'INVITO BOLERO" ("SOIRÉES MUSICALES").

(3) "L'Invita," Bolero. Pretty, attractive and sparkling. A useful educational piece.

(4) "La Gita in Gondonola," Barcarole. In this the gentle, rocking theme is well varied in simple and attractive style. The left hand extensions require care.

(5) "Il Rimprovero." Canzonetta ("The Reproach"). In similar style—with an energetic and impassioned episode.

(6) "La Pastorella dell 'Alpi" (Tirolese), ("The Shepherdess"). This is in the style of a Tyrolese waltz, quite simple and pretty.

(7) "La Partenza" ("The Departure"). Canzonetta. Light and ingenious and tuneful, with sections of the theme for left hand. A useful study for left hand.

(8) "La Pesca" ("The Fisher"). Nocturne. Pleasant, Italian and sentimental.

These eight numbers constitute Part I, Schott Ed. Collection, the remainder Part II.

(9) "La Danza." Tarentelle. A once very popular air in Naples. Merry and bright. Not so easy as it appears, but a useful velocity study.

(10) "La Serenata" is technically well decked out (Cadenza and arp.). Sentimental in style, as the original is somewhat weak.

(11) "L'Orgia" ("Merriment") is a gay waltz, varied and attractive in treatment—a good educational piece.

(12) "Le Marinari" ("The Sailors"). Duetto. A minor key melody with stormy interludes ending in the major. The best numbers are Nos. 2, 3, 6, 9 and 11. (Separate in Ricordi and Schott Ed.)*

These numbers are educationally useful, and No. 6 is quite easy. Liszt also made Fantasias of some numbers, extending and modifying them to make a satisfactory work, and these appeared in 1837, as Op. 8, No. 1, "La Pastorella" and "Le Marinari" (Nos. 6 and 12), and Op. 8, No. 2, "La Serenata" and "L'Orgia" (Nos. 10 and 11), (Schott—old prints). Nos. 9 to 12 had been previously published separately—before the Collection as a whole.

There are two other Rossini transcriptions:

(1) Air, "Cujus Animam" ("Stabat Mater").

(2) "La Charité."

---

* The Litolff Rossini Album (2644) contains Nos. 1, 2, 4, 9, with "Cujus Animam" and "La Charité." Ricordi Ed. 1 to 12.

These belong to a later period, 1840-50. In "Cujus Animam" we have the dramatic and effective presentation of a great theme with advanced left hand octave work—a good Etude. "La Charité" presents a simple theme with good variety of florid technique—eight kinds in all, but the result is restless. It is not too difficult.

"SOIRÉES ITALIENNES."

Another series of works originating in Italy, are the transcriptions known as "Les Soirées Italiennes" (Edition Classique, Durand), comprising "Six Amusements" on Mercadente themes, and three based on airs of Donizetti.

The Mercadente Album was dedicated to Elizabeth of Austria, vice-Queen of the Lombard-Venice Province, and the Donizetti Album to the Marchioness Sophie de Medici.

These Albums are masterly in their own way. They combine attractive Italian melody and Lisztian technique—a combination that would be difficult to surpass, and may be looked upon as a souvenir of his five years' stay in Italy, 1835-40, at an impressionable time of his life (aged 24-9), during which he gained experience both as virtuoso and composer.

In a letter—on leaving Italy, he writes that he had worked enormously during his sojourn in Italy, and he trusted he had become more accomplished as an artist.

The first of the Mercadente themes:

(1) "La Primavera" ("Spring") is an artistic, graceful, and not too difficult work, introducing left hand theme and easy interlocking—a refined and expressive composition for the *salon.*

(2) "The Galop." A galop resembles a quick march in form and style, and this is a capital example with simple bright-spirited melody (in F), giving splendid practice on chords and octaves.

(3) "Il Pastore Svizzero." ("The Swiss Shepherd"). A Tyrolese sketch. Resembles No. 1 in style—with echo effects. The quasi Presto with right hand accompaniment shake and left hand tenths and the Finale are very effective.

(4) "La Serenata del Marinari" ("The Sailor's Serenata"). This is an energetic composition, melodious, bright, effective—a capital educational work (mostly wrist, with left hand arpeggios), and not really difficult. Liszt is always pianistic and effective in the various styles, and what looks difficult usually falls easily under the hands.

(5) "The Brindisi" (Rondoletto), ("Drinking Song"). A merry and bright piece in educational style, in A flat, using sixths and double thirds—both attractive and useful.

(6) "La Zingarella Spagnola" ("The Spanish Gipsy"). An effective Bolero—energetic and brilliant like No. 4, but twice the length and rather more advanced, with more varied technique.

DONIZETTI ALBUM (Schott, separate Nos.).

(7) "Il Barcajuolo" ("The Barcarolle"), (Doni-

zetti). An agreeable composition which does not enchant, until Liszt in the Piu Animato, begins to spin attractive embroideries which give an interest to the close.

(8) "L'Alito di Bice" ("A Breath of Bice"), out of print.

(9) "La Toree di Biasino" ("The Tower of Biasino"). A typically light, Italian air with an introduction in the minor—which Liszt makes the most of.

THE SCHUBERT SONG TRANSCRIPTION.

The Liszt transcription may be valuable as a preparation for the higher technique, and also for keeping mere technique in its right (and subordinate) place, as the attention has naturally to be concentrated on the theme and its appropriate expression.

Some aspects of the Lisztian technique are not difficult in themselves, but just require greater activity or agility—an aspect which should come by concentrated practice.

What looks really difficult to read, especially in sight reading, often becomes quite easy, in practice, the mentally difficult may be technically easy—*if pianistic*—while the reverse is true sometimes, the mentally easy may be ungrateful and awkward from the practical aspect.

In the concert halls of Vienna Liszt's greatest success was made through his Schubert Song Transcriptions. The "Praise of Tears" and "Hark, the

Lark," and the "Serenade" were hailed with delight. The following are the various Schubert Collections transcribed: (1) "Four Songs" (1839), (2) "Twelve Songs," (3) "Four Sacred Songs," (4) "Six Songs," (5) "Six Miller's Songs," (6) "Fourteen Swan Songs," (7) "The Winter Journey"—eleven songs. There are fifty-seven in all of these. Also four songs are arranged for voice and orchestra, and "Die Allmacht," for voice, chorus and orchestra, in 1870.

Liszt's method of transcribing differs according to inspiration. In the Schubert "Serenade" he takes the first two verses and simply fills in the chords more fully with some interlocking or overlapping with the second verse, as a quasi violoncello solo; then follows an imitative section, with the melody treated in echo fashion. In the third verse the original accompaniment given already echoes the melody, but here it is made fuller, with an added cadenza and a final *ppp* arabesque cadence.

In "The Trout" we find much more elaboration:

(1) A new Introduction with Cadenza.

(2) Verse 1. Acpt. alternating an octave higher, with melody in the middle.

(3) Verse. 2. Melody above.

(4) Verse 3. Melody in left hand with playful two-octave skips above throughout. At the *Piu animato* the figure leaps continually above, ending with a cadenza in tenths.

(5) The last verse enters simply, and there a florid

figure is echoed from left to right, closing with cadenzas. As has been mentioned, the form and limitations of the song transcriptions make them one of the best ways of acquiring the extended Liszt technique, and the following descriptive list is made in *progressive order.*

(1) "Serenade." A moderately easy setting of the immortal theme. Useful as an introduction to Liszt's mode of interlocking of melody and accompaniment.

(2) "Wandering." Pretty (and mod. diff. only) setting. The second verse has the melody in the left hand with a right hand arabesque above.

(3) "Litany." One of the sacred songs. Noble theme. Example of doubled or thickened harmonisation.

(4) "Impatience." Animated work. Crossing of hands and octaves. Rhythmical and impetuous.

(5) "The Post." Makes a light, attractive piece with loose wrist extensions and crossing.

(6) "Praise of Tears." Famous melody—straightforward setting, opening theme may be taken as a left hand solo. The Finale is in big (but not difficult) style.

(7) "The Wayside Inn." Simple, expressive song. The tremolando rises to a climax. Quiet ending.

(8) "Farewell." Noble setting. Crossing. The contrary chord passages require concentration.

(9) "Withered Flowers." Dignified and medita-

tive. Arpeggiando extensions. Sweeping, bardic style.

(10) "Hark, Hark, the Lark" (Shakespeare's Serenade). Light and piquant theme, moves between the hands. A feature is the brilliant passages above in the final section representing the song of the lark. "A slight pause separates the last call, 'Sweet maid, arise!'—the warbling of the lark ceases and the call melts into chords full of devotion" (Ramann).

(11) "Barcarolle" ("On the Water"). A charming and effective piece, played with loose wrist, and educationally useful. The melody wanders. Not difficult.

(12) "Sweet Repose." Beautiful melody. Valuable crossing etude, with tumultuous climax—and dramatic soft close.

(13) "Faith in Spring." Charming setting. The left hand setting (second verse) requires concentration.

(14) "Resting Place." Characteristic and dramatic. Rushing torrents and waving woods are depicted. A powerful but straightforward setting requiring energy.

(15) "Whither?" Pretty song. Good example of Liszt's extension and overlapping, left hand solo and rotatory work.

(16) "The Wanderer." Favourite and impressive. Chords, octaves and general technique. Schubert's Op. 15. "The Wanderer" Fantasia is founded on this theme, and was re-written in modern form. (See

Chapter XXIII.) The Fantasia by Liszt is for orchestra and piano, also two pianos.

(17) "The Linden Tree." Effective and pretty. Not difficult until the last half—or four pages. Study in rotatory and scale work, and especially in shakes.

(18) "The Erl King." Of great dramatic interest. Useful wrist etude, requiring endurance. Rather difficult.

(19) "Ave Maria." The lovely melody set to Scott's poem wanders amid florid *pp* chord passages and later in left hand with brilliant superimposed *pp* arpeggios.

(20) "The Maiden's Lament." Powerful and dramatic setting. Florid and agitato, tremolando work.

(21) "Angel of Beauty." A good example of thumbing the melody between two hands. Pretty and effective in a refined way. Not too difficult.

(22) "The Trout." Pretty and effective setting on black keys, increasing the difficulty. Final section has double octaves leaping against left hand setting and cadenzas.

The following, while interesting as transcriptions, are not so effective as solos. They are also in progressive order:

(23) "The Organ Player and Illusion." Light and delicate style, interpreting the will o' the wisp. Mod. difficult.

(24) "The Counterfeit." In mystic, declamatory vein.

(25) "By the Sea." Sustained, tremolando and left hand extensions are the features.

(26) "Gretchen at the Spinning Wheel." Expressive, characteristic setting; but not effective until the impassioned Finale is reached.

(27) "The Miller and the Brook." A quiet Pastorale, left hand tenths and arpeggios, also tremolo work.

(28) "The Pigeon." Florid, energetic and rather difficult setting, though good and varied technical practice, with an attractive, simple melody.

(29) "The Young Nun." Dramatic. Tremolando setting of 9 pages, requiring endurance.

(30) "Longings for Spring." Piquant and light, attractive setting, taken *prestissimo* with extensions. Rather difficult.

(31) "Benumbed." Expressive but with restless energy. Rotatory work with syncopatory effects.

The foregoing are all published separately by Augener. The Litolff Album comprises Nos. 19, 17, 16, 12, 18, 13, 25, 6, 10, 1, 9.

The following are Schubert transcriptions other than those already mentioned, and to be had in the Cranz Ed. of five volumes.

Those given here are effective as solos:

"Restless Love," Vol. I. Vol. II, "Die Stadt." "In der Ferne" ("Lamentation"—somewhat difficult.

Vol. III. "Krieger's Ahnung" ("The Warrior's Warning").

Vol. IV. "Gute Nacht" ("Good-night"). "The Stormy Morn." (Good study.) "In Dorfe" ("The Village"). (Good study.)

Vol. V. "Das Sterbe Glöcklein" ("The Passing Bell"). Difficult.

Most of these and of the next section are rather difficult. The Cranz Ed. includes forty-six transcriptions in all.

The Schubert Transcriptions here given are those which, while useful as piano representations, are *not* suitable as solos. Cranz Ed. Vols.:

Vol. I. "Calm Sea" ("Meerstille").

Vol. II. "The Fisher Maiden." "Abschied" ("Departure").

Vol. III. "Ihr Bild" ("Your Picture"). "Love's Message." "Atlas."

Vol. IV. "Die neben sonnen" ("The Mock Sun"). "Mut" ("Courage"). "Wasserflut" ("The Flood"). "Der Leierman" ("The Hurdy Gurdy"). "Tauschung" ("Illusion").

Vol. V. "The Rose."

THE LISZT SONG TRANSCRIPTIONS.

Transcriptions of Liszt's own songs. These include Liszt's arrangements of his own songs, as follows:

(1) Three "Liebesträume" ("Love Dreams"). 1850.

(2) Three Sonnets of Petrarca. 1839.

(3) Three Chansons—Male Part Songs. 1850.

(4) Six Songs. "Lorlei," etc. 1860.

Of these songs, the beautiful "Lorlei," "Mignon" and "Love Dreams" are unique—and the three latter in their rearranged form are among the finest lyrical and original compositions for the piano. Liszt's transcriptions of his own works naturally rank as original compositions. There are two settings of Liszt's "Lorlei," the easier one (Universum) having also the words. It begins simply and though effective is not difficult. The other one (Universum) sets out in more florid style and presents the full battery of Lisztian technique without being too difficult.

"The Liebesträum." No. 1, "Hohe liebe; No. 2, "Seliger Tod"; No. 3, "O Lieb."* No. 3, the most popular, is the most difficult. No. 1 is graceful and poetic; No. 2 is tragic and passionate; while No. 3 works up to a fine frenzy in the middle section.

It is interesting to compare the universally popular No. 3 in A flat with the transcription made by Raff (Liszt's pupil) of the same (with the title of Notturno, Op. 37), (Ricordi). Liszt's transcription of his own song is much more artistic, and allowing for the cadenzas, more concise. Raff, for instance, inserts an introduction and other matter, and commences the song an octave higher.

The settings of the "Petrarca Sonnets" were rearranged and became Nos. 4 and 6 of the "Années de Pélerinage," i.e., second year or Italian album.

---

* Ernest Austin has made an English words setting of this song, No. 3 (Ascherberg).

Liszt's collected songs, some fifty-seven in number, have been transcribed by Otto Singer in ten books (Kahnt). It is interesting to note the difference in result regarding the "Lorlei." Herr Singer's is a representative transcription (Book II), Liszt's own is a piano solo, with added matter including cadenzas. The difference is characteristic—though one cannot rank it among the effective solos. Another of the Singer collection, "Die zelle in Nonnenwerth"* ("The Convent Cell") ("Ach, nun taucht die Kloster-zelle"), No. 35, Book VII—a pathetic and expressive, attractive transcription in A minor which appears in Liszt's own version in a more florid solo guise. ("Die Zelle," Hoffmeister). The Hoffmeister Edition presents two versions with alternative fuller (and more difficult) passages. This appears as No. 2 in "Two Album Leaves." No. 1 being usually the "Valse Mélancolique" in E major. Note No. 1 in the Steingräber Edition is another Valse in A flat ("Valse Elegante"). Finck, in his "Songs and Song Writers," points out that in the characteristic feature of the art song—i.e., word painting—"Liszt goes beyond Schubert and his followers and substitutes for the regular strophic form of the poem a continuous musical plot." Liszt's best songs "belong to the Weimar period." He wrote six French settings, six settings, "Cällgemso," of Goethe's poems, of which Finck says: "'The King of Thule' is a ballad which

---

* Nonnenwerth—an island on the Rhine containing a half ruined convent and a chapel—a romantic summer home occupied by Liszt.

would be heard a dozen times in our concert halls every season, if singers were more enterprising." "To be sure," he adds, "it takes an artist to play Liszt's piano parts properly." There are settings also of Schiller's and six of Heine's, including "Lorely," abounding in "exquisite details of melody and harmony."

He says finally that: "With Liszt the development of the lied apparently reached its end."

"Geharnische Lieder" ("Armour Songs"), (Kahnt). These are male part song transcriptions.

No. 1, "Before the Battle"—stirring, dramatic and effective sketch. No. 2, "Nicht Gezagt" ("Dauntless"); and No. 3, "Es rufet Gott" ("God Warns Us").

Another version in concertante style appears separately under different titles. No. 1 being named "Esperance"; No. 2, "La Consolation"; and No. 3, "Avant la Bataille." These three being entitled "Trois Chansons."

The "Geharnischte Lieder" form Nos. 4 to 6 of Liszt's Twelve Male Part Songs, so that all items in this section rank as original. Liszt's "El Contrabandista," entitled "Rondo Fantastique," was an early work and is now out of print. It was based on a song by Manuel Garcia and published in 1837. The composition of this during the Swiss travels with Georges Sand and Daniel Stern—the two *littérateures*—inspired the former to write her lyrical story, "Le Contrabandier."

"Faribolo Pastour" (French song by Jasmin).

This is a quaint and interesting paraphrase; educationally useful and of moderate difficulty (Schott).

"Chanson du Bearn" (Schott). Out of print.

POLISH SONG TRANSCRIPTIONS.

"Glanes de Woronince" ("Gleanings from Woronince"), 1849 (Kistner). Woronince was the Polish estate of the Princess Sayn-Wittgenstein with whom Liszt became acquainted at Kieff in Russia in February, 1857. She was of Polish descent.* The above work consists of paraphrases of three Polish melodies and is dedicated to the princess. No. 1, a Ukraine ballad in B minor—a quaint and expressive melody—is treated somewhat in variation form, first one with shake accompaniment, and then in florid but attractive diversity. No. 2, in A flat, a Chopin melody (and treated also in the "Chants Polonais") begins as a waltz, and then runs off into quaver movement with right hand skips—a favourite item. No. 3, "Complainte" (a dumka) is a lento in the minor with introduction, transformed into a polonaise in the major with left hand arpeggio work.

When Liszt for the last time touched the piano, he played his favourite "Liebesträume," No. 3, and the No. 2 of the "Woronince Ballads"; this was on the occasion of his visit to Munkaczy, the Hungarian painter, on July 19, 1886.

---

* See the interesting sketch of the Princess in Sacheverell Sitwell's "Liszt," p. 155 f.

"GLANES DE WORONINCE," No. 2.

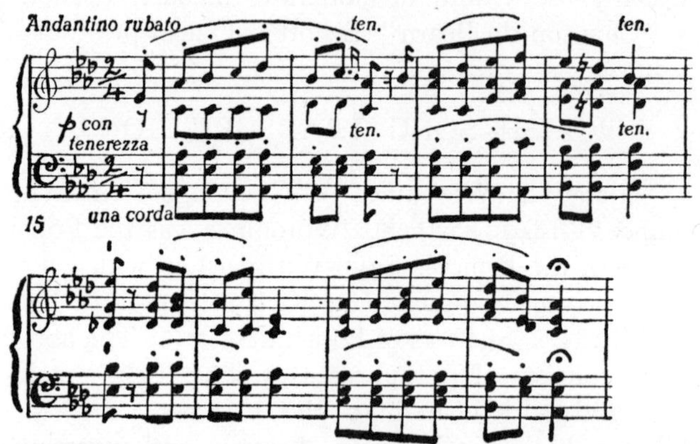

Polish colour is prominent in these three works, they are artistic, individual and attractive.

"CHANTS POLONAIS" (1860).

Chopin composed seventeen Polish songs (1824-44), and, of these there are six transcriptions made by Liszt under the above title. They are of easier grade than the "Soirees de Vienne." Taken in progressive order, they are:

(No. 4), "Hulanka" ("Drinking Song"), a mazurka in C. Easy and effective with glissandos thrown in.

(No. 2), "Wiosna" ("Spring"), in G minor—is an easy "song without words" in folk-song style.

(No. 3), "Pierscien" ("The Ring") in E flat. Expressive and effective.

(No. 1), "Zyezenie" ("Maiden's Fancy"). Pretty melody with three variations in key of G.

(No. 6), "Narzeczony" ("The Return"). A prestissimo or velocity étude of a stormy character.

(No. 5), "Mosa Pieszczotka" ("Nocturne") in G flat. Six pages. Popular in style. Includes cadenzas and a climax.

The first three being easy, they form an easy introduction to Liszt's modern technique.

EDITIONS. "Six Polish Songs" (Litolff 2600; Augener 5003). "Glanes de Woronince" (Augener and Kistner Editions).

VARIOUS SONG TRANSCRIPTIONS.

"Hussite Song" (fifteenth century). Paraphrase (Hoffmeister). This has the form of a Rhapsody. Of Bohemian origin, the allegro section is followed by the theme in the minor, as a *Lento*, succeeded by the Allegro in the major brilliantly treated. An effective work and not too difficult. This theme was to have been used for his youthful Revolutionary Symphony.

"Abschied." "Russian Folk Song" (Fritzsch). A simple characteristic short song and a simple setting.

"Three Lieder" from Wolff's "Tannhäuser," originally set by Lessmann (Junne):

(1) "Der Lenz is Gekommen" ("Spring is Come").

This makes a pretty piece with Lisztian technique of moderate difficulty.

(2) "Trinklied" ("Drinking Song"). Bold and melodious and attractive. Good practice in mod. diff. octaves; the melody is curiously the same as part of a once popular song, "The Midshipmite."

(3) "Du schaust mich an." Expressive and sentimental melody.

Liszt transcribed fourteen songs by Robert and Clara Schumann. Of these there are the:

"Schumann Album"—Nine Song Transcriptions (Tagliapietra Ed., Ricordi). Schumann composed both fine pianoforte music and songs, and it is interesting to see Liszt's treatment. Not every song lends itself to effective transcription. Out of the nine songs three make effective solos, and two of the three are little amplified, viz., "'Tis the Spring" and "Spring Night." Schumann himself tells in these. In "Devotion" ("Canto d'Amour"—"Widmung") we have more of Liszt and a favourite concert work.

There is also the provincial "Minnelied."

A popular collection of Transcriptions is found in Litolff Album, 2627, which includes:

Beethoven's "Adelaide" (1841). As a solo this is not very effective until we come to the three-page cadenza, where Liszt naturally comes to the front. He relates in 1840: "I have played it all without being hissed at the concert given at the Paris Conservatoire for the Beethoven monument." Liszt was devoted to Beethoven, who, however, did not excel as a composer of songs.

Schumann's "Widmung" ("Devotion"), 1849. This, on the other hand, is one of the finest Transcriptions in existence. There is not too much variety of technique, and the whole is artistic, but then Schumann's nature was essentially lyrical.

Schumann's "Fruhlingsnacht" ("Spring Night"), 1872. An effective number, technically and musically, in the key of F sharp, with wrist work, chordal shakes and arpeggios. Practical, impassioned and brilliant. The two following works are entitled "Two Arabesques."

(1) Alabiev's "Nightingale" ("Le Rossignol"), 1853. This Russian song is one not generally known, but the transcription is, and it makes a delightful little piece. The accompaniment trill forms a useful study.

(2) Alabiev's "Bohemian Song," 1853. In this gipsy air we wish at first for more of Liszt and less of Alabiev. The last 4 pages (out of 9) are effective. Canonic imitation is a feature of the middle section, and the allegro begins the development in florid, arabesque style, with a climax at the *ff* and a *pp* coda. Sitwell remarks: "A complete virtuoso piece in miniature: nothing better with which to end a recital."

Mendelssohn's "On Wings of Song." A favourite and popular melody. This is more of a transcription than a solo. The overlapping in the second verse is not easy but yields to practice. There are nine Mendelssohn Song Transcriptions in all. The Augener selection of three includes the above, also the "Gondola Song" and "Hunter's Farewell," taken in one—and laid out as a solo, varied in treatment, graceful and effective. Of the seven in Breitkopf's "Forty-two Lieder," the "Frühlingslied" stands out as a brilliant solo. The song itself is No. 38 in Augener's volume.

The "Zuleika" transcription is an instance of Liszt's wonderful power of enhancement of the original (No. 34 in the same collection), the transcription glows with beauty.

Liszt had a fondness for Beethoven's compositions, the Beethoven Song Transcriptions are in two vols. in B. and H. Edition: Six Sacred Songs, and six others, with "Adelaide" and "An die ferne Geliebte," the Augener Ed. of the Six Sacred Songs contains only one, No. 3 ("Against Thee Only"), which is laid out as a solo, this one making effective use of chromatic thirds and octaves.

"Hallop, Jagdchor und Steyrer," from the opera "Tony" (Kistner), 14 pages. A vivacious and tuneful hunting chorus and Styrian valse effectively presented.

"Oh, wenn es doch immer so bliebe" (Rubinstein), 13 pages (Kistner). An undistinguished theme, but one much improved by the variety of technique presented.

"God Save the Queen" (Schuberth), 9 pages. This makes a very effective solo, presents the theme in a new light, and ennobles it. It was issued also under the German title "Heil dir." The melody has become national also in Germany and America.

"La Marseillaise" (Schuberth). This also is effective, though not so varied as "God Save the Queen," it is useful for wrist and octave work—8 pages.

"Confutatis and Lacrymosa" (Mozart's "Requiem"), (Kistner). Impressive, short and effective transcriptions.

Lassen's "Hagen und Kriemhild," and (2) "Bechlarn" (1879), Hainauer, Breslau, from the "Nibelungen." These contain charming, refined music, the second being in idyllic mood.

Lassen's "Faust" (Hainauer), out of print.

Lassen's "Löse Himmel, meine seele" ("Deliver my Soul"). Edited by Tagliapietra (Ricordi). A very expressive and beautiful work in F sharp, fully florid but yet not too difficult.

Franz's "Es ist gekommen" (Kistner). A most attractive work of 6 pages, and not unduly difficult. Educationally valuable, it should be well worth reprinting.

This No. in Novello's Ed. of Franz's thirty songs is "Lo! he has come," of the thirteen Franz Transcriptions in the Breitkopf Ed. (forty-two Lieder). "Der Schalk" is very pretty and effective, as is also "Der Bote."

Beethoven's Op. 98. "Au die ferne Geliebte." Song cycle (B. and H.). From a pianistic point of view we do not recognise here the hand of Liszt. The settings are simple and practical as transcriptions. This applies also to the six Lieder, which, with "Adelaide," are in the Breitkopf "Forty-two Lieder Transcriptions"—now out of print.

Other transcriptions are "La Romanesca" (sixteenth century melody) and (Schles.) Bülow's "Tanto Gentile," Meyerbeer's "Le Moine," and Wielhorsky's "Autre Fois" (Fürstner), also out of print.

There are transcriptions of the Arcadelt "Allelieua" and "Ave Maria" (Peters), and "A la Chapelle Sixtine" (Peters), which are better as organ transcriptions; also of Weber's "Schlummerlied" (out of print) and "Einsam bin ich" ("Preciosa", of thirteen songs by Franz, and three by Dessauer; also Goldschmidt's two songs from "Die sieben Todensünden."

Weber, "Leier und Schwerdt" (Schles.). The transcriptions of the "Sword Song," "Prayer" and "Lutzows Wild Hunt" are of interest, but not as solos. (Out of print.)

An English Song.

An article in the "Musical Record"* draws attention to a hitherto unnoticed vocal work by Liszt: "Liszt's cosmopolitanism shows itself in his songs. Of his eighty-one songs, the majority, sixty-three in number, have German words, ten are settings of French texts, four of Italian, three of Hungarian. Only one little song—a masterpiece—is in English.

---

* "Musical Record," September, 1934. "An English Song"—Schrapp.

Oddly enough it has remained almost entirely unknown. It is not in the collected edition of Liszt's songs—nor in later collections." Sir William Cusins, Master of the King's Music (whom I met about 1890), had asked Liszt in May, 1879, for a contribution to the new edition of "Tennyson Songs." Three months later Liszt sent him a setting of "Go not, happy day." Cusins greeted it as a "gem of the first water"—and it is published in Kegan Paul and Co.'s "Tennyson Songs."

CHAPTER XXII.

INSTRUMENTAL TRANSCRIPTIONS.

From Bach. Liszt and the organ. Berlioz paraphrases, Hungarian Works, etc.

"A musican that with flying finger startles the voice of some new instrument."—ROSCOE.

Transcriptions, "They are poetical resettings seen through the medium of the piano."—OSCAR BIE.

Liszt was not only the first to revive interest in the old Italian and other piano classics, but he also was the first to transcribe some of the organ works of Bach. The "Six Preludes and Fugues" transcribed by him are those in A minor, C major,, $\frac{4}{4}$ time, the big C minor, C major, $\frac{9}{8}$ time, E minor (Wedge), B minor (Univ. Ed.). The piano cannot hope to compete with the organ, and Liszt, the Thunderer, recognised this, his filling in is not extravagant compared with that of some later transcribers. The very fine Fantasia and Fugue in G minor (Schles.) was also transcribed by him. It appears along with Liszt's original Prelude and Fugue on "B A C H" (B flat, A, C, B natural) in the Litolff Ed. and in Peters, Vol. 10.

LISZT AND THE ORGAN.

Here it should be said that Liszt was familiar, to some extent, with the organ of his day, and some of his compositions for the organ, for instance, the Fantasia and Fugue on "B A C H" (see Chapter XVIII) and the "Ad Nos" Fantasia, though pianistic, are amongst the important works for the King of Instruments.

During a Swiss tour in 1836, with Mons. Pictet and the *littérateures*, George Sand and the Countess d'Agoult, Liszt tried the organ in the Cathedral of Fribourg.

"Liszt sat before the organ; near him stood Mooser (the organ builder) to work the stops. His fingers began to intone Mozart's 'Dies Iræ' with modulations that died like shadows in the deep. Suddenly the tones of the organ sounded *fortissimo* and the harmonies rolled like an unchained deluge through the precincts of the sacred edifice." Pictet describes in detail the progress of the master's improvisation, "unfolded with all the verve of genius" (Ramann).

Liszt's interest in the organ was aroused and Liszt was the first to presume that an organist should have a manual technique equal to that of the virtuoso pianist.

By 1835 he had written organ pieces, but it was not until 1851 that his "Ad Nos" Fantasia was sent to the publisher. Dr. Eaglefield Hull (in the

"Rotunda," April, 1928) was of the opinion that: "The 'Ad Nos' Fantasia exhausts all the technique of the modern organist, just as Liszt's one and only piano Sonata is even to-day the greatest achievement for the modern pianist."

It is interesting to quote here from an article on Transcriptions by Franklin Peterson ("Musical Record," January, 1895). He asks:

"How can the puny pianoforte hope to rival the Great Organ? How can a weak hand hold the reins of Sol's chariot or grasp the thunderbolts of Jove? Compare the dignity of the G minor Fantasia as it sounds on the organ with the fussy, self-important and entirely inadequate effect it has on the pianoforte."

One might reply that as regards magnitude of sound the organ is supreme—and yet an organ transcription as rendered on the piano may be quite impressive.

Liszt had visions of a piano with greatly increased powers and facilities. Writing in 1837 in the "Gazette Musicale," he says:

"The keyboard of the organ, with its capabilities of expression, will show the natural way to the invention of pianos with two* or three keyboards, and so complete the peaceful victory. The pianos with bass pedal, the polyplectrum, the spinet, and other

---

* In the autumn of 1934 Miss Winifred Christie gave a recital in London on a double-keyboard piano.

imperfect attempts, are a proof of the generally felt necessity for its extension."

We may remind the reader that features of the eighteenth century harpsichord were double keyboards, with various stops (harp, lute, etc.) for influencing the quality of the tone and swell shutters as with the Swell in the organ. A later development was the piano-violin, in which the strings were actuated by a rosined bow contrivance, and having the effect of a string quartet. The writer's first delightful introduction, as a youth, to the sonatas of Beethoven, which are frequently orchestral in thought, was through one of these instruments—no ordinary piano being there available. A piano which would combine string quartet tone with various percussive effects and in different pitches is quite possible, and would tend to make up for the lack in the piano of varied tone colour such as we hear in the organ and the orchestra.*

Prelude on "Weinen Klagen" motive (Augener Edition), 5 pages. This is built by Liszt on the theme from Bach's cantata: "Weinen Klagen" (weeping, lamenting), used by Bach as a ground bass (basso ostinato) for the "Crucifixion" chorus. A poignant theme and composition of moderate difficulty. Liszt worked it up to a passionate climax —but with a soft ending. Liszt has also taken the same theme for his

* For an interesting account of such inventions, see Weitzmann's "History of Piano Playing" (trans.), (Schirmer).

Bach Theme (Weinen, Klagen) as a Basso Ostinato.

Variations on "Weinen Klagen" (17 pages), in the same key (F minor). Here Liszt lets himself go in alternating chords, chromatic octaves and arpeggios. It is a powerful work in sad and pessimistic mood. (Univ. Ed., also Peters, Vol. 10.) He has arranged the same for organ, and it is interesting to see how he limits his naturally exuberant technique (Peters and Univ. Ed.) in the process.

With the above I link also the: Fantasie and Fugue on "Ad Nos" (B. and H.), the Chorale used in Meyerbeer's "Prophet." This fine work, 42 pages in length, appears as a piano transcription by Busoni. Originally written for the organ, it was probably planned out first on the piano. The Fantasia consists of a Moderato of 14 pages, in C minor. II, an Adagio in F major, of 11 pages, with variations on the theme in a freer manner. As a solo it is best to take the 17 page section from the Allegro deciso, which forms a short introduction to the Fugue itself. It is from this Allegro that Dr. Fricker's organ edition (B. and H.) begins, from which point, with modifications, contractions and expansions, the piano work proceeds. A two-page cut is also suggested before the Vivace molto. Except in the second or third part, purely polyphonic work, massiveness and brilliance are the characteristics, and it is not too difficult. Other smaller works for organ are included in the two vols. in the Peters Edition.

BERLIOZ PARAPHRASES.

"Un Bal"—Symphonie Fantastique (Berlioz), (Hofmeister). This is one of the earliest works Liszt tried his wings on, the theme is from one of his friend, Berlioz's, symphonies. Written on a dance theme, this paraphrase is both practical and effective—though the theme itself is not individualistic. It dates 1832-33, but was not published until 1836. Liszt did a Transcription of the whole work, and Berlioz, writing in November, 1834, states: "The 'Symphonie Fantastique' is out, and as our poor Liszt has dropped a terrible lot of money over it, we arranged with Schlesinger that not one copy was to be given away."

Ernest Newman, writing in the "Sunday Times," says: "If any young musician wants to get to the innermost secret of this art, I would recommend to him the close study of Liszt's piano arrangement of

Berlioz's 'Symphonie Fantastique'—a masterpiece, if ever there was one, not only of poetic understanding, but of technical ingenuity."

Berlioz had a genius for orchestral colouring, but he lacked melodic inspiration and to some extent the power of characterisation.

Someone asked Liszt for his opinion on Berlioz's symphony, "Harold in Italy." Liszt replied:

"I really don't believe that Harold ever saw Italy; I find no traces in the symphony of a single Italian impression. . . . Perhaps Harold took the wrong route and travelled through Palestine without knowing it."*

"L'Idée Fixe." "Andante Amoroso" (Berlioz), (Cranz). This has charm. The melody and Liszt's filigree work suit each other (5 pages), key A. This and the following are from the Symphonie, "Marche au Supplice" (Schles.). Interesting in Berlioz's orchestration this may be, but lack of the orchestral colouring leaves it somewhat unattractive. The same may be said of the "Marche des Pélerins" (Joubert), from the symphony, "Harold in Italy."

Fantasia on the Tyrolienne from "La Fiancée" (Auber), (Cranz). (Published in Paris by Troupenas.) This is marked Op. 1, and, therefore, is an early work. It shows brilliancy, and on the whole individuality in technique—but lengthy as it is (21 pages), requires cuts to make an acceptable modern solo. D'Artigue wrote of this: "It dis-

* "Personal Recollections." Donajowsky.

plays marked earnestness and Byronic spirit; it is coquettish and brilliantly written in Herz's style."

THE "SOIRÉES DE VIENNE" (VALSES CAPRICES).*

These charming works associated with Vienna, consist of nine numbers founded on various Viennese waltzes by Schubert. The round or whirling dance known as the waltz (valse) seems to have developed mainly in Austria, and at first, in Vienna, was a slow dance, but quicker forms were introduced. Mozart and Beethoven wrote these "Deutsche Tänzen"—German dances, as they were termed, but Schubert was the founder of the artistic modern waltz. In the collections of Schubert's dances (Peters) are eleven under the titles of "Walzer," "Ländler," "Deutsche Tänzen," "Valses Sentimentales" and "Valses Nobles." They are in quite simple sixteen-bar form and are, as mentioned, intended for dancing.

Liszt's association with these consisted in taking various numbers from here and there, and turning them into artistic *salon* compositions. The plain $\frac{3}{4}$ time (mm. tum. tum.) is converted by flowery quaver movement, changed harmonies, interludes and imitative passages, into something essentially

* Though sometimes termed "Valses Caprices," the term originally belongs to three pieces, "Grande Valse de Bravoura," in B flat, "Valse Melancolique" and "Valse de Concert" ("Lucia" and "Parisina" motives), (Schles.), Op. 6.

different in aspect, and yet with the Schubert foundation.

The best of the series are No. 2, in A flat (founded on Schubert's Op. 9, No. 1), and the "Ländler," No. 3, with the Op. 9a (No. 6), written in the style of a moderately difficult Chopin waltz.

No. 3, in E. More brilliant, more advanced right hand arpeggios, imitative passages, octaves and sixths, velocity scales. 12 pages and a long Presto Coda.

No. 4, in D flat. In capriccio style with working out, chords and octaves. Easier than No. 3.

No. 5, in G flat. 8 pages. Artistic, mostly in quaver movement with left hand solo. Grade with No. 4.

No. 6, in A minor. First Version, 7 pages. Fairly easy, with a triplet variation form. Based on the "Valses Nobles," Nos. 9 and 10. Second Version, 11 pages, with cadenza and development of No. 10 added.

The Bote and Bock (Ashdown) Ed. (Vol. 3) gives Liszt's later additions in smaller type.

No. 7, A major. 5 pages, with left hand arpeggio work.

No. 8, in D. 11 pages. More massive. Capital wrist practice in chords and octaves.

No. 9, in A flat, is founded on the lovely "Sehnsucht Waltz," and presents six variations in chromatic work, sixths and arpeggios.

No. 1, in A flat, is lacking in interest.

The "Soirées" also make a good introduction to

Liszt's style. Nos. 3 and 9 require higher technique, No. 8 is less difficult. None are really difficult. No. 6, first version, is about the easiest.

HUNGARIAN MUSIC.

Liszt's Hungarian compositions form a class to themselves.

"I, too," he said, "am a member of that ancient race."

Liszt wrote his Hungarian pieces *con amore*, and his work on Gipsy Music is proof of his great interest in the music of his native land. We must remember, however, the dual nationality represented, the Magyar and the Gipsy. The other day, a leading Hungarian composer, Prof. Bartok, protested against the "prevailing misconception which regarded gipsy music as representative of Hungarian musical genius." "There are," he says, "at least 10,000 genuine Hungarian folk songs in existence." Much reputed Hungarian music is "the work of anonymous amateur composers embroidered by gipsy performers with their traditional flourishes." (See Chapter XII: "Hungary and the Rhapsodies," also Musical Association Lecture, November, 1902, "Hungarian Music of a Thousand Years," by Ilona de Gyory.)

YOLANDO MERO *says* ("Etude," April, 1926) that "the famous Second Rhapsody of Liszt is far more Slavic in type than Hungarian. The Sixth Rhapsody, however, is typically Hungarian." She continues: "The Liszt tradition in Hungary is immense. He ranks with the greatest of Hungarian national heroes."

REMENYI, the Hungarian violinist, claims that the theme treated in No. 7 is by himself, and that the one in No. 4 is not Hungarian, but an imitation of Schubert's "Serenade" (Remenyi, "Biography," page 93).

Recently a violin Rhapsody written for Remenyi was performed by Szigeti for the first time in England, in February, 1934.

DOHNANYI states ("Etude," April, 1926) that the folk tunes used by Brahms in the "Hungarian Dances" "were written by known composers shortly before the time of Brahms. It is reported that Remenyi gave them to Brahms." See also end of Chapter XII.

HUNGARIAN TRANSCRIPTIONS.

"Scenes from Hungary" (Univ. Ed.). This comprises five folk songs, short and simple, of which No. 4 is the best. In addition, there are three other pieces. No. 2, "Puszta Wehmuth" ("The Lonesome Heath"), in easy rhapsody form, with expressive *Lassan* and lively *Friska*—an attractive piece; also No. 1, "Memorial Music for death of Mosonye," and No. 3, "To the Memory of Petofi."

"Ungarisch in A." David (Hammond). This is one of a series of violin pieces by David, "Bunte Reihe." An easy and tuneful transcription.

"Album d'un Voyageur," seven Hungarian melodies (Leduc). Also "Trois Melodies Hongroises" (Leduc), which contains two items from this Album. No. 3 of the Album is a short, slow movement in D flat, in rhapsody style. Nos. 4 and 5 are from the Sixth Rhapsody with cadenza work omitted. No. 6, in G minor, is in the style of a rhapsody. No. 7 is a fuller and improved version of the Fourth Rhapsody. No. 1 in the album is a hymn introduction. No. 2, is a short, attractive, moderately easy dance-form. The so-called "Three Melodies" are the

"Szozat."

three movements from the Sixth Rhapsody—including the Finale—which is also published separately as a "Melodie" in B flat.

"Szozat and Ungarischer Hymnus" (Rozsavolgyi). This consists of an effective Czardas movement, the Andante or Hymnus, and the Czardas resumed. This is one of the best Liszt works in rhapsody style. It is named Rhapsody No. 16—but that No. is claimed in the Nos. 16 to 19 issued by the Universal Ed. It is not difficult, mainly octaves and chords in technique.

Attention here might be drawn to the moderately easy "Trois Morceaux," in old Hungarian dance form (Rozs), by Liszt, which are typical, interesting and educationally useful. No. 1 is the best. Nos. 2 and 3 are Czardas in style.

HUNGARIAN RHAPSODIES (1-15).

It is asserted that the airs represented in the Rhapsodies originated, *generally speaking*, with the Magyar peasants, not the gipsies who played them. In the Thirteenth Rhapsody "Come in, my Rose," and a drinking song are used; in the twelfth an air entitled "We will Dance Together." Other melodies used are:

"In Heaven there Shine One Thousand Stars."
"The sleigh is flying."
"The bulrushes are ripe," etc.

Some of the airs are used by Brahms in his "Hungarian Dances."

We can now treat in progressive order and describe those most interesting works.

No. 3, E flat major. 5 pages. Moderately difficult. Well known air in bass. Easy cimbalom (dulcimer) effects.

No. 5, E minor. 8 pages. Fine, impassioned elegiac work. Octaves and general technique. A non-gipsy work.

No. 7, D minor. 11 pages. Showing vivace. Left hand octave leaping passages. No. 18 could follow here.

No. 13, A minor. 11 pages. A beautiful "oriental" slow movement here interprets the saying: "The Magyar weepingly rejoices"—a true rhapsody followed by true rousing gipsy music.

No. 4, in E flat. 8 pages. Begins nobly rubato and develops "florid poetic style." Concludes with a merry-go-round in octaves.

No. 6, D flat. 10 pages. Opens in march style, in alternating rhapsody. Finale resembles No. 4. Begins piano. Last two pages brilliant and exciting.

No. 8, F sharp minor. 11 pages. The dignified *lento* taken *mesto* (sadly) is the best movement. The allegretto is in F major.

No. 1, in E major. 17 pages. The least characteristic so far, the best section being the "quasi improvisato."

No. 15, in A minor. 12 pages. "The Rakoczy March." This is a traditional march, and one of the most characteristic Hungarian themes. A very effective work, employing glissando and free octave work. Writing on November 6, 1882, Liszt says:

"The real title of my transcription of the 'Rakoczy March' should be 'Paraphrase Symphonique.' It has more than double the pages of Berlioz's well known one, and was written *before* his. From delicacy of feeling for my illustrious friend I delayed the publication of it until after his death; for he had dedicated to me his orchestral version of the 'Rakoczy,' for which, however, one of my previous transcriptions had served him."

No. 14, in F minor. 16 pages. Somewhat patchy at beginning as a funeral march, leading to an "heroic" allegro followed then by a capriccio, and gipsy music, and a lively finale.

No. 11, in A minor. 8 pages. Begins with zimbalom effects. Free and varied technique. Ends with a prestissimo in octaves in key of F sharp.

No. 2, C minor. 17 pages. This is the best known and perhaps the best liked rhapsody. The zimbalom effects are well to the fore in the Friska and the whole goes with a swing.

No. 10, in E. 13 pages. This requires neat playing. Velocity scales and cadenza accompaniments, also glissandos are features.

No. 9, in E flat. 25 pages. The "Carnaval de Pesth." This is the longest, a brilliant and a merry piece. In its various presentations of the theme, the gipsy element is almost absent.

No. 12, in C minor. 13 pages. This is the finest of the set and the most typical, with its zimbalom *campanella*, tremolando, shakes, sprightly and bravura style.

The best are Nos. 5, 13, 15, 2, 9 and 12.

RHAPSODIES 16-19 (UNIVERSAL EDITION).

Taking these four also in progressive order, they fall thus:

No. 18, F sharp minor. 6 pages. Moderately difficult. Octave on black keys in F sharp.

No. 17, D minor. 5 pages. Moderately difficult. Octaves with thirds, ends in B flat.

No. 16, A minor. 11 pages. More difficult. Cadenzas, octaves, augmented intervals.

No. 19, D minor. 21 pages. Difficult. Skips, thirds, general technique.

They are published (Nos. 16 and 17, 18 and 19) in two books. Of the others there are many editions: one volume, Ashdown; two volumes, Schott's Library Edition, etc.

The author of "Personal Recollections" (Reeves) once mentioned to Liszt that a Liszt rhapsody brought up visions of "a demon let loose, trying to smash a piano," and that when he had heard Liszt play the "Pester Carnival" (No. 9) he could hardly realise that he was listening to one of the "Rhapsodies." Liszt laughed and attributed the impression to the Leipzig school, one originated by Mendelssohn, who apparently was somewhat jealous of Liszt. He further avows that "Liszt *hardly* ever used his muscular powers" and that "the great charm of his playing lay in the delicate and subtle, and not in the muscular and powerful."

"Marche Hongroise" (Schubert), duet and solo (Leduc). This is much more than a transcription.

The opening theme and trio of the march (second movement) in Schubert's duet, "Divertissement à la Hongroise"* are given and filled out, and on the return of the chief theme follows new matter brilliantly presented and ending in C major. Schubert's weak points, discursiveness and "heavenly length" avoided, the work makes an acceptable whole.

"Marche Hongroise" (Szabady-Massenet), (Heugel). This transcription is made from Massenet's orchestral version. A very forcible work, in real Hungarian style, it is effective and not difficult.

"Hungarian Storm March," 1843 (Litolff), five pieces. This also is very impetuous and in popular style. It is very effective but more difficult than the previous work with passages in thirds and eighths, and with optional more brilliant passages.

Other compositions utilising Hungarian national airs are the "Coronation Hungarian March" (Schuberth), "Hungarian Geschwind" (quick march), "Introduction and March" by Szechenyi (Rozs).

RUSSIAN TRANSCRIPTIONS.

"Tarentella," Dargomijski (Rahter), in A minor. This is a brilliant work with Russian flavouring. The original—as Liszt tells in a note, was for three hands, one playing the bass

---

* Schubert, "Duet Divertissement," Op 53 and 54 (Lit.).

"TARENTELLE" (DARGOMIJSKY).

throughout. Liszt makes a break in this and adds "petites variantes et amplifications." It is good practice, effective and not difficult. Sixteen pages.

"Polonaise," Tchaïkovsky's "Onegin" (Rahter). This is more cosmopolitan, but it makes a good concert work. The episode in C makes grateful contrast. Mainly octaves and arpeggios. Brilliant and not really difficult. Eighteen pages.

VARIOUS TRANSCRIPTIONS.

In addition there are transcriptions of themes from Wielhorsky's "Romance" (out of print); Bulbakov's "Russian Galop" (Schles); Conradi's "Gipsy Polka"; "Elegie," "Prince Louis" (Schles), now out of print; also "Gaudeamus"; "God Save the King" and the "Marsellaise" (Schuberth); "Tscherkessen March," Glinka (Schuberth); and the well known "Schiller March," Meyerbeer (Schles.); with Lassen's "Symphonic Intermezzo," 1883.

"Marche Funebre" ("Le Dom Sebastian," Donizetti (Cranz). A fine theme to work on, and Liszt's artistic restraint makes this an acceptable work—one more nearly a paraphrase than varied. Liszt reaches out as usual in the technique—which can, however, be kept subordinate. Thirteen pages. Another Donizetti transcription is the "Elegy d'apres Sorriano," "Feuille morte" (Troupenas, Paris).

"Valse de Concert" on two motives from "Lucia" and "Parisina." Nineteen pages. In A (Schles). A piquant work, though not on distinguished themes, it requires a cut (pp. 13-18) to make it effective. This, with two other valses ("Valse di Bravura" and "Valse Mélancolique" were classed as "Valses Caprices" (1840).

"Valse de Concert" (from the suite in valse form by De Vegh). There is a good deal of effective concert material here if its twenty-one pages are reduced by omitting pages 6 to 11. Liszt is sometimes apt to wander and gets diffuse like other great composers who could be mentioned. It is not difficult and worthy of being preserved in abbreviated form.

"Bunte Reihe" (Kistner). These consist of twenty-four pieces for violin and piano by Ferd. David, transcribed in simple, straightforward style. Two only of these require special notice.

No. 19, the well known "Ungarisch," in its simple first form; the second version has much more Liszt in it—nine pages as compared with five of the first version—and is well worthy of separate publication. It is a miniature rhapsody.

No. 20. Tarentelle," in A minor, also makes an individual and pianistic work, melodious and effective for concert or educational work of moderate difficulty.

"Sarabande and Chaconne" from Handel's

"Almira" (Kistner). This is one of the best transcriptions in sound classic style. Of moderate difficulty it is best for concert purposes to omit the chaconne and proceed to the grandioso and omit twelve bars of the final allegro. The introduction of the chaconne weakens the effect of the whole.

"Schiller March," Meyerbeer (Joubert). This also is one of the best and most effective transcriptions. Liszt seems to have been happy in the Meyerbeer transcription. At a time when Meyerbeer as a successful composer of opera was looked down upon in high musical circles because he was a Jew, Liszt stood by, and by his effective transcriptions helped the cause of music, and of Meyerbeer. A most attractive work for general use, without being really difficult, it is well worth issuing in a good edition.

TWO EPISODES FROM LENAU'S "FAUST."

(1) "Der Nächtliche Zug" ("The Night Ride"). This is from Liszt's incidental orchestral music to Lenau's "Faust." First episode (J. Schuberth). It consists of five connected sections, but little emerges that can be of separate use for the piano. For the piano and organ (or orchestra) sections 3, 4 and 5 are very effective. In No. 3 we hear the church bell and the distant chant of monks. In the next the church theme, "Pange Lingua," appears, treated with increasing interest. The finale yields a passionate outburst but ends softly with resignation.

The scene supposed is a dark gloomy night in

spring. Faust enters on horseback, nightingales are singing in the trees and lights are showing in the distance. A religious procession singing "Pange Lingua" passes by and Faust relapses into tears.

(2) The first "Mephisto Valse" (second episode), "The Dance in the Inn" (Schuberth). This is much played as a piano solo and is taken from the same work. Here the slight theme and the syncopated section in D spin out to twenty-three pages. It is good practice but needs more than one cut to make the best impression (Hofmeister Edition). Other editions of this are found in Litolff, Augener Edition and Peters, Vol. 5. A mystical atmosphere prevails. Mephisto plays the violin for the peasants and there is an air of abandonment.

"Mephisto Valse," No. 2 (Fürstner). Written at the Villa d'Este. This number, occupying twenty-nine pages, is again more suited as incidental music than as a solo, unless considerably abbreviated. It was orchestrated in 1880-1 by Liszt. It is vivacious but "thin." This applies also the "Mephisto Polka" (fifteen pages) which is incidental music only. There is an out of print third "Mephisto Valse" (Fürstner), which was orchestrated by Reisenauer. A fourth "Mephisto Valse" also—the latter is unpublished. The "Mephisto Valses" were written in the "eighties." To the same period belongs the "Valse Elegiaque" ("Valse Oubliée," No. 1).

The "Tanz Momente," of Herbeck (Doblinger). These are light, short movements in the style of Schubert's valses. Nos. 4, 7 and 8 would make a good suite. No. 8, of seven pages' length, needs one and a half pages cut before the *sempre accelerando.* These are effective and of moderate difficulty.

"Three Marches," Schubert. (1) "Trauer " (Funeral) March. (2) March in B minor. (3) "Reiter" (Trooper) March in C. 1845 (Peters, Vol. X).

These are solo paraphrases of Schubert's "Duet." Marches No. 1 is No. 5 of the Op. 40. No. 2 is No. 3 of the same; and No. 3 is No. 1 of the Op. 121.

Liszt's plan in No. 1 seems to have been to present the duet march as a solo in amplified and enriched form up to the trio and then to increase the florid ornamentation or technical development up to the climax. In No. 2, however, he introduces *a new episode* in A flat in the grand manner, returns to the B minor theme, but finishes tumultuously in B major—instead of the minor.

In No. 3, episodes in A minor, F minor and major are introduced at length, and a coda in the return portion. The simple duets have become powerful—almost orchestral—and difficult solo presentations.

"Gretchen," second movement, Liszt's "Faust" Symphony. This transcription is one of those useful as a souvenir. Much of the acceptableness of orchestral music depends on orchestral colouring which cannot be supplied on the piano. Other transcriptions are those of Saint-Saëns's "Danse Macabre" (Durand)* and Cui's "Tarentelle" and Liszt's own violin work, "Epithalam," arranged for piano.

* Liszt's own "Totentanz" is also named "Danse Macabre."

Saint-Saëns was a pupil of Liszt's. Liszt, writing him regarding the "Danse Macabre" (Durand) says:

"I beg you to excuse my unskilfulness in reducing the marvellous colouring of the score to the possibilities of the piano. No one is bound by the impossible. To play an orchestra on the piano is not yet given to anyone." Notwithstanding the above Liszt's transcription possesses atmosphere. It is not gruesome, for that depends on orchestral colouring, but is light and playful in spirit, pianistic, effective and not too difficult—in length twenty-one pages.

"Valse d'Adéle," Zichy (Heugel). This is a paraphrase of a valse for left hand in E flat, by Count Zichy, the one armed pianist. Of moderate difficulty it begins quite simply; its middle section is in imitative form and the conclusion is brilliant.

"La Fête Villageoise" in G (Heugel). This is a mod. diff. re-arrangement of the composer's early "Pastorale" in E, given in the Swiss Album ("Années de Pélerinage") extended by episodes from 2 to 5 pages—a better and more artistic whole.

Andante, Finale and March, Raff's "King Alfred." These themes, though not outstanding, are brilliantly dealt with. Raff was a pupil of Liszt.

Interlude from Liszt's "St. Elizabeth" (Kahnt). This is neither outstanding nor effective, apart from the whole.

"Salve Polonia," Interlude. Liszt's "Stanislaus" (Kahnt). Like the two previous works, it is of little attraction, except to those interested in the works as a whole. The extract is 34 pages long.

LISZT

Overture, "Les Franc-Juges" (Berlioz), (Schott). This is quite in the orthodox style, with little extended technique. On the other hand, the Overture to "William Tell" (Rossini), (Schott), shows interlocking and crossing of hands and other extensions with brilliant effect. Overture to "Tannhäuser" (Wagner), Peters (Vol. 12), and Univ. Ed. (Vol. 12) —a well-known virtuoso setting.

Liszt was early enamoured of Weber's works, and he made paraphrases of Weber's Overture to "Der Freischütz" and "Oberon," and the "Jubel" Overture.

"Bülow March" (Schles.). This is Liszt's transcription of an orchestral march by him dedicated to Von Bülow—his son-in-law. One must almost look on this as a musical joke. In mock academic but pompous style it struts along. It does not achieve distinction. Other transcriptions of Marches were those of the Goethe "Festmarsch," "Huldigungs March,"* the "Künstler Festzug," the "Hungarian Storm March" and "Coronation Marches," and "Vom Fels zum Meer" ("From Crag to Sea").

To the above transcriptions may be added the piano scores or "Partitions de Piano," of Beethoven's and Hummel's "Septetto" (Schubert), Beethoven, Symphonies (B. and H.), Berlioz's "Symphonie Fantastique," "Marche des Pélerins" and "Danse des Sylphs" (Simrock).

---

* The piano version is dated 1853 (published in 1858); the orchestral arrangement was published in 1860.

CHAPTER XXIII.

PIANO WORKS WITH ORCHESTRA.

Hungarian and "Wanderer" Fantasias. Spanish Rhapsody. "Totentanz," Concertos.

"Now strike the golden lyre again,
A louder yet, and yet a louder strain."—DRYDEN.

A new element is introduced here. It has been said that when the organ is opposed to the orchestra, one is the Emperor and the other the Pope.

As associated with the piano the orchestra assumes a still more commanding aspect, and much depends on its management in a concerted work. Liszt proved himself a master of the orchestra. Calvocoressi says here: "Liszt has been perhaps the most admirable orchestrator who has ever lived," so we may be sure that with him the piano does not suffer by its association with the many-voiced and powerful modern orchestra.

There is another aspect, and that is timbre or colour.

"Instrumentation is in music what colouring is in painting" (Berlioz), and thus the association of the piano with the orchestra by the added colouring makes a more artistic whole. In a musical composition the pictorial outline is represented by melody, the light and shade by varied harmonies, and the colouring by acoustical timbre or tone colour. Possibly a string quartet may be likened to a sketch in sepia, a septet with wind instruments to a water colour, and a symphony to a glowing picture in oils.

The works for piano and orchestra which demand first consideration are the Hungarian Rhapsodies. Liszt arranged fourteen of these, under the title of "Fantasias on Hungarian Melodies," and they were dedicated to Von Bülow. He also orchestrated six others, between 1858 and 1860, and greatly extended them in symphonic style, in which work he was assisted by Doppler, of Buda Pesth. In the Apponyi Rhapsody the national *cimbalom* is used, but in the others its place is taken by the harp.

The most popular of these orchestral compositions with piano is the

HUNGARIAN FANTASIA, 1860.

This is a delightful work, based on two national melodies, and a typical example of Liszt's genius. It is based on the fourteenth Rhapsody, re-written and extended. A slow introduction leads to the main theme, Allegro eroica.

After the manner of the Rhapsodies, with their alternate slow *(Lassan)* and quick *(Friska)* sections, a Molto adagio and Moderato with cadenzas leads

HUNGARIAN FANTASIA.

to a gipsy Allegretto with the usual arabesque embroidery, the re-entry of the Allegro is characterised by sweeping velocity scales. The Vivace assai—light and fleeting—hurries to the close. The difficulty is about that of the average solo rhapsodies. Edition (Litolff), (two pianos), Peters.

"The Wanderer" Fantasia, 1851 (Schubert's Op. 15). This is so-called because the Adagio is based on the "Wanderer" *lied* by Schubert. Schubert was more orchestral in style than pianistic, and generally lyrical in aspect. It is instructive to see how Liszt turns mere accompaniment work into an entity, and how the comparatively feeble technical figuration is amplified and made brilliant. While the orchestra breathes out lovely Schubert melody, the pianist is kept extended at times—and the result is surpassing.

Liszt was enamoured of Schubert's work. He speaks of him in a letter to Prof. Lebert as "my cherished hero of the Heaven of youth."

Writing of the above "splendid 'Wanderer' Dithyramb," he says: "Several passages and the whole of the conclusion of the C major Fantasia I have re-written in modern pianoforte form, and I flatter myself that Schubert would not be displeased with it."

"Rhapsodie Espagnole," for piano and orchestra. This is an arrangement made by Busoni from the original Liszt solo. The sub-title is "Folies d'Espagne et Jota Aragonese," the former appearing as the Andante moderato—and the Jota in the Allegro. The brilliant orchestration greatly adds to this attractive work. It forms "a fine piece of pyrotechnics" (Sitwell). Universal Ed. (Friedman), for two pianos—also Peters, Vol. XI.

"Polonaise," Weber, Op. 72 (1851). Here Liszt utilises the Largo from the Polonaise (Op. 21) in E flat minor as an Introduction, transposing it to E minor, thirteen bars of this, with forty-seven bars of Cadenza and new material (quasi Andante) prepare the way for the otherwise abrupt entry of the theme, the amplifying is left till the sextolet portion enters. With a supporting orchestra, Liszt is able to double the passage work, and, when the climax comes, to pile "Pelion on Ossa." While effective, this work is not really difficult. (Edition Peters, Vol. XI.)

The "Totentanz" ("Dance of Death"), 1849-50. This somewhat gruesome composition consists of variations on the old chant, "Dies Iræ," and had its origin, according to Liszt himself, on beholding the fresco entitled "Triumph of Death"—Death the Reaper.

Berlioz also utilised the theme in the "Witches' Sabbath" of his "Fantastic Symphony."

For sheer musical interest the variation form is in itself handicapped from the beginning. Much depends on the theme. In this case one could hardly select one less promising, but

THEME OF "DIES IRÆ."

association comes to the rescue, and only one variation seems to suggest the church (Canonique), otherwise the 33 pages are replete with the brilliant and bizarre. In imagination we hear the gibbering of ghosts and the *ignis fatui* of the spirit world flutters by. (Edition Peters, Vol. XI.) As an impressive masterpiece of sardonic and demoniac aspect, this claims a niche of its own. Borodin considered this the most powerful of all Liszt's works for piano and orchestra for its originality and beauty. The alternative title, "Danse Macabre," has also been used by Saint-Saëns in a work of which Liszt has also made a transcription (Durand).

THE CONCERTOS.

No. 1, in E flat. Editions, Litolff, Peters, Vol. IX, etc.

This popular work is in four movements, and is constructed in style something after the freer form of the Symphonic Poems. Written in 1848, it was first performed during the Berlioz week at Weimar in 1855.

Allegro. The very striking and dramatic theme opens as follows.

CONCERTO IN E FLAT.

Cadenzas are early in evidence—the virtuoso is to the fore, leading to a beautiful but transitory Nocturne melody in E flat. Battalions rush in to reinforce the main theme, and then the lovely Quasi Adagio appears.

Allegretto vivace. This is a piquant gipsy movement. In 1855 schools of national colour were hardly in existence, and the very appropriate use of the triangle in the orchestra, though used by Beethoven in the Choral Symphony, by Haydn, Schumann, Berlioz and Wagner, considerably astonished the unthinking and hide-bound critics, one of whom dubbed it the Triangle Concerto.

The sparkling and capricious motive is ornamentally developed by the soloist, and the Allegro animato leads to the Marziale, where the previous Quasi Adagio now appears as a march.

Liszt himself says: "It is only an urgent recapitulation of the earlier subject-matter, with quickened, livelier rhythm." "This kind of binding together and rounding off a whole piece at its close is somewhat of my own."

Arthur Johnstone, the well-known critic of thirty years ago, writing in 1903, speaks of "the superb Liszt Concerto in E flat—quite the most brilliant and entertaining of concertos. No person genuinely fond of music was ever known to approach it with an unprejudiced mind and not like it."

Concerto No. 2, in A. Also written about 1848, this was not performed until 1857 at Weimar. Liszt has the forward mood. The Concerto is all in one movement and dominated by one theme. It is not a democracy but an autocracy. Liszt skilfully uses his method of metamorphosis. It has been said that the effect is kaleidoscopic, and that it is daring and audacious. "And ever and anon the first wailing melody returns in one shape or another."

Apart, however, from matters of form and mode of

CONCERTO IN A.

workmanship—and the latter is skilfully concealed—the Concerto is a charming work. One attractive movement is where, after the *crescendo* on a dominant pedal, the theme appears in the form of a bravado march dominated by the orchestra (see Ex.), after which Liszt follows with his glittering ornamental showers up to the massive and closing climax. Notable editions, Steingräber (annotated) and Litolff, 26476.

The "Concerto Pathétique" (1850), (B. and H.) deserves attention here. Originally written as a piano solo for a competition at the Paris Conservatoire, it appeared as re-cast for two pianos, requiring two virtuosi, and with an added slow movement. In this form it was not quite a success. It has been arranged by Burmeister for piano solo and orchestra—necessarily making some alterations and additions. In this form it was played at the London Promenade Concert in 1907. It is also published as a grand Solo de Concert in E minor (Grosses Konzert-Solo), (B. and H.), which in Weitzmann is ranked with the sonata. An orchestral arrangement was made also by Ed. Reuss, and Liszt, writing Breitkopf in November, 1885, says:

"Although your firm is already saddled with two editions of my 'Concerto Pathétique,' I recommend to you most particularly the excellent orchestral arrangement of the same piece to which I have added some bars for completion, which should also be included in the possible (?) later piano editions." This two piano Concerto is a most attractive work. The Allegro emerges in classic style, leads to a romantic Andante in which the first piano has a bird-like cadenza and the second piano later billowy waves in the bass. In the following Allegro the familiar Wagnerian theme appears, in various forms. The whole is effective.

Pathetic Concerto.

Concerto, "Malédiction." Liszt left a work with this title in MS., but unfinished, as not completed for orchestra.* Otto Lessman (in Weitzmann's work) reports that it contains "many beautiful poetic touches."

* Lists of the unpublished compositions are given in Grove (some since published) and in Sitwell, p. 338.

Chapter XXIV.

ORCHESTRAL WORKS, SYMPHONIC POEMS AND THE SYMPHONIES.

"Instrumental music, alone of all the arts, expresses sentiment without presenting their direct representation."—Liszt ("The Gipsies and their Music").

"Divine art strives incessantly to reproduce the unity of Infinite Form—or the absolutely Beautiful."—Lamennais.

The Symphonic Poems.*

These are orchestral works, but they had their origin in the piano, and as Liszt arranged versions for solo piano, two pianos and piano duet, the student of Liszt's piano works will be interested.

The poems are most important examples of orchestral music, as based on or influenced by a programme. As the creator of the symphonic poem, Liszt extended the ideas of his predecessor, Berlioz, and these orchestral works are still unsurpassed in their own domain.

Liszt himself has said: "The programme has no other object than to indicate the spiritual moments which impelled the composer to create his work; the thought which he endeavoured to incorporate in it."

* See Huneker, p. 107.

Liszt decided his own "form," declaring unanswerably that "the return, change, modification and modulation of the motives are conditioned by their relation to a poetic idea."

(1) "Cé qu'on entend sur la montagne," 1849, is a study of nature based on Victor Hugo's "Les feuilles d'automne." It is otherwise entitled the Berg (Mountain) Symphony; unlike descriptive music of a prior age, it was not drawn as a picture—but an exposition of spirit or feeling.

Editions. The Symphonic Poems are arranged in the B. and H. Edition for solo duet and two pianos. The Litolff selection for solo consists of Nos. 2, 3, 4 and 6. Miniature scores of the Symphonic Poems and Concertos are to be found in the Eulenberg Edition.

(2) "Tasso" (1849), Lament and Triumph. This commemorates the sufferings and triumph of Tasso, the Italian poet. Liszt avowed that he was strongly influenced in this Lament by Byron's poem.

The work opens in a depressed and tragic mood. With the Adagio we have the Gondolier's Song, while the Minuet expresses life at the Court of Ferrara. The second part from the Allegro in C, depicts the glory of his martyrdom. Years afterwards, in 1866, Liszt was moved to add an epilogue: "Le Triomphe Funèbre de Tasse" (B. and H.). It describes the approach of the cortège in lyrical, rhythmical style—in alternative elegy and triumph.

(3) "Les Préludes." This was inspired by Lamartine's "Meditations Poétiques." "What is life but a

series of Preludes to that unknown song of which Death gives the first solemn note?" Manliness is succeeded by "the enchanted demon of love." The storm of destiny arises only to be succeeded by the peace of the Pastorale. And yet again the trumpet's call to arms is heard, and the work ends in supreme confidence.

(4) "Orpheus" celebrates the triumph of art in its civilising aspect over humanity.

The hymn-like theme opens loftily, and the tender persuasive Lento, followed by the hymn, rises to a climax and finally subsides in a calm *dolcissimo*. Wagner esteemed this as the best of Liszt's works.

(5) "Prometheus"—suggested by "Prometheus Unbound"—depicts the Titan in defiance—a classic theme represented in a romantic manner. Liszt sums it up as "Sorrow and Glory," a "triumphant desolation"—represents the musical character of this theme. Olivier, the French statesman, and son-in-law of Liszt, writing in his Journal in 1861, speaks of the "ravishing chorus" in "Prometheus," and hails Liszt's "Faust" as "a real masterpiece."

(6) "Mazeppa." The ballad of "Mazeppa" consists of two songs built upon a single *motif*. Wagner wrote about "Mazeppa": "When I ran through it the first time I gasped for breath. The poor horse made me unhappy. Nature and the world are still a terrible thing." This symphonic poem was based upon the piano etude of that name, but it was greatly extended. The impetuous Allegro agitato interprets the mad three days bound to a wild horse.

The martial movement stands for Mazeppa when rescued—and instated as leader of the warriors of the Steppe.

(7) "Fest klänge." "Festal Sounds" was written about 1853, when the projected marriage with his patroness and helper, Princess Witgenstein, seemed to be a possibility twice, and finally was thwarted through political and family influence.

It may be said to depict the guests in procession, a love scene, a dance, and finally a national anthem. The "Polonaise" gives it also national colour.

(8) "Héroïde Funèbre." Liszt introduced into this a part of his early Revolutionary Symphony of twenty years previous. It is intended to consecrate the Tomb of the Brave. A Hungarian atmosphere pervades the work. It was performed at the Liszt "Memorials" in 1886.

(9) "Hungaria" is a national tribute to the struggles and aspirations of his countrymen, and is redolent of national melody and rhythms.

(10) "Hamlet." An original work, lofty, serious and emotional. A mood and tone picture of the immortal drama.

(11) "The Battle of the Huns" was suggested by a picture portraying a battlefield near Rome between Pagans and those professing Christianity. In the finale he introduces and develops the chorale, "Crux fidelis"—thereby "the Victory of the Cross, with which I," as he says in a letter, "both as a Catholic and as a man, could not dispense."

Liszt writing August Manns, then conductor of

the Crystal Palace Concerts (in 1879) says that the picture "represents two battles—one on earth and the other beyond—according to the legend that the warriors continue to fight after their death as spirits. In the centre of the picture the Cross is seen with its mysterious illumination, and upon this my symphonic poem is based."

Sitwell says: "The beginning of 'Hunnen-schlachet' is terrifying—it has to be heard to be believed."

(12) "Die Ideale" is intended as an illustration of Schiller's poem, an "elegy on departed youth." Liszt, however, strives, he says, for "the continued realisation of the highest ideals in life."

Bülow preferred this to "'Tasso,' the Preludes and the other Symphonic Poems."

Wagner, writing to Liszt, refers to a male chorus, "The Artists," in "The Ideal," and describes his appeal to artists as a great, beautiful and admirable gesture of your true life as an artist." Wagner is profoundly moved, and says: "I do not know a soul to-day who would be capable of doing anything like it, of doing it with such power."

(13) "From the Cradle to the Grave." This was a work of Liszt's old age, and lacks somewhat in freshness and vigour, but it is concise, and worthy of performance.

Liszt writes: "It was suggested by a drawing of Michel Zichy." It is divided into three parts (Edition Bote and Bock).

Of a similar nature and with all movements developed out of one characteristic all-embracing theme in each, are:

THE SYMPHONIES.

"The eternal feminine leads us onward and upward."

The Symphonies are two of Liszt's greatest works.

In the "Faust" Symphony—Liszt's masterpiece (1861), we have three character pictures: the delineation of Faust, Gretchen and Mephistopheles—the Margaret movement being extraordinarily beautiful.

It has been well said that the "Faust" Symphony is the climax of the Romantic Age.

Arthur Johnstone, the critic, says regarding the "Faust" Symphony: "Many composers have made 'Faust' music of one kind or another"—"Wagner's "Faust" Overture is the nearest akin to Liszt's Symphony. But it is much too one-sided to vie in interest with Liszt's tremendous composition, which seems to grasp the whole subject and tear the very heart out of it."

The less known but very fine (1856) "Dante" Symphony is descriptive, in a similar manner, as manifested in (1) the dramatic "Inferno," (2) "Purgatorio" and Magnificat, (3) "Paradise." These include the Prayer and Repentance melodies, also the Magnificat and Hosanna for women's voices. Weingartner speaks of its "thrilling representations of the torments of Hell and the "Purgatorio"—"the summit of his creative power." Both symphonies were given by the B.B.C. Orchestra in the season 1934-5.

The other ORIGINAL ORCHESTRAL WORKS are:

Lenau's "Faust," two episodes: the "Nächtliche Zug" ("Night Ride") and "Mephisto Valse," No. 1.

"Les Morts," Oraison.

"Salve Polonia" and two Polonaises from "St. Stanislaus."

Goethe, "Fest March," "Huldigungs March."

Künstler, "Festzug," Hungarian Storm March.

Hungarian Coronation March and "Vom Fels zum Meer" ("From Crag to Sea").

Transcriptions from these have been mentioned.

ORCHESTRAL ARRANGEMENTS made by Liszt:

The Hungarian Rhapsodies. Six of them, aided by Döppler, also Nos. 17, 18 and 19.

"Szozat" and "Hymnus," "Marche Funèbre" ("Third Year").

Bülow's Mazurka Fantasie.

Zarembski's two "Dances Galiciennes."

Schubert, "Four Songs" and "Four Marches."

MISCELLANEOUS WORKS include:

"Epithalamium" and "Romance Oubliée," for

piano and violin, and "Ein Grabe," Elegy for string quartet, and 12 Books of Technical Studies.

Of the Breitkopf Complete Edition of the works of Liszt:

"GESAMMTAUSGABE,"

31 vols. have been published (price £32 10s.), viz.:

Orchestra, 13; piano solo, 12; church and sacred vocal, 1; songs, 3; piano transcriptions, 3.

CHAPTER XXV.

LISZT'S POSITION AS A COMPOSER.

The bird's-eye view. Critics repelled. Choral and organ works. A summary.

"It is time that the critique of defects should be followed by a critique of excellencies."—CHATEAUBRIAND.

"Both teacher and taught should turn more and more to this mighty teacher—by taking as a model the unselfishness of Liszt's life and his ideal conception of art."—EUGEN D'ALBERT.

Music, like the other arts, has its periods of advance and recession, its fashions and fancies. From the historically crude it is progressing ever and anon to something better, breaking out in new directions here and there, gaining perfection in one aspect and losing ground in another.

Liszt, in his personal life, experienced the usual vagaries of fortune. He was popular until the next star came along. When Thalberg appeared in Paris, the fickle Parisians promptly forgot about Liszt, and Liszt's music was little played until he appeared again.

Then there were short-sighted people who worshipped Liszt as a pianist, but who could not imagine him as a composer.

In his own words (written in 1865), people had for some fifteen years been saying:

"Be a pianist and nothing but that,"

and he laments in Chamfort's words that:

"*Celebrity is the punishment of talent* and the chastisement of merit."

Again, in writing Louis Köhler in 1859, he refers to the latter's observation that people cannot immediately "label and catalogue me correctly and place me in an already existing drawer." While he always advised friends not to perform his works, he admits (in 1867), frankly, "that it would be very agreeable to me to stand in a somewhat better light in Vienna as a composer than I have hitherto done. But the time has not come for that—and if it should ever come, half a dozen of my compositions, for instance, the 13th Psalm, the 'Faust' and 'Dante' Symphonies, some of the Symphonic Poems and even *horribile dictu:* the 'Prometheus' chorus, would have to be introduced to the public in proper style."

THE BIRD'S EYE VIEW.

There is ground indeed for the failure of the public and critics to "place" Liszt.

Like Wagner, his position was, and is, for many people, hard to ascertain. His piano works in general are still a closed book for the average amateur pianist, his beautiful songs (sixty) are not sung, and his symphonies and choral works heard occasionally only—and how can the position of any composer be estimated without at least a bird's eye view of his works? Apply this condition to those for the piano and we find that but a few are heard in public occasionally. Notwithstanding this, there are a few bold spirits with the larger vision, who place him among our greatest composers; others again deny this, saying thus: "(1) He was lacking in originality and spontaneity, (2) proper development of ideas, and (3) his creations were *neither abundant nor varied enough.*"

CRITICISM REPELLED.

As regards the last (No. 3) it is difficult how such an attitude can be maintained for a moment.

First, get together all Liszt's original piano works, estimated at about 375. Hear, and, much better still —play them. Result—not proven.

Secondly—originality and *inspiration.* No composer was ever inspired or original always—as the schoolboy put it, "No man is sane at all times." The inspired works will remain—the others die out.

We should also remember that Liszt did not seek publicity for his works. Writing to von Herbeck in 1859, he thus protests: "My intimate friends know perfectly well that it is not by any means my desire to push myself into any concert programme whatever." Later he advises von Bülow to lessen the number of his works put forward. "People," he says, "do not want to hear so many of my things."

Thirdly—development of ideas. This is a matter of choice. Music has progressed in development from the fugal style to the sonata style, and from that to the process of metamorphosis—invented, and developed, by Liszt—and each time it has made a step forward.

Liszt, like all great men, was an innovator—we are indebted, as Prof. Niecks puts it, "for the many impulses and suggestions he has given to his contemporary composers and successors by his innovations in harmony, form, orchestration, pianoforte style, etc. Wagner confessed himself a debtor to Liszt, the harmonist." Prof. Niecks continues: "We are indebted also to Liszt for perfect art works, many beautiful little things, some beautiful large ones, and innumerable beautiful parts of large ones which as *wholes* fail to reach perfection."

It is good to read this, for exactly the same criticism can be applied to Bach, Handel, Beethoven, Mozart, and all the great composers. Let us then first seek to *know* Liszt, and

"Prove all things—hold fast to that which *is* good."

Huneker ("Liszt," p. 142 f.) points out where Wagner is indebted to Liszt for his themes, whereby "Liszt was the loser, the world of dramatic music the gainer." Nor was Wagner the only one. If Liszt learned much from Chopin, Meyerbeer and Berlioz, the younger men, Tchaïkovsky, Rubinstein and Richard Strauss, made free use of Liszt.

Cecil Gray also says: "It is not only Strauss and

other modern composers of symphonic poems who are directly and profoundly indebted to him, but also the great Russian composers of the last century, particularly Balakirev, their leader, and Borodine." French impressionism "is already to be found in such pieces as "Jeux d'eau" or "Au Bord d'un Source" ("Heritage of Music"—Oxford Press). In addition, Debussy speaks of "the undeniable beauty of Liszt's work."

In 1911 came the centenary of the year of Liszt's birth, and numerous Liszt festivals, at which his works were performed, were organised. "No longer," said Saint-Saëns, "was it possible to affirm that the composer of 'Christus,' the 'Legend of St. Elizabeth,' the symphonies 'Dante' and 'Faust,' and of the Symphonic Poems was simply a writer of 'pianist's music.'"*

This work does not pretend to deal with any but the piano works of Liszt, it will suffice therefore to give merely a list of his other works.

CHORAL WORKS†—SACRED WORKS.

The Wagnerian "Missa Solemnis," known as the "Graner" Mass, performed at Gran, in Hungary, in 1856. Hungarian Coronation Mass, 1866-7. Psalms 18 and 116 (all published by Schuberth). Choral Mass in A minor, 1886. Requiem for men's voices, The "superb" Psalm 13, and Psalms 23, 129 and

* "Liszt, the Pianist," "Musical Times," Sept., 1921.

† Masses and Psalms. See Huneker, "Liszt," p. 187.

137—(all Kahnt). Mass for men's voices, 1848. "St. Cecilia's Day" (female voices, 1875). "St. Elizabeth," the "Opera Sacra"—the second part and Crusaders' March are very effective. "St. Stanislaus," 1874 (all Kahnt). His *magnum opus*, the church oratorio, "Christus"* (Schuberth). Various publishers: Ten Church Hymns. Also an ethereal and fascinating "Angelus," or "Chorus of Angels," 1849. "Contentis Organis," alto solo and chorus, 1881; "St. Francis d'Assisi," male chorus and orchestra, 1885; "Nun Danket," "An den Heiligen Franciscus," 1862; "Natus est Christus"; "Christus est geboren"; "Hymn de l'Enfant"; "Pax vobiscum"; "Septem Sacramenta"; "Qui Mariam"; a Mass in C minor (B. and H.); and "Le Dieu des Magyars," for male voices (Petofi and Liszt), 1881.

CHORAL WORKS—SECULAR.

"An die Künstler" (male ch.); choruses, "Prometheus"; "Festival Album"; "Festgesang"; "Festlied"; "Mariengarten"; "Morgenlied"; "Die Allmacht" (Schubert); "Zur Säcular Feier"; twelve and sixteen Male Part Songs; also "Angels' Chorus" from "Faust," and "Bells of Strasburg" (Schuberth).

SONGS.

Fifty-five Collected Songs, 1860. Six Songs, 1843, including "Loreley," "Mignon's Song" and "Angio-

* "Christus." See Mohl, Chapter VIII. "Christus" was performed at the Leeds Festival in October, 1934.

lin du Viando crin" (transcribed in 1860 as piano solos). Three sonnets and three Liebesträume—later transcribed as piano solos. Five other songs, ("Go not Happy Day." "Il m'aimait tant"—also transcribed). "Joan of Arc," "Crucifix," Psalms 129 (baritone) and 13 for alto. "Ungarns Gott" (baritone), "Threnodie" and "Wartburg Lieder." See Kahnt's collection of fifty-seven songs, in ten books; Breitkopf and Härtel, sixty songs, in three volumes.

"Christus"* was performed at the Leeds Festival in October, 1934.

Mr. Ralph Hill says: "There are a dozen or so of Liszt's songs that may with every justification be called first rate. 'Mignon's Lied,' 'Du der von dem Himmel,' 'Ueber allen gipfeln,' 'Wo welt er' and 'Lorlei,' may be cited as conspicuous examples."—("Sackbut," October, 1932.)

WORKS FOR ORGAN.

The Peters Edition collection contains in:

Vol. I. (1) Variations on "Weinen Klagen," built upon the ground bass taken from the Bach cantata of that name. The *piano version* is dated 1862, that for the organ, 1863—nineteen pages. (See Chapter XXII.) (2) "Evocation à la Chapelle Sixtine." (a) "Allegri's Miserere"; (b) Mozart's "Ave Verum." (3) "Litany, Ora pro nobis." (4) Hymn, "Der Papst."

Vol. II. (1) Fantasia and fugue on "Ad nos"—

---

* "Christus." See Mohl, Chapter VIII.

the chorale in Meyerbeer's "Prophet"—fifty pages, forty-five minutes in performance. An abbreviated version is in general use. (2) Prelude and fugue on B.A.C.H. (B flat, A. C. B natural). These are both very fine standard organ recital works. (3) Adagio in D flat. (4 and 5) Church hymns, "Salve Regina" and "Ave maria stella." (6) Organ mass for church use—eight numbers (short). (7) "Requiem"—seven numbers. (8) "Zur Trauung" (marriage ceremony).

Besides the above there is "Rosario," three organ pieces published posthumously, and about thirty arrangements of other works. (See Göllerich for list.)

Of arrangements of organ works for piano there are:

(1) The Prelude and Fugue on B.A.C.H.

(2) Six Organ Preludes and Fugues and the Fantasia and Fugue in G minor of Bach.

(3) An arrangement by Busoni of the "Ad nos Fantasia." For a description see Chapter XXII.

PIANO ACCOMPANIMENT AND DECLAMATION.

Mozart was one of the first to point out the charming effect of beautiful speech or declamation to appropriate music. Liszt had the dramatic instinct and the ear for colour, and it is most instructive to see how, for instance, he fits in with the sentiment of the "Mournful Monk." As the poem is declaimed:

"In Sweden stands an old grey tower,
Sheltering owls and eagles,
Sport of lightning, storm and shower,
For some nine hundred years or more," etc.

We hear the rising storm in hurrying triplets over a whole tone scale in the bass.

"Der Traurige Mönch" ("The Mournful Monk"), Ballade by Lenau, 1872, (Kahnt).

"Lenore," Ballade by Burger, (Kahnt), 1860.

"Des todten Dichters Lieb," poem by Jokai. ("The Dead Poet's Love," 1876 (Taborsky).

"Der Blinde Sänger" ("The Blind Bard"). Ballade by Tolstoy. (Bessel), 1877.

"Hilges Treue," by Dräsecke, 1859-70.

"Der Ewige Jude," by Victor Hugo (posthumous)*

Ralph Hill in "Some Reflections on Liszt"† says, "The declamatory style of Liszt's music appears to reflect the power of the spoken word. The texts, the exposition, the peroration, the continuous climaxes express the personality of the man. Few composers have put more of themselves into their music than Liszt has."

---

* More detail as to the above general works by Liszt may be gained from the catalogue given in Göllerich, Grove's "Dictionary," and Corder's "Liszt" (Kegan Paul), though neither of the latter seems to be quite complete.

† "Sackbut," October, 1932.

LISZT'S WORKS—A SUMMARY.

There are various estimates as to the number of Liszt's works. The detail as to this has been gained mostly from Ramann and Breitkopf and Härtel's catalogue. It is said that out of 1,300 works about 400 are original—another says 375, while Sir Alex. Mackenzie says, "There exist some 700 original works (large and small) not counting transcriptions and arrangements." A catalogue—but not complete —will be found in Grove, while Göllerich devotes fifty-five pages to the list of the composer's works. For Liszt's literary works see Part II, Chapter 26, "Liszt the Writer."

The following list is summarised from Göllerich. It excludes works for piano solo and includes printed works only.

(1) Orchestra. Original works.

Symphonic poems	13
Episodes, Lenau's "Faust"	2
Second "Mephisto Waltz"	1
"Faust" and "Dante" symphonies ...	2
Legends	2
Marches	5
Fest-Vorspiel and Künstler Festzug ...	2

(2) Arrangements for Orchestra.

6 Rhapsodies, 2 marches and 5 others ...	13

(3) Piano and Orchestra.

Concertos and Totentanz	3
Arrangements, 3 fantasias, polonaise and	

the "Pathetic" Concerto	5
(4) Other composers' works orchestrated (Schubert 4 marches)	9
(5) Arrangements for small orchestra (elegies, etc.)	7
(6) For strings (arrangements), 30; organ and trombone, 2	32
(7) Piano Duets, arrangements	54
(8) Piano Duet and Klavier Scores, works ...	25
(9) Arrts. for two pianos	35
(10) Melodrama for klavier	5
(11) For Organ, original and arrangements	32
(12) For Harmonium, arrangements ...	19
(13) Vocal, oratorios, etc., 5; masses, 5 ...	10
(14) Choral Works with orchestra, arrts. ...	19
(15) Psalms, 7; and sacred songs, 24; with organ or orchestra	31
(16) Secular, male choruses, 26; female, 2 ...	28
(17) Songs, set with orchestra, 16; with klavier, Fr., Ital. and German, 23	39
(18) Collected Lieder, 57; others, 7	63
	456
Add Piano Solo works, original and transcriptions	716
	1272

Yes truly Liszt "*was* something more than a mere virtuoso."

CHAPTER XXVI.

LISZT THE WRITER—LISZT THE MAN.

Liszt in England. The Liszt Centenary.

"Music unites those arts which appeal to the senses, with those which belong to the spirit."—LAMENNAIS.

"Liszt was the most enamoured of literature of all musicians who have ever lived."—ANTCLIFFE.

We have seen how in the days of his youth Liszt was an ardent revolutionist. Like his son-in-law, Wagner, he sought new paths in the musical world; and he was not content to preach reform, but the written word was accompanied by deeds. Pianists are apt to forget that Liszt was the most literary of the great musicians. Schumann was the next; but it is surprising how great or voluminous a writer Liszt was. Liszt's collected writings occupy seven volumes in the edition published (in German) by Breitkopf and Härtel, as follows:

(1) "Frederic Chopin, Life of. Translation. (William Reeves Bookseller Limited). 1852. (Very poetical.)

(2) Essays (nine) and twelve letters. The essays are on works by Thalberg, Schumann, etc.

(3) "Dramatic Essays" (seventeen) on various operas, etc., including those of Wagner.

(4) Articles on Berlioz.—John Field and his nocturnes. (1859.)

(5) Criticisms, various (six).

(6) "The Gipsies and their Music in Hungary. Translated by Edwin Evans. Two volumes. (William Reeves Bookseller Limited.)

(7) Prefaces to Liszt's musical works, etc. As mentioned English translations are available in Nos. 1 and 6.

Liszt took a practical interest in outside matters. The working of the various musical institutions deeply interested him and his essays include some on church music. He also edited several issues of the piano classics.

LISZT'S LETTERS.

These are computed in number at seven hundred, but new collections keep on appearing.

"If you have ever read the two-volume 'Correspondence' between Wagner and Liszt you will see that Liszt was the most unselfish person in the world. Great as he was, he was willing to sacrifice himself for the sake of advancing the interests of the greater man, Wagner."—CLAYTON JOHNS, "Etude," April, 1926.

The principal Liszt correspondence is comprised in some ten volumes, as edited by La Mara.

Liszt and Wagner, two volumes.

Liszt and Bülow, one volume.

Liszt and the Grand Duke of Saxony.

Liszt and Carl Gille.

Liszt and contemporaries.

Also four volumes general correspondence.

Two volumes of an English translation appeared in 1894 (Grevel, etc.). The "Correspondance de Madame D'Agoult" extends only to 1840. (Paris, 1933, seven shillings and sixpence.)

Liszt was a cosmopolitan. A Hungarian father, German speaking mother and a Parisian upbringing, contributed energy, insight and tact to his humanity. He forgot his native tongue, and preferred always to speak and write in French, and he also became acquainted with the best French literature in its various branches. His magnanimity towards rivals and friends was well known. Prof. Niecks says: "The study of the letters fill us with ever increasing wonder. What sympathy, what *savoire faire*, what wisdom, what practical usefulness, what diplomacy, what courtesy, what art? An extraordinary man."

LISZT THE MAN.

"Sorrow is hard to bear, and doubt is slow to clear."—BROWNING.

This is the age of nationality in music. With Chopin the Pole, Liszt the Hungarian, Grieg the Norwegian, and others entered the influence of local colour. We do not expect followers of this school to mould their thoughts after the models of Bach and Beethoven. The standard is different. "He belonged to a race endowed with different—almost opposite characteristics.* He sprang from noble

* Sir Alexander Mackenzie's "Liszt" (Murdoch).

LISZT

Hungarian lineage, was cultured, dignified and open handed, his recognised position was that of a prince among artists."

His purse was ever open to those in distress and his help, instruction and guidance as an artist to those less fortunately endowed. He not only gave a "tremendous impetus" to the art of piano execution, but raised the level of the artist enormously.

Of all nineteenth century composers he was perhaps the most subject to violent prejudice and misrepresentation and the worst features are, as the eminent critic, Calvocoressi, says:

"The disdain and total ignorance still to-day usually manifested in nearly every land towards the magnificent artistic work of Liszt."*

Not only did he accomplish and open out a new world in the art of piano composition and execution and in symphonic music, but in the psalms and masses he wrote, he brought about as great and important a change in sacred music.

That his faith was simple and sincere is evident in the letter he wrote to the Princess Sayn-Wittgenstein in 1860, at the age of forty-nine (nearly). He says:

"Yes, Jesus Christ on the Cross, a yearning longing after the Cross and the raising of the Cross, this was ever my true inner calling; I have felt it in my innermost heart ever since my seventeenth year, in which I implored with humility and tears that I

* Calvocoressi's "Liszt" (Laurens, Paris)

might be permitted to enter the Paris Seminary. In spite of the transgressions and errors which I have committed and for which I feel sincere repentance and contrition, the holy light of the Cross has never been entirely withdrawn from me." This was in a letter directing the disposal of some of his belongings.

He mentioned "the redeeming word *caritas*," charity, and charity was surely the motto of his life. In all his actions and writings there was no trace of jealousy or spite.

From those who really knew both the man and his work, nothing but love and admiration ever came.

Liszt's point of view is aptly illustrated in his letters. Writing to Von Schober, friend of Schubert, on April 3, 1840, he says: "I have sent back Kiss of Dresden. He is a good fellow, but a little awkward and wanting in a *certain point of honour*, without which a man is not a man as *I* understand the word." And again, in asking D. Brendel not to protest against a song by Hiller, he says: "Regardless of the fact that we must not expect that they on their side will deal thus with us, we must consistently and faithfully carry out and fulfil this simple *justice and fairness*, and thus show the gentlemen how people of a nobler mind and more proper cultivation behave."

LISZT IN ENGLAND.

Constance Bache, the sister of Walter Bache, gives an interesting comparison of Liszt's visit to England in 1840, when on his fourth visit he appeared at a concert in Sunderland. (See "Musical Record," June, 1902.) The occasion was related by a musician who was present. Apparently the concert had not been well organised.

A "thundering rap" was heard, and the writer heard a loud voice ask: "Is dere a concert here?" In strode Liszt. "His hair was long and somewhat sandy, and he wore a dark blue and ragged coat. He carried a book in his hand at which he glanced from time to time." During the concert the writer looked at the book and found it to be a German translation of Shakespeare's "Tempest"—at the opening of a description of a storm. "It at once struck me he had been attempting to reproduce that storm on the piano."

Miss Bache compares this visit with Liszt's first visit to St. Petersburg in April, 1842, before three thousand people in the Salle de la Noblesse: "His breast decorated with innumerable orders from the crowned heads of Europe, and his great mane of fair hair tossed back as he always wore it."

Again we see Liszt in April, 1886—forty-four years later, at Walter Bache's reception in London —where "bent in body, but not broken in spirit, with the same great mane of hair, silvered, though hardly turned by age, he stood up once more, and for well nigh the last time before an expectant audience of some four hundred guests "he played that night the finale of Schubert's 'Divertissement à la

Hongroise,' and his own Rhapsodie Hongroise in A minor."

Constance Bache, in her "Brother Musicians" (page 296) says: "The fortnight of Liszt's stay in England was one continued succession of concerts, dinners and other *reunions.* The excitement of the musical world was at its height; it spread amongst all classes; the very cabmen talked of the 'habby Liszt'; the whole air was full of the Liszt-fever."

A feature of the celebrations was a performance of Liszt's "St. Elizabeth." Miss Bache writes (page 290): "Well, the performance was splendid; Albani is simply perfect as St. Elizabeth. I never heard anything more beautiful and refined."

At the Grosvenor Gallery concert the Liszt programme was: "Angelus," for strings; "Angels' Chorus" from Goethe's "Faust," sung by R.A.M. students; "Bénédiction de Dieu," played by Walter Bache; three songs from Schiller's "Tell."

Liszt left England on April 20, 1886, and passed away on August 1. (See end of Chapter XIII.) As Constance Bache remarks:

"Between 1842 and 1886 a life's history had been enacted, so strange, eventful and marvellous that the stories current about it seem almost to approach the fabulous."

Again we look forward—this time from 1886 to 1911 (a step of twenty-five years)—to the Liszt centenary, which was celebrated everywhere in musical circles in honour of the master.

THE LISZT CENTENARY, 1811-1911.*

The Liszt centenary was, as mentioned, celebrated in 1911. Liszt was born on October 23, 1811.

The chief celebrations were at Buda Pesth and Heidelberg. At Buda Pesth Siegfried Wagner, Liszt's grandson, conducted at the five days' festival. The oratorios, "St. Elizabeth" and "Christus," were performed and four eminent pupil pianists took part, viz., D'Albert, Lamond, Rosenthal and Sauer. At Heidelberg four great programmes were given with the help of Saint-Saëns, Strauss, Busoni, Risler and Von Possart. The "Requiem," "Gran" and "Coronation" Masses were given at Pozsony, near Raiding, his birthplace, while the symphonies and chief symphonic poems were performed in many continental centres.

No Liszt festival was given in England, but various works, the preludes, Hungarian fantasia, etc., were rendered; at the Norwich Festival the E flat Concerto, in Bath the "Dante" Symphony and piano sonata. Thus celebrated musical Europe "the centenary of the benefactor of us all—Franz Liszt."

WHAT OF THE FUTURE.

Liszt died in 1886. What about the future? Is there no one to carry forward the banner of Liszt?

One can say in reply that as a *school* of piano

---

* A. Sallès, "Le cententaire de Liszt" (Paris, Fremont, 1911). "Musical Record," October, 1911. The Liszt Centenary.

composition, only the modern Russians, Glazounov, Scriabin (early works), Liadov, Balakirev, Stcherbachev, Blumenfeld, Wihtol and others, have followed in his train. They have secured the modern technique with new and beautiful effects—but are not always inspired. Gerald Abraham points out "Liszt's influence on the Russian nationalists" ("Musical Record," March, 1934), "and how that Liszt's two Lenau episodes and 'Danse Macabre' had a strong influence on Borodin and Rimsky-Korsakoff. They learnt something also of his sonorous and bold style of orchestration." Finally, we have to remember that "art is long and time is fleeting," and that whatever the future may bring forth we can only cry:—EXCELSIOR.

"He was an artist to the heart's core."—GRILLPARZER on Beethoven.

Programme of B.B.C. Promenade Concert in London on Thursday, September 20, 1934:

"March of the Crusaders" ("The Legend of St. Elizabeth"); Pianoforte Concerto No. 1, in E flat; song with orchestra, "The Lorelei"; "A Faust Symphony" *(a)* "Faust," *(b)* "Margarita," *(c)* "Mephistopheles"; Pianoforte Concerto No. 2, in A; symphonic poem, "Les Préludes."

PART III.

CHAPTER XXVII.

A PRACTICAL INTRODUCTION TO LISZT.

GRADED SETS AND REPERTOIRES.

MASTER WORKS.

"The greatest of all Liszt's achievements is his recreation of the technique of piano playing."—ERIC BLOM.

"Certain of Liszt's compositions, which were once regarded as impossible of execution, are now everyday performances of the young pupils of the Conservatoire. On the piano, as on all other instruments, virtuosity has made gigantic strides all along the line."—SAINT SAËNS.

GRADED PREPARATORY COURSES.

The best way of acquiring Lisztian or modern technique is (presuming a sound general foundation, with mastery of the weak fingers and of the black keys)* to work through a graded series of Liszt's works.

The following three sets of pieces begin with easy works, and in each case work through to moderately

---

* See condition at head of Set VI.

See also O'Neill's "Exercises for the Weaker Fingers" (Novello).

difficult ones. They differ slightly in aim and difficulty—and the student or teacher must choose which to adopt. Having finished one of the preparatory courses, further material for a repertoire of moderately difficult pieces can be selected from sets IV and V, or the direct bid for the higher grade can be made through set VI. A still shorter cut towards virtuosity can be made through set VII—this requiring, of course, greater concentration. All the following suggested courses can be re-inforced from other works described in other chapters. There are no repetitions in the first six courses.

In contemplating such a preparatory course as the following, it is interesting to know Liszt's

PRINCIPLES OF TECHNIQUE

as set forth by Mme. Boissier—a pupil of Liszt in the "Etude" of August, 1931.

(1) Octaves to be played entirely and without exception with the wrist and without using the arm.

(2) Irreproachable evenness in execution.

(3) Weaker fingers to be equal in strength to the thumb.

(4) Slow practice for exercises—always listening to oneself.

(5) Scales separately and slowly.

(6) Practise many diminished seventh arpeggios.

Liszt was, however, not satisfied with technique

alone. In order to get the poetical atmosphere "he loved to read some fine pages of poetry or prose—Vigny or Chateaubriand—to his pupil," and above all he said, "One should only express what one felt." ("La Revue Musical," Liszt number.)

The writer of "Personal Recollections or Chats with Liszt" (Reeves) reports Liszt as saying that he knew that his friend Chopin "spent many hours a day working simply on technical studies"; and for myself, in reply to a further question Liszt said: "I never kept count of the hours I practised, but I am sure that for *many years* it was never less than *ten hours* a day."

SET I.

EASY INTRODUCTORY PIECES—GRADED.

"Some day I shall make a list of all Liszt's pieces for piano, which most amateurs will find much easier to master and digest than the chaff of Thalberg or the wheat of Henselt or Chopin."—VON BULOW.

(1) No. 2 of Three Pieces in old Hungarian Dance Form in G. (13 pages). Phrasing and staccato. (Rozsavolgyi.)

(2) "Puszta Wehmuth" (Lonesome Heath), D minor. (4 pages.) "Hungarian Pictures," octaves and phrasing. (Universal.)

(3) "Wiosna" (Spring), "Chants Polonais No. 2," in G minor. (2 pages.) Broken chords, legato octaves. (Augener.)

(4) "Ungarisch," in A (Bunte Reihe No. 19. (5 pages.) Phrasing. (Hammond.)

(5) "Tanz Momente," No. 5, in F. (2 pages.) Easy thirds, sixths and octaves. (Doblinger.)

(6) "Consolation," No. 5, in E. (2 pages.) Cantabile. (Litolff Edition.)

(7) "Polonaise" (Polish), ("Christmas Tree," No. 12), in B flat. (5½ pages.) Abbreviated, octaves and phrasing. (Heugel.)

SET II.

(1) "Hungarian Scenes," Nos. 2 and 4, in G and E. (3 pages.) Chords and octaves. (Universal.)

(2) "Chant Polonaise," No. 3 in E flat. (The Ring). (2 pages.) Chords. (Augener.)

(3) No. 1 of Three Pieces in old Hungarian Dance form, in A minor. (2 pages.) Velocity, octaves, chords. (Rozsavolgyi.)

(4) "Old Noel" ("Christmas Tree," No. 8), B minor. (3 pages.) Octaves and thirds. (Heugel.)

(5) "Consolation," No. 2, in E. (3 pages.) Broken chords and octaves. (Litolff Edition.)

(6) "Hongroise" ("Christmas Tree," No. 11), F minor. (3 pages.) Octaves. (Heugel.)

(7) "Valse D'Adele," in B flat. (7 pages.) Octaves, broken chords and rep. (Heugel.)

SET III.

(1) "La Pastorella dell' Alpi," in C (Soirées Musicales, No. 6). (2 pages.) Easy wrist work. (Ricordi, Schott.)

(2) No. 2, "Album d'un Voyageur," in C. (1 page.) Chords and octaves. (Leduc.)

(3) Presto in C from Sixth Rhapsody. (1 page.) Chords.

(4) "Lohengrin's Reproach" (Wagner Trans., No. 8), in C. (5 pages.) Octaves, chords. (Litolff.)

(5) "Les Cloches du Soir" (Christmas Tree), $3\frac{1}{2}$ pages.) Left hand independence. (Heugel.)

(6) "Consolation" in E, No. 6. (4 pages.) Arpeggiando. (Litolff.)

(7) "Album Leaf" in A flat ("Valse Elégante"). (3 pages.) Octaves, broken chords. (Schott.)

SET IV.

Repertoire I. Moderately Difficult Pieces Graded.

"Study first with the head and then with the fingers."—
Von Bulow.

(1) "Soirée de Vienne," No. 6, in A (Schubert trans.). (8 pages.) Octaves and sixths. (Universal), single work.*

---

* In some cases single (and not collective) editions are given.

(2) "Hymn de l'enfant" ("Harmonies Poétiques"), in A flat. (9 pages.) Sixths, chords and octaves. (Ricordi.)

(3) "Elsa's Dream," in A flat (Wagner trans.). (3 pages.) Broken chords. (Litolff, Universum Edition.)

(4) "Carillon" ("Christmas Tree"), in A. (6 pages.) Independent hands. (Heugel.)

(5) "Canzone" ("Venice and Naples"), E flat minor. (4 pages.) Tremolo and left hand arpeggios. (Universal.)

(6) "Barcarolle" in A (Schubert trans.). (8 pages.) Sixths and chords. (Augener.)

(7) "Spinnerlied" in A (Wagner trans.). (9 pages.) Alternative hands, fluency. (Universal.)

(8) "Trinklied" in C (Lessmann trans.). Octaves. (Junne.)

(9) "The Miller and the Brook" in G (Schubert trans.). (6 pages.) Extensions. (Augener.)

(10) "Soirée de Vienne," No. 9, in A flat. (7 pages.) Chopinesque variations.

(11) "Second Apparition," in A (Book I). (4 pages.) Delicacy. (Hofmeister.)

(12) "Chanson Bohémienne," in A ("Arabesque"). (11 pages.) Octaves and chords. (Augener.)

(13) Rhapsody No. 18, in F minor. (6 pages.) Octaves and chords. (Universal.)

(14) Impromptu in F sharp. (4 pages.) Great delicacy, black keys. (Litolff.)

(15) Invocation in E ("Harmonies Poétiques"). (4 pages.) Massed chords and octaves. (Litolff.)

SET V.

Repertoire II of Moderately Difficult Pieces Graded.

"Endeavour to sing on the piano."—Rubinstein.

(1) "En Rêve," Nocturne in B. (2 pages.) Cantabile style. (Doblinger.)

(2) First "Valse Oubliée," in F sharp. (7 pages.) left hand arpeggios. (Bote.)

(3) "Mazurka Brillante," in A. (8 pages.) Sixths. (Litolff.)

(4) "Soirée de Vienne," No. 4, in D flat. (6 pages.) Chords. (Litolff.)

(5) "Valse Impromptu," in A flat. (12 pages.) Arpeggios and octaves. (Universum, Peters.)

(6) "Valse Mélancolique," in E. (6 pages.) Broken chords. (Universum.)

(7) "L'Invito Bolero," in A minor ("Soirées Musicales"). (4 pages.) Fluency. (Ricordi.)

(8) Second "Valse Oubliée," in A flat (abbreviated). Sixths and octaves. (Bote.)

(9) "The Sailor's Serenade" in G minor ("Soirées Ital."). (12 pages.) Wrist and arpeggios. (Schott.)

(10) "Album Leaf," in A minor. (4 pages.) Octaves, interl. and arpeggios. (Schott.)

(11) "Introduction and Bridal Chorus," in G (Wagner.) (18 pages.) Wrist and arpeggios. (Universum.)

(12) "La Danza Tarentelle," in A minor. (16 pages.) Velocity. (Ricordi.)

(13) "Chromatic Galop," in E flat. (9 pages.) Wrist. (Universum, Leduc.)

(14) Introduction and Polonaise in D ("Puritani"). (9 pages.) Chords and octaves. (Schott.)

(15) "Löse Himmel," in F sharp (Lassen). (7 pages.) Arpeggios and chords. (Ricordi.)

(16) First "Mephisto Valse," in F minor. (23 pages.) Requires abbreviation, octaves and arpeggios. (Litolff.)

(17) Rhapsody No. 15, in A minor ("Rakoczy March"). (12 pages.) Octaves and chords, chromatic scales, etc. (Universum Edition.)

(18) "Storm March," in E minor ("Marche Hongroise"). (12 pages.) Thirds, chords and octaves. (Litolff.)

SET VI.

STANDARD GRADED COURSE.

(See Preparatory Courses I, II and III.)

"Technical perfection is nothing more than an artist's accursed (enforced) duty, but not a special merit."—LISZT.

This may be described as a standard course for those possessing a good technical foundation. It uses the black keys from the first. The first piece is only of moderate difficulty and the last enters the highest grade.

(1) "Au lac de Wallenstadt," in A flat ("Années I"). (3 pages.) Right hand skips, left hand on black keys. (Litolff 2624.)

(2) "Eclogue," in A flat ("Années I"). (5 pages.) Right hand broken chords. (Ricordi Edition.)

(3) "Berceuse," in F sharp ("Christmas Tree"). (5 pages.) Broken chords. (Heugel.)

(4) "Melodie Polonaise," in A flat ("Woronince"). (5 pages.) Sixths and skips. (Augener, Kistner.)

(5) "Chant Polonais," No. 5, in G flat (Chopin trans.). (5 pages.) Broken chords and cadenza. (Augener Edition.)

(6) "Consolation," in D flat. (3 pages.) Left hand broken chords. (Litolff.)

(7) "Soirée Vienne," No. 5, in G flat. (8 pages.) Left hand solo, right hand octaves and thirds (Litolff.)

(8) Rhapsody No. 5, in E. Arpeggios and octaves.

(9) "Liebestraum," No. 1, in A flat. (6 pages.) Right hand broken chords and cadenza. (Universum Edition.)

(10) "Sonetto 123," in A flat. (5 pages.) Sixths and cadenza. (Litolff 2624.)

(11) "Devotion," in A flat ("Liebeslied," Schumann trans.). (4 pages.) Sixths and arpeggios. (Universum Edition.)

(12) "La Regata," in C ("Soirées Musicales"). (7 pages.) Easy bravura and arpeggios. (Universum Edition.)

(13) Rhapsody No. 13, in A. (11 pages.) Tremolo, left hand octaves.

(14) "Les Cloches de Geneve," in B. (6 pages.) Arpeggios. (Litolff.)

(15) "The Nightingale," in C sharp minor ("Arabesque," trans.). (5 pages.) Shake. (Augener.)

(16) "Paganini Etude," No. 6, in A. (10 pages.) Six variations, general technique. (Litolff.)

(17) "Sposalizio," in E ("Années II"). (6 pages.) Left hand octaves. (Litolff.)

(18) "Liebestraum," No. 3, in A flat. (6 pages.) Broken chords and cadenza. (Universum, Beal.)

(19) "Cantique d'Amour," in E ("Harmonies Poétiques"). (9 pages.) Chords and arpeggios. (Universum.)

(20) "Au Bord d'une Source," in A flat. (7 pages.)

Cadenzas, cross hands. (Universum.) In the Edition Nationale Française (Lemoine), the version given is more difficult, more extended, in fact, a virtuoso paraphrase of the same work.

(21) "Orage," in C minor. (9 pages.) Octaves, thirds, arpeggios. (Litolff.)

(22) "Waldesrauschen," in A flat. (8 pages.) Left hand octaves and bravura, alternate hands. (Universum.)

(23) Concert Etude in A flat, No. 1 ("Il Lamento"). (15 pages.) Arpeggios and alternate hands. (Augener.)

(24) Rhapsodie No. 12, in C minor. (13 pages.) Octaves, thirds, shakes and alternate hands. (Universum.)

(25) "Les Jeux D'eau," in F sharp. (13 pages.) Alternate hands, left hand arpeggios, octaves, shake, thirds. (Litolff.)

(26) Second Polonaise in E. (14 pages.) Scales, runs, chords, cadenzas, left hand and staccato. (Litolff.)

(27) First Paganini Etude in G. (9 pages.) Left hand solo, extensions, scales. (Litolff.)

(28) "La Campanella," in G sharp minor. (12 pages.) Skips, shakes, alternate hands, left hand octaves. (Litolff, Ashdown.)

"Yesterday Liszt played us his 'Campanella.' Liszt gave it with a velvety softness, clearness, brilliancy and pearliness of touch that were inimitable."—Amy Fay.

(29) Trans. of Schubert March in B. (12 pages.) Massed chords, good introduction. (Peters, Vol. 12.)

(30) "Rigoletto" Fantasia in C sharp. (11 pages.) Left hand arpeggios, octaves and cadenzas. (Peters.)

(31) Concert Etude in D flat. (10 pages.) Alternate arpeggios, extensions, cadenzas, etc. (Augener.)

(32) "Ricordanza," in A flat ("Etudes Transcendentale," No. 9). (14 pages.) Arpeggios and runs. (Augener.)

(33) "Mazeppa," in D minor ("Etudes Transcendentale," No. 4). (14 pages.) Alternate hands, octaves, right hand shakes, chords. (Augener.)

(34) "Wedding March and Elves Dance," in C. (21 pages.) Alternate hands, left hand work and repetition. (Augener.)

SET VII.

THE GATEWAY TO LISZT'S HIGHER TECHNIQUE.

"Liszt is the father of modern virtuosity."—PROSNIZ.

This is an independent course, and the works selected are, with one exception, those which make progressively yet rapidly the necessary big style and power required. The first is of moderate difficulty, the last may well lead to the most difficult of Liszt's works.

(1) "Praise of Tears," in D (Schubert's trans.). (5 pages. The last two introduce a big, expanding style.) (Augener.)

(2) "Thou art Repose," in E flat (Schubert trans.). (6 pages.) Three pages of leaping chords. (Augener.)

(3) "Cujus Animan," in A flat (Rossini trans.). (6 pages.) Octaves in arpeggio. (Universum.)

(4) "Fruhlingsnacht," in F ("Spring Night," Schumann trans.). Chords and arpeggios. (Litolff or Augener.)

(5) "Die Forelle," in D flat ("The Trout," Schubert trans.). (10 pages.) Black keys, broken chords and octaves. (Augener.)

(6) Sixth Rhapsody in D flat. ($3\frac{1}{2}$ pages.) First movement massed chords, finale in B flat, in octaves.

(7) "Gnomenreigen," two Concert Studies in F ("Ronde des Lutins"). (11 pages.) A study in delicacy, broken chords and scale work. (Universum, Heugel or Litolff.)

(8) "Eroica," in E flat ("Etudes Transcendantes," No. 7). (8 pages.) Octaves in arpeggios. (Augener.)

(9) "Harmonies du Soir," in D flat ("Etudes Transcendantes," No. 11). (10 pages.) Massed chords and arpeggios. (Augener.)

(10) "Ab Irato," in E. (14 pages.) Massed chords and arpeggios. (Augener.)

The student could now go on to No. 19 of Set VI and work through the rest of that series, or attack the next set.

As an instance of Liszt's energy, and that at the

age of seventy-three, Hueffer recounts how he had called on Liszt at Bayreuth during the busy Wagner Festival week in 1882, and "did not expect to see him again, but the next morning, at a little after seven, I heard a loud knock at my bedroom door, and in came Liszt with many excuses for his early call. He always rose, he said, at four in the morning, and his time for visits was from six to eight a.m."

SET VIII.

Master Works.

"Nobility of line, purity of conception that amounted to a sort of religion in itself and heroism in playing—these were the characteristics of Liszt's music—these were the essentials he taught." —Rosenthal.

The works given below are selected from those which require the highest developed technique.

Set VII forms a technical introduction to the more difficult of Set VI (taking from No. 19 onwards) or it may be used as a short cut—where the pianist's powers are fully developed in every direction—and go on to the following. The various works are described elsewhere. (See index.) They are given, roughly speaking, in progressive order.

(1) Concert Study No. 1, in A flat ("Il Lamento"). (13 pages.) Chopinesque velocity. (Edition, Six Etudes, No. 4, Ricordi, Augener.)

(2) Berceuse in D flat. (8 pages.) Delicacy, cadenzas, etc. (Litolff.)

(3) "Ab Irato," in E (second version). (6 pages.) Octaves and arpeggios. (Ricordi, 3 bis., Augener.)

(4) "Ernani" Fantasia, in A flat. Massed chords, interlocking, etc. (Peters.)

(5) Concert Study No. 2, in A flat (La Leggierezza). Chopinesque velocity. (Ricordi.)

(6) Legend, "St. Francis's Sermon to the Birds," in A. (11 pages.) Shakes, delicacy. (Litolff.)

(7) Fantasia on "Santo Spiritu," in B ("Rienzi"). (17 pages.) Alternate hands, massed chords. (Litolff.)

(8) Legend, "St. Francis Walking on the Waves," in E. (11 pages.) Scales, arpeggios, alternate hands, massed chords. (Litolff.)

(9) Etude, in F minor ("Etudes Transcendantes," No. 10). (12 pages.) Interlocking, etc. (Augener.)

(10) Second Ballade in B minor. (19 pages.) Chords, scales, arpeggios, alternate hands, etc. (Litolff.)

(11) "Mazeppa," in D minor ("Etudes Transcendantes," No. 4). (14 pages.) Alternate and interlocking hands. (Augener.)

(12) "Bénédiction de Dieu," in F sharp ("Harmonies Poétiques"). (29 pages.) Black keys, arpeggios. (Litolff 2625, Augener.)

(13) Sonata in B minor. (37 pages.) Chords, arpeggios, velocity. (Heugel.)

(14) "Après un Lecture de Dante," in D ("Années

II"). (22 pages.) Alternating hands, arpeggios, chords, octaves. (Ricordi.)

(15) Variations on "Weinen, Klagen," in F minor. (16 pages.) Alternating hands, arpeggios. (Universal.)

(16) "Vision," in G minor ("Etudes Transcendantes," No. 6). (10 pages.) Arpeggios. (Augener.)

(17) Concert Study in D flat ("Un Sospiro"). (10 pages.) Arpeggios. (Ricordi, Augener.)

(18) Fantasia and Fugue on "Bach," in B flat. Interlocking. (Litolff.)

(19) "Wedding March and Dance of Elves," in C. (21 pages.) Repetition, interlocking, thirds, octaves, shakes. (Augener.)

(20) "Don Giovanni ("Juan") Fantasia, in D. (42 pages.) Abbreviate, chromatic work, thirds. (Augener.)

(21) "Figaro" Fantasia in C. (30 pages). Thirds, scales, alternative hands. Edited by Busoni (Breitkopf and Härtel).

WORKS WITH ORCHESTRA (OR TWO PIANOS).

(1) Hungarian Fantasia. (Litolff.)

(2) Concerto in E flat. (Litolff.)

(3) Concerto in A. (Litolff, and Steingraber.)

Facilitated Editions.

The frequent use of extensions and other features requiring unusual stretch and energy has induced the use of facilitated editions of Liszt's works. In this the Universum Edition with eleven numbers (including the first, second, twelfth, fourteenth and fifteenth Rhapsodies) leads the way. Other similar instances are "Rakoczy March" (Schubert), "Don Juan" Fantasia (Schles), albums of ten pieces (Schles.), Rhapsodies 1 and 2 (Simrock), "Spanish" Rhapsody (Kistner), Rhapsody 2 (Augener), and "Chromatic Gallop" (Leduc). Leduc also publishes an amended version of the Sixth Rhapsody with the cadenza and andante omitted, as "Trois Melodies Hongroises."

The better way, of course, is to work through a series of graded Liszt pieces, from easy to difficult, employing characteristic Lisztian technique. The previous section, giving various graded courses, is intended to help towards this consummation.

The essential features of Lisztian technique are:

(1) The use of black key positions.

(2) Graded technical work: (a) skips; (b) extensions; (c) alternate hands; (d) interlocking hands; (e) wrist chords and octaves; (f) cadenzas.

CHAPTER XXVIII.

THE SEEKER AFTER LISZT.

MODERN EDITIONS AND PUBLICATIONS.

"Correctness is an indispensable requisite in a musical phrase."—HAUPTMANN.

Except for purposes of research both the concert artist and the student will require the best and most modern edition of Liszt's works, and it goes without saying that if the lover of music, whether amateur or professional, seeks to know more of Liszt, he must know where to find it. Possibly he hears, say, the "Cantique d'Amour" at a recital, and afterwards interviews his music seller, who probably has never heard of it. Neither the collection nor publisher being known, the music seller refers it to his collector in London, who again probably refers to an importer.

Disappointment and delay will be saved if in the present work both the publisher and the collection (if any) are looked up before ordering. Some collections are incomplete, while some older publications are in small print, and it is best to order a modern edition.

Well known pieces like No. 3 of the "Liebesträume" are published by many firms, others perhaps can only be got from one or two continental firms, so that it is best to be exact in ordering.

MODERN EDITIONS. SOME ITEMS OF NOTE.

Litolff Edition (London agent, Piena).—New edition, Max Pauer. Wagner Trans., complete (14). Rossini Trans. (6). Wagner Trans., complete. "Soirées de Vienne" (9) complete. Fantasia and Fugue on Bach. Two Bach Trans., Ballads, Legendes, Polonaises. Spanish Rhapsody Sonata. For two pianos: Hungarian Fantasia and two Concertos. Four Symphonic Poems for piano solo, etc.

Augener, London (Thümer Edition).—6 "Chants Polonais" ("Melodies Polonaises"). Two Arabesques. 3 "Liebesträume." Mendelssohn's "Wedding March" Trans. "Mephisto" Waltz No. 1. "Polonaises" (Scharwenka). "Soirées de Vienne." "Venezia and Napoli." Concert Studies and "Bénédiction de Dieu" (Thümer). "Etudes Transcendantes" and 3 Concert Studies (Dannreuther). "Ab Irato" (Dannreuther). "Don Giovanni" (Pauer). Legends. Beethoven, Six Sacred Songs Trans. Bach, Fantasia and Fugue in G minor; and Bach, Prelude on "Weinen" (Dunhill). "Rigoletto" and "Les Patineurs" Paraphrases. 30 Schubert Song Trans., separate (Thümer). Hungarian Rhapsodies and "Rapsodie Espagnol." Hungarian Fantasia (two pianos). Wagner albums, etc.

Costallat, Paris (Philipp Edition of Select Works).—Variations on Bach motive. Cadenzas for Beethoven Concerto, Op. 37. Cantique, Funerailles, etc.

Heugel, Paris (Banks of York), Ed. Française (Moskovski Edition).—(3) "Etudes de Concert," titles (1) "Lamento"; (2) "La Leggierezza"; (3) "Il Sospiro." Two "Etudes de Concert," etc.

Lemoine (Paris).—Three volumes, 49 Standard Pieces, edited by Lack. Collective Edition, quarto. Earlier Virtuoso Edition of Paganini. Etudes and E flat Concerto, etc.

Leduc, Paris.—"Album d'un Voyageur." Seven Hungarian Melodies.

Ricordi, London and Milan (Edition Tagliapietra).—"Années de Pélerinage," three volumes and supplement (24 pieces complete). "Harmonies Poétique," 10 pièces complètes. Six Concert Studies (edited Brugnoli): Two Concert Studies, Three Concert Studies and "Ab Irato," with introduction and notes. Op. 6, "Grande Valse de Bravura. Six Paganini Etudes and Grand Fantasia (Brugnoli). Twelve "Soirées Musicales" (separate and complete), etc.

Peters Edition (Augener, London).—"Rigoletto," "Trovatore" and "Ernani" Fant. Vol. 10, Bach, Six Organ Preludes and Fugues; the G minor Fantasia and Fugue; Variations on "Weinen," "Klagen." Vol. 11, Concertos, "Todtentanz"; Hungarian Fantasia; Schubert, Op. 15; Weber, Op. 72. Vol. 12, Three Schubert March Trans.; Scherzo and March; Fantasia and Fugue on BACH.

Schott, London and Mainz.—Folio library edition

in twelve volumes. Rhapsodies, Vols. 1 and 2, edited by D'Albert. Vols. 5 and 6, "Années de Pélerinage," complete (Klindworth Edition). Vol. 9, "Two Apparitions," Berceuse, Valse, Impromptu, etc. "Soirées Musicales," two volumes. Overtures, "Franc Juges" and "William Tell."

Universal Edition. Vienna (London agent, Cranz), (edited by Friedman).—Great Variations on Bach-Motive. Schubert, "Wanderer" Fantasia, Op. 15. Vol. 12, "Tannhäuser" Overture; "Wedding March"; Gounod, Waltz; "Rigoletto" and "Trovatore" Paraphrases.

Breitkopf (Busoni Edition).—Fantasia and Fugue on "Ad Nos." Fantasia on "Figaro." Fantasia on Two Swiss Melodies. Twelve Symphonic Poems and "Triomphe de Tasse" (for piano solo). Concert Solo ("Pathetic" Concerto, two pianos).

Kistner, Leipzig (Bosworth, London).—"Spanish" Rhapsody (with orchestra, Busoni). "Glanes de Woronince." "Todtentanz." "Allegro de Bravura."

Bosworth, London (Steingräber Edition).—Concerto in A. Liszt, Album (Album Leaf in A).

Lengnick, London.—D'Albert Edition of Rhapsodies.

Rozsavolgyi, Budapest.—D'Albert Edition of the "Legendes."

Cranz, Leipzig and London.—Schubert Song Trans., four volumes (forty-six numbers). Fantasia on the Tyrolienne "La Fiancée," Op. 1.

Simrock, Leipzig (Benjamin).—Second Polonaise (Busoni Edition).

Bote and Bock, Berlin (Ashdown, London), (D'Albert Edition).—Three volumes, Selected Pieces. Three "Valses Oubliées." "Les Adieux" (Gounod).

Ashdown, London.—Rhapsodies, complete, one volume. Liszt Album.

J. Schuberth, Leipzig.—Technical Studies, twelve books. Symphonic poem, "Von der Wiege."

G. Schirmer, New York.—Joseffy Edition of Rhapsodies, "Années," Sonata, Transcriptions, etc., "Valse d'Adèle," Gounod valse, "Der Asra," "Slumber Song," etc., also "Pathetic" Concerto for two pianos, or piano and orchestra, the two Concertos, etc.

Hofmeister, Leipzig.—Early editions see List. Henselt Edition of "Lucia" Fantasia, etc.

Kahnt, Leipzig.—"Three Swiss Pieces." Two Elegies, etc.

Schlesinger, Berlin.—Bach, G minor Fantasia and Fugue. Busoni Edition and "Heroic" March. Burmeister Edition of Rhapsodies.

Fürstner, Berlin.—"Weihnachtsbaum" ("Christmas Tree").

Durand, Paris.—"Soirées Italiennes" (1 to 6). Trans. "Danse Macabre" (Saint-Saëns). Trans. "Tarantelle" (Cui).

POPULAR EDITIONS.

Benjamin's Universum Edition, Hamburg and Leipzig.—Excellent cheap edition of forty-six separate numbers (revised by Singer), including "Valse Mélancolique," "Cantique d'Amour," six Rhapsodies and ten Wagner transcriptions, also nine facilitated numbers. Other well produced Liszt items are found in the

Tonmeister Edition (by Rosenthal) of 89 numbers (Ulstein, Berlin), very clear print. Agent, Oxford University Press; also in the Music Lovers' Library (Liszt, Vol. 7, No. 63). Hammond's Academic and Examination Series, Beal Edition, "Liebesträume."

Ditson.—Three Liszt Albums (I, Original; II, Trans.; and III, Rhapsodies). (Spanuth Edition), First and Second "Apparitions." Trans. "The Messenger" (Franz).

Lemoine.—Three volumes, Forty-nine Standard Pieces (Lack Edition). No. 1141 is a virtuoso edition of "Au bord d'une source."

Bote and Bock.—Three volumes, thirty-three pieces (D'Albert Edition).

Schirmer, New York.—Two volumes, fifteen pieces.

Bosworth.—Thirteen Pieces.

Steingräber.—Eight Pieces.

For other firms, see Original Publications List in the next chapter.

Chapter XXIX.

LISZT RESEARCH.

ORIGINAL PUBLISHERS, EARLY WORKS, ETC.

"The sole aim of the composer should be the progress of his art."—Gluck.

There are various works by Liszt which are scarce, or have gone out of print. This is to some extent proof of past popularity, and for the benefit of those interested in tracing such works, the following list of original publishers and editions has been compiled.

Mr. Dannreuther, in his edition of the "Transcendental Etudes" (Augener) aptly points out in 1899: "There are few opus numbers on the title pages of Liszt's earlier pieces; none on his latter. No dates of composition, publication or republication. In course of time copyrights have expired or changed hands, and there is no uniform edition. Pieces almost identical are on the market *under different headings;* others differing as much as a pencil sketch from a finished picture are offered for sale *under the same title*—arrangements and adaptations cannot readily be distinguished from originals, and work, not Liszt's own, is current under his name."

Liszt had the faculty which distinguishes genius—that of taking pains. He did not rush into print, and when his work was published he would revise and revise again, and republish, so that the unravelling of the various original issues of his works proves to be no easy task. Many publishers were involved and sometimes two or more different versions were issued by different publishers. Many changes have taken place since that time, and some firms have been taken over by others. The following firms were acquired: Haslinger by *Schlesinger;* Mechetti, Schreiber, Spina and Diabelli, by *Cranz;* Licht and Siegel, by *Kistner;* Wetzler by *Doblinger;* Simrock and Rahter and Senff, by *Benjamin;* Trautwein by *Bahn;* Heinze by *Peters;* Taborsky and Parsch (Budapesth), by *Weinberger*, of Vienna; Brandus and Maquet (Paris), by *Joubert.* Others publishing Liszt's works, as mentioned by Ramann, were Dunkl (Pesth), Hoffmann (Prague), Korner (Erfurt), and Muller (Mayence).

Liszt's works are now out of copyright except special editions. The best known works are issued by several publishers. *Leipzig firms:* Breitkopf and Härtel (Breitkopf, Cranz, Hoffmeister, Kahnt), Leuckart, Peters, Benjamin (Simrock and Rahter and Senff), J. Schuberth, Kistner, Steingräber. *Breslau:* Hainauer. *Mainz:* Schott. *Berlin:* Bote and Bock, Furstner, Schlesinger, Ullstein (Tonmeister Edition by Rosenthal). *Magdebourg:* Heinrichsofen, Bahn. *Budapesth:* Rozsavolgyi. *Vienna:* Doblinger, Universum Edition. *Paris:* Heugel, Leduc, Joubert, Lemoine, Durand. *Milan:* Ricordi.

London agents: Augener for Peters; *Bosworth* for Kistner and Steingräber; *Cranz* for Universum Edition; *Ashdown* for Bote and Bock; *Banks of York* for Heugel; *Oxford University Press* for Tonmeister Edition; *London branches,* Breitkopf and Härtel, Schott, Ricordi, Litolff (Piena).

The Early Works of Liszt.

The classification of the works of Liszt is a difficult task. Dates of composition and publication do not coincide, often there is a brief gap between.

There are two Ops. 1 and 2, and no Op. 10, and his opus numbers did not go beyond Op. 13.

Some of Liszt's works were improved and sold to other publishers. Some publications have gone out of print, some are "old prints," some are well worth reprinting, and others not. Add to this the fact that Liszt's publications were first printed by French firms, and later by German, and that they are very much scattered, sometimes under various titles. It has therefore been quite an undertaking to get them together. Liszt had a habit of rewriting works for publication anew. See the "Au bord d'une source," from the "Années" in Lemoine's "Pantheon," which reappears as a virtuoso paraphrase of the usual version.

The following list will help to make the early period clear:

Liszt's works may be roughly divided into periods.

I. EARLY VIRTUOSO.—Mostly virtuoso paraphrases.

II. 1840-50, SONG TRANSCRIPTIONS.—Paraphrases.

III. 1850-60, ORCHESTRAL WORK.—Concert studies, sonata, ballads, etc.

IV. 1860-86, ORATORIOS AND MASSES.

EARLY WORKS.

With the name of present publisher, date, and Liszt's age in parenthesis.

"An interpreter should be the opposite of a gravedigger, he should bring to light what is hidden and buried."—
VON BULOW.

Opus 3. Impromptu on themes by Rossini and Spontini. Kistner, 1824. (13.)

Opus 4. Allegro di Bravura. Kistner, 1825. (14.)

Opus 1. Etudes en douze Exercises Repr. 1830 withdrawn. Out of print, 1826. (15.)

Opus 1. Fantasia on "Tyrolienne" ("La Fiancée"). Cranz, 1829. (18.)

Opus 2. Fant., "L'Idée fixè," 1833. La Clochette de Paganini," original. Cranz, 1834. (23.)

"Three Apparitions." No. 3 was on a Schubert waltz. Hofmeister, 1835. (24.)

Transcription of Berlioz, "Symphonie Fantastique." A, "Un Bal," B, "Marche au supplice." Schlesinger, 1836. (25.)

Trans. of Schubert's song, "The Rose." Hofmeister, 1834-5. (24.)

Trans. of Schubert's songs. Sets of three and twelve. Schlesinger, 1837-8. (26.)

"Pensée des Morts" Comp. d. 1834. 1835.

Six Caprices de Paganini. Schlesinger, 1839. (28.)

Liszt goes to Geneva, 1835 to end of 1836.

"Album d'un Voyageur." I, Impressions, seven numbers; II, "Fleurs Mélodiques," three; III, Paraphrases, later as "Three Airs Suisses." Schlesinger, 1842.

"Album d'un Voyageur." A selection appeared in the "Années," Vol. I, nine pieces. 1852.

Opus 5. No. 1, "Niobe" Fantasia, Pacini. Schlesinger, 1837. (26.)

Opus 5. No. 2, "Fantasia Romantique" on two melodies. Hofmeister, 1839. (28.)

Opus 5. No. 3, Rondo Fantastique, "El Contrabandista." Hofmeister, 1837. (26.)

Opus 6. "Grande Valse Bravura," in B flat. Schlesinger, 1836.

Opus 7. "Puritani" Fantasia. Schott, 1837.

No. 2, "Soirées Italiennes," Mercadente and Donizetti. Schott, 1838-9.

Opus 8. (No. 1) "Serenata," (No. 2) "Pastorella" (Rossini). Schott, 1837. "Les Soirées Musicales" (Rossini). Schott, 1838.

Opus 9. "La Juive" Fantasia. Hofmeister, 1836.

Opus 11. "Les Huguenots" Fantasia. Hofmeister, 1837-9.

Opus 12. Chromatic Gallop. Hofmeister, 1838.

Opus 13. "Lucia" Fantasia. Hofmeister, 1840.

"Lucia" March and Cavatina. Schott, 1840.

"Lyon," compl. 18 pages. Out of print, 1842.

Overture, "Franc Juges," completed 1833. Schott, 1845.

Overture, "William Tell," completed 1838. Schott, 1846.

ORIGINAL PUBLICATIONS.

Scarce or Out of Prints.

Hoffmeister, Leipzig.

Op. 5, "Pacini" Cavatina; (2) Swiss Fantasia on two melodies; (3) Rondo, "El Contrabandista." O.P. (O.P. signifies out of print.) 1837.

Op. 9, Fantasia, "La Juive." (O.P.) 1836.

Op. 13, Fantasia, "Lucia." (Henselt Edition, modern.) 1840.

"Hussitenlied." 1841.

"Du Zelle in Nonnenwerth." (With alternative more difficult version.)

Schlesinger, Berlin.

Trans. "Russian Galop." (O.P.) 1846.

Donizetti, March. 1847.

Op. 6, "Three Valses Caprices," 1847.

Bulow, "Tanto Gentile," Canzonetta. (O.P.) 1860.

Meyerbeer's song, "Le Moine," 1870, and "Roberto" Fantasia (1841). (O.P.)

"La Romanesca" (sixteenth century melody. (O.P.) 1860.

Breitkopf.

"Trauer" (Funeral) Vorspiel and March. (O.P.)

Kistner.

Op. 4. Allegro de Bravura.

"Sarabande" (Almira).

Hunting Chorus and "Styrienne" from "Tony," 1841.

Kahnt—Leipzig.

Two Elegies, Moukhanoff (1868) and Ramann. 1870.

"Festzug" (Schiller Festival), two and four hands. 1859.

Three Pieces from Liszt's "St. Elizabeth."

"Geharnischte Lieder" (Liszt's Male Part-songs). 1861.

Fürstner.

Two new "Mephisto Walzes," No. 2 (No. 3 O.P.). 1883.

"Weihnacht-baum" ("Christmas Tree"), 1882. (See Heugel, Paris Ed.)

Wielhorsky's "Romance." (O.P.) 1885.

Meser, now *Fürstner.*

Trans. Schubert Four Marches for Duet. 1836-46.

Rieter-Biedermann, now *Peters.*

Trans. Berlioz, "L'Idée Fixe," "Andante Amoroso." (See Cranz.) 1840.

"Marche au supplice. 1836. "Pilgrim's March" ("Harold"). 1840.

"Danse des Sylphes" (now discontinued). 1866.

Simrock, now *Benjamin (Leipzig).*

Impromptu on Rossini and Spontini Themes. (O.P.)

Rahter, now *Benjamin.*

Trans. Polonaise ("Onegin"), Tchaïkovsky. 1880.
Trans. "Tarantelle" (Dargomischsky). 1880.

Fritsch (Leipzig).

Trans. "Abschied" (Russian Theme).

Trautwein, now *Bahn, of Magdeburg.*

"Elégie d'après Sorriano" (Donizetti). 1849.

Cranz.

Funeral March, Dom Sebastian.

Mechetti (Vienna), now *Cranz.*

Paraphrase, Capriccio ("Ruins of Athens").
"Andante Amoroso" (Berlioz). 1840.

Diabelli, now *Cranz.*

Op. 1. Fantasia, "La Fiancée" (Auber). 1829.
Var. on Waltz by Diabelli. 1823.

Schreiber, now *Cranz.*

Op. 2. Fant. on Paganini's "Clochette." 1834.

Leuckart (Leipzig).

Trans. Berlioz, "Harold." 1840.
Trans. Berlioz, "Symph. Fantastique." 1840.

Schott.

Int. and March, "Les Puritains." 1837.
Fantasia, "Norma." 1841.
Op. 13. March and Cavatina ("Lucia"). 1840.
"Salve Maria" (Verdi). 1870.
Berceuse ("La Reine de Saba"). 1864.
I, "Faribolo," II, "Chanson du Bearn." (O.P.)
"William Tell" Overture. 1846.
"Les Franc Juges" Overture. 1845.
"Il m'aimait tant," trans. of song by Liszt. 1886.

Heinrichsofen (Magdeburg).

Trans. Andante, Finale and March ("King Alfred"), (Raff). 1853-4.

Bote and Bock.

"Huldigungs March" (orch. and piano), also two hands. 1858.
Three "Valses Oubliées."

"Illustrations," "The African," No. 1, "The Sailor's Prayer." 1865.

"Les Adieux" ("Romeo et Juliette"), (Gounod). 1868.

Hainauer (Breslau).

Trans. Par. Lassen's "Nibelungen" (2). 1879.
Lassen's "Faust" (Hymn, March and Polonaise).

Otto Junne.

Trans. Lessmann's "Lieder," 1, 2 and 3.

Doblinger.

Trans. "Dance Moments" (Herbeck). 1881.

Wetzler, now *Doblinger.*

"En Rêve"—Nocturne.

Schindler (Pressburg).

Hungarian "Geschwind March."

Lemoine.

Ed. of "Soirées Italiennes," 5 Nos. Nos. 1 and 2 together.

J. Schuberth (Leipzig).

"Technical Studies," 12 Bks. (2 vols).
Prelude, "Strasburg Chimes," Liszt. (O.P.)
"Hungarian Coronation March," Liszt. 1867.
Fest. March ("Säkular feir"). (O.P.)
Symp. Poem, "Von der Wiege," Liszt. 1883.
"March de Rakoczy," Symphonic Ed. 1852.
Trans., "God Save the King." (O.P.) 1841.

"Marseillaise." (O.P.) 1841.

"Tscherkessen March." (O.P.)

Fest. March (Herz). (O.P.)

Rozsavalgyi (Budapest).

Three Pieces in the style of old Hungarian Dances. Appeared 1850. Republished 1909.

Trans., "Szozat," and Hungarian Hymns (Beni and Erkel). 1872-5.

Introduction and Hungarian March (Szechenyi).

"Interlude" (Lassen). 1883.

Fantasia, "Ilonka" (Mosonyi), opera. 1868.

Leduc.

"Album d'un Voyageur," consists of seven Hungarian Melodies. (Nos. 4 to 7 are from the Rhapsodies.)

Heugel.

"La Fête Vilageoise."

"L'Arbré de Noel" ("Christmas Tree"), 12 pieces. 1882.

No. 7. Berceuse (see "Schlummerlied"), (Schirmer).

Trans. "Marche Hongriose" (Szabady-Massenet).

"Salve Maria," Verdi's "Jerusalem." 1870.

"Valse d'Adele" (Zichy). 1877.

Maquet, now *Joubert.*

"Hexameron." 1837.

"Pilgrims' Chorus," Berlioz, "Harold." 1840.

Ricordi.

"Années" and Supplement—Complete.
"Harmonies Poetiques" (10 Nos.), Complete.
"Soirées Musicales," Complete. 1838.
"Aïda" (Verdi), (Dance and Duet).
"Don Carlo" (Verdi), (Chorus and March). 1867.
Requiem (Verdi), ("Agnus Dei"). 1838.

Litolff.

Scherzo and March.

WORKS FOR ORCHESTRA AND PIANO.

Concerto No. 1, in E flat. *Schlesinger.* 1857. Two pianos. *Litolff.*

Concerto No. 2, in A. *Schott.* 1865. Two pianos.

Litolff, Steingraber.

Hungarian Fantasia (Rhapsody 14). *Heinze.* Two pianos. *Litolff.*

"Todtentanz" (Var. on "Dies Iræ" or "Danse Macabre"). *(Siegel) Kistner.* 1850-5. Two pianos.

Kistner. Peters.

Fant. on theme from Beethoven's "Ruins of Athens." *(Siegel) Kistner.* 1865. Two pianos.

Kistner.

"Hexameron" Var. (Introd., one Var., Tutti and Finale, by Liszt). *Schlesinger.* 1837.

Weber's Polonaise in E, arr. (Op. 72). *Schuberth.* 1852. Two pianos. *Schlesinger.*

Schubert's Fantasia (Op. 15), in C. *(Schreiber) Cranz.* Two pianos. Vol. II. *Peters.*

Spanish Rhapsody (arr. Busoni from the solo). *Kistner.* Duet.

Kistner.

Two new "Mephisto Waltzes," Nos. 2 and 3 (two or four hands). *Fürstner.* No. 3 is out of print.

Concerto, "Malédiction," for piano and strings (unfinished work). 185—?

Cadenza for Beethoven's Concerto, Op. 37. *Costallat, Paris.*

Pathetic Concerto (two piano work orch. by Burmeister for solo piano and orch.). *Breitkopf.* 1850.

LISZT'S ORCHESTRAL WORKS ARRANGED FOR THE PIANO.

As Arranged by the Composer these are Practically Original Piano Works.

"I have now convinced myself that you are the greatest musician of all times."—Wagner, letter to Liszt, 1856.

1. Dante Symphony, two pianos. *Breitkopf.*

2. "Faust" Symphony, two pianos and duet. *Schuberth.* Part II, "Gretchen," for piano solo. *Schuberth.*

3. Two Episodes (Lenau's "Faust"), two and

four hands, also two pianos. I, "Der Nächtliche Zug"; II, "Mephisto Valse." *Schuberth.* 1862.

4. Symphonic Poems (12), for two and four hands and two pianos. *B. and H.*

5. Goethe Fest March, two hands. *Schuberth.* 1849.

6. "Huldigungs March," two hands. *B. and H.* 1853.

7. "Vom Fels zum Meer-March," two hands. *Schlesinger.* 1865.

8. "Künstler Fest-Zug" (Schiller), two and four hands. *Kahnt.* 1859.

9. "Gaudeamus Igitur," two hands. *Schuberth.*

10. Bulow March, 1883. *Schuberth.*

11. Fest Vorspiel for the Schiller and Goethe Festival. 1857-8.

12. "Salve Polonia." 1882.

13. "Les Morts," Oraison pour Orchestra. 1860.

ORCHESTRAL ARRANGEMENTS BY LISZT OF OTHER WORKS FOR PIANO.

Hungarian Rhapsodies, Nos. 1 to 6, for four hands. *Schuberth.* 1886.

Hungarian Coronation March, two and four hands. *Schuberth.* 1867.

Rakoczy March, symphonic arr., two, four and eight hands. *Schuberth.* 1867.

Hungarian Storm March, two and four hands. *Schlesinger.* 1876.

"Szozat and Hymnus," by Beni and Erkel, piano solo. *Rozsavölgyi.* 1872-5.

Sacheverel Sitwell, in his Biography (1934), p. 326, says regarding Liszt: "There is no one who loves music who will not admire some side of his talent."

"Things which are completely unknown to the public are legion. There is so much of the highest possible interest lying completely unknown and forgotten. His last symphonic poem, 'From the Cradle to the Grave,' his 'Triomph funèbre de Tasso' (Symphonic Poem No. 2, the Martyrdom of Tasso the poet), his last 'Mephisto Waltzes,' the 'Salve Polonia' interlude from the projected oratorio, 'St. Stanislaus,' and the Malédiction Concerto, could fill an orchestral programme, and would all be first performances so far as the living public is concerned."

Breitkopf's "Gesamtausgabe."

This critical edition is being issued in 31 volumes. Vol. XIII, Works for piano and orchestra.

For choral and vocal works, see Pt. II, Chapter XXV.

A list of Liszt's *Unpublished Works* is mentioned in Grove (1927), and a later one in Sacheverell Sitwell's Biography, p. 339.

In Göllerich's 55 page Catalogue of Works those unpublished are distinguished by lighter type.

ENVOI.

"Since Liszt opened new paths there has been no writer for the instrument who has not been a greater composer for the *orchestra* than for the pianoforte." —Krehbiel.

CHAPTER XXX.

THE LISZT RECITAL. SIX RECITAL PROGRAMMES AND A REPERTOIRE.

"Liszt's first consideration was the essentially noble and heroic interpretation."—ROSENTHAL.

The piano music of Liszt is not always suitable for the quiet seclusion of one's own hearth. It is not usually introspective, as much of Schumann and of Brahms is, it calls for the ear of the multitude. Liszt is an orator, and therefore we look for effect —in the best sense. The following programmes are intended as an effort in the difficult task of programme building—with an eye to contrast of key and of style, not forgetting the climax and to some extent grading of difficulty in each.

(1) EASY CLUB PROGRAMME. Suited to ordinary capacities, either for one or several performers: interspersed with short anecdotes or sketches of Liszt or some of Liszt's songs, this would be quite effective.

(2) STUDENTS' GRADED RECITAL. Would suit an ambitious student who wishes to work by degrees for a Liszt recital. It can, of course, also be divided among students of different capacity.

(3) HISTORIC EARLY VIRTUOSO RECITAL. As representing the virtuoso pieces with which Liszt built

up his reputation as a virtuoso—this also with a biographical sketch makes an interesting evening.

(4) LISZT RECITAL. ORIGINAL WORKS. Well contrasted and attractive. The Twelfth Rhapsody is included as largely original.

(5) LISZT RECITAL—with Transcriptions. Includes two effective transcriptions and the Fantasia and Fugue.

Programme notes can be made from other references. See INDEX OF WORKS.

These programmes could be extended by a Master Programme, consisting of the Sonata, "Lecture de Dante," Concerto Rondo in E minor, "Mazeppa," Hungarian Fantasia, Concertos, "Vallée d'Obermann," "Funérailles," "Ricordanza," and so forth.

I.—EASY CLUB PROGRAMME.

"His playing is the living, breathing impersonation of poetry, passion, grace, wit, coquetry, daring and tenderness."—AMY FAY on Liszt.

"No artist ever began as a master."—SCHUMANN.

(1) "The Maiden's Fancy" (Chopin Paraphrase), Chants, Polonaise.
(2) Trois Morceaux (Nos. 1 and 3) in Hungarian style.

(3) "Polish" (Christmas Tree).
(4) "Ave Maria" (in E). *Rosavölgyi and Universum.*
(5) "Album Leaf" in A flat ("Valse Elégante").
(6) 18th Rhapsodie, or "L'invito Bolero," No. 3 ("Soirées Musicales").
(7) "Liebesträume," No. 1.
(8) "La Regata" ("Soirées Musicales," No. 2).

II.—The Student's Programme.

Graded Liszt Recital.

"That is the way Liszt teaches you. He presents an *idea* to you, and it takes first hold of your mind and sticks there."—Amy Fay.

"Never seek success in mere brilliancy of execution but endeavour to produce the effect which the composer intended."
—Liszt.

(1) "Consolation," No. 6.
(2) "Carillon" ("Christmas Tree").
(3) Impromptu in F sharp.
(4) "Valse Oubliée," No. 2.
(5) Hungarian Storm March.
(6) "Liebesträume," No. 3, in A flat.
(7) "Waldesrauschen."
(8) "Cantique D'Amour."
(9) Polonaise No. 2.

III.—Historic.

Early Virtuoso Recital.

"May the artist of the future place his goal *within* and without himself, making virtuosity a means, never an end."
—Liszt, 1841.

"All new phenomena in music are the work of genius."—
Schumann.

The early Impromptu and Allegro di Bravura are out of print. The "Douze Exercises" of 1826 (Op. 1) were withdrawn and then reprinted in 1830, and now exist in a French edition *(Costallat).* The first concert work existing is the

(1) Fantasia on the Tyrolienne ("La Fiancée"), 1829, Auber-Liszt *(Cranz).*

(2) Liszt's next compositions were the Berlioz transcriptions, "Un Bal," "Marche au Supplice," and "L'Idée Fixe" (1833), and "Pensée des Morts" (Harmonies Poétiques), 1834.

"L'Idée Fixe" (Andante Amoroso)—one of Liszt's *salon* pieces at this time, later attached to the Berlioz-Liszt March.

(3) Fantasia ("La Clochette"). The Bell Rondo is also the theme of one of the Paganini studies. This opens the series of his great virtuoso concert pieces.

The delicate "Apparitions," "Pensée des Morts" and "Lyon" form the next group. Then came the works of the Genevan period. The best are:

(4) Divertissement, "Niobe," Cavatina (Pacini-Liszt). Played at the Thalberg Competition, 1836.

The "Niobe" and "Lucia" Fantasias were Clara Wieck's favourites.

(5) "Puritani" Fantasia.

(6) Fant., "La Serenata et l'Orgia" (Op. 8), 1835-6 (Rossini-Liszt). Played in Milan, 1837.

(7) "Lucia" Fantasia, Op. 13 (Bellini-Liszt), *Henselt Ed.* (1835-6).

(8) "Chromatic Galop," 1838.

IV.—Liszt Recital (Original Works).

"His touch and his peculiar use of the pedal are two secrets of his playing, and then he seems to dive down into the most hidden thoughts of the composer."—Amy Fay.

"The end of mastery of style is to enable an artist to execute the most intricate and difficult compositions."—Liszt.

"Nobody will equal him with those rolling basses and those flowing trebles. And then his *adagios!* When you hear him in one of those you feel that his playing has got to that point where it is purified from all earthly dross and is an exhalation of the soul that mounts straight to heaven."—Amy Fay.

(1) "Invocation" ("Harmonies Poétiques").

(2) "Album Leaf" in A.

(3) First Ballade (D flat).

(4) "Apparition," No. 2, in A.

(5) "St. Francis Walks on the Waves" (E), (Legend No. 2).

(6) "Gnomenreigen" (F).
(7) Sonnet, 123, A flat.
(8) Twelfth Rhapsody.

V.—Liszt Recital.

"The virtuoso is called upon to let these (works) speak, weep, sing, sigh—to render these to his own consciousness."
—Liszt.

"The first requisite in a musician is that he should respect, acknowledge and do homage to what is great and sublime in his art."—Mendelssohn.

Programme includes transcriptions.

(1) "Ab Irato" (E), Etude de Salon.
(2) "Il Lamento" (A flat), No. 1 of three Concert Studies.
(3) "Le Rossignol" (C minor), Two Arabesques.
(4) "Orage" (C minor), Années I.
(5) "Chant Polonais," No. 5 in G flat, Chopin-Liszt.
(6) Fant. and Fugue on BACH, B flat.
(7) "St. Francis' Sermon to the Birds," F sharp (Legend No. 1).
(8) "Ernani" Fantasia, F minor.

VI.—Rubinstein's Liszt Recital, 1886.

(1) D flat Etude.
(2) Valse Caprice (?).

(3) "Consolations" in E and D flat.
(4) "Au bord d'une source."
(5) Rhapsodies Nos. 6 and 12.
(6) "Soirées Musicales de Rossini": "La Gita in Gondola." "La Serenata." "La Regata Veneziana." "La Danza"—Tarentella.
(7) Schubert-Liszt, "Auf dem Wasser," "Ständchen," "Erl König."
(8) Schubert-Liszt, "Soirée de Vienne."
(9) Meyerbeer-Liszt, "Robert le Diable" Fantasia.

A Repertoire of Original Works. A Study of Styles.

This selection of original works—as excluding transcriptions—avoids the *heavier* works, such as the Sonata, "Bénédiction de Dieu," etc., and hackneyed items as the "Liebestraum," No. 3, in A flat, "Mephisto Valse," Second Polonaise, Hungarian Rhapsodies, and "Soirées de Vienne." The items are put in historical order; they can be selected so as to give contrast in style and key, and they are all effective (but not extraordinarily difficult), and lead to an impressive climax. For descriptions and publisher refer to the Index.

Nocturnes.

Liszt was strongly influenced, as was Chopin, by the Nocturnes of John Field (1782-1837), the virtuoso composer of his time—as Liszt was of his.

A placid *nobilamente* strain runs through Field's works. Liszt hails Field's Nocturnes as "the very essence of all Idylls and Eclogues." The following selection of ten Nocturnes gives us this essence, ornamented by the ethereal cadenzas of Liszt.

LISZT NOCTURNES.

* Cuts are possible.

"On Wallenstadt Lake." A flat. Placid and restful. 4 pages. 1835.

"The Chimes of Geneva." B. Impassioned. 7 pages. 1835.

"Eclogue." A flat. A lovely Pastorale. 4 pages. 1835.

"Apparition," No. 1. F sharp. Original. Anticipates Debussy. 6 pages. 1835.

"Valse Mélancolique." E. Ethereal Cadenzas. 6 pages. 1840.

"Albumblatt"—"Nonnenwerth." A minor. Fond recollections. 4 pages. 1840.

Petrarca Sonnet, No. 104. E. Impassioned episode. 5 pages. 1848.

"Consolation," No. 3. D flat. Charming, Fieldesque. 3 pages. 1850.

"Seliger Tod" "Liebestraum," (Nocturne), No. 2. E. Ecstatic. 4 pages. 1850.

*Berceuse. D flat. A florid and somewhat Chopinesque Arabesque. 10 pages. 1854.

The Art Lied.

Liszt's art songs are among the most beautiful of their kind. Entrancing melody is their foundation. This selection presents works in this *form* adorned with evanescent cadential embroidery.

"Ricordanza" ("Memories"). A flat. Etude Transcendental. 14 pages. 1831-54.

"Cantique d'Amour" ("Harmonies Poétiques"). E. Impressive climax. 8 pages. 1851.

Impromptu in F sharp. (Meditation—passion—resignation.) 4 pages. 1877.

Storms.

Here again Field, in his Fifth Concerto (1817), "L'incendie par Orage," which was heard all over Europe in its time, probably inspired Liszt. Liszt's fiery nature impelled him to say "Storms are my *métier*," and his series of storm pictures are unrivalled on the piano.

"Orage" ("The Storm"). C minor. Very dramatic. 9 pages. 1835.

*Ballade No. 2 ("Tragedy at Sea!"). B minor. 19 pages. 1854.

"Legend," No. 2, "St. Francis Walks the Waves." E. 11 pages. 1866.

Storm March (Hungarian). E minor. Very effective. 12 pages. 1876.

THE BRAVURA ELEMENT.

In his earlier bravura period Liszt, through his operatic Paraphrases, set out to astonish by the amazing brilliance of his execution. The early Valse di Bravura is in Chopin's style and merits comparison.

BRAVURA WORKS.

*Valse di Bravura. B. Closes *presto* in $\frac{2}{4}$ time. 12 pages. 1836.

"Waldesrauschen." D flat. A descriptive nature study. 8 pages. 1849-63.

*"Tarentella" (Italian Supplement). G minor. Introduces Italian folk song. 17 pages. 1861.

*"Les Jeux d'Eaux" ("Fountains"). B, F sharp. Sparkling. 13 pages. Posth.

BUSONI'S REPERTOIRE.*

The following is the repertoire of Busoni (d. 1924), the famous virtuoso editor of Bach and Liszt.

ORIGINAL WORKS.

"Etudes Transcendental," complete. Années I, II and III, complete. Paganini Etudes, complete. Hungarian Rhapsodies, Nos. 5, 6, 12, 13, 19 and 20. Hungarian March. "Melodies Hongroises," No. 1. Spanish Rhapsody. Two Concertos. Two Polonaises. Two Legends. Fant. and Fugue on B.A.C.H. Two Ballades. Sonata. "Totentanz." Variations on "Weinen." "Hexameron." "Apparition," No. 1. "Valse Mélancolique." "Venezia e Napoli." Two "Valses Oubliées." "Die Zelle in Nonnenwerth." Chromatic Galop. "Christmas Tree." Études: "Gnomenreigen" and "Waldesrauschen." "Mephisto Valse," No. 1. "Bénédiction de Dieu."

TRANSCRIPTIONS.

Operatic: "Norma," "Portici," "Sonnambula," "Lucrezia," "Lucia," "Figaro," "Don Juan," "Rigoletto," "Il Trovatore," "Roberto," "Tannhäuser" and Donizetti March, Bach's Fant. and Fugue in G minor; "Ruins of Athens," "Chants Polonais,"

---

* From Prof. Dent's "Biography of Busoni" (Oxford University Press, 1933).

Gounod Waltz, Mendelssohn's "Wedding March," Rossini's "Serenata," Schubert's "Wanderer" Fantasia, and four songs, Schubert's Hungarian March, two "Soirées de Vienné" and "Valse Caprice," Schumann's "Widmung."

Mr. Sacheverell suggests an *Orchestral Programme* of works for *first performance* in Great Britain, viz., the symphonic poems "Von der Wiege" and the "Triomphe Funèbre," the last "Mephisto Valses," the "Salve Polonia" Interlude and the "Malédiction" Concerto.

GREAT SAYINGS.

"Don't imitate anyone. Keep yourself true to yourself. Cultivate your individuality.—LISZT.

"Originality is in oneself, it is the true voice of the heart."

"You never heard Liszt?"

"Ah, it was the great Liszt who listened—listened to his inner voice. They said he was inspired—he was simply listening to himself."—DE PACHMANN.

"I consider Liszt the greatest man I ever met—a man with mental grasp, splendid disposition and glorious genius. Liszt's personality can only be expressed by one word—'Colossal.'"—REISENAUER.

"Every individual needs a different technical system."

"It is often perfection in little things which distinguishes the performance of the great pianist from that of the novice."—BUSONI.

"The greatest thing in the artist's life is—W-O-R-K."—J. FRANCIS COOKE.

THE LISZT PROGRAMME.

"The Queen's Hall was packed for the Liszt programme. Liszt," Sir Henry said, "was definitely returning to favour. I think people are beginning to realise what a very great work the 'Faust' Symphony is."—Interview with Sir Henry Wood, "Belfast News Letter," October 13, 1934.

FOR ALL TIME.

Cecil Austin, writing in "Musical Opinion," December, 1924:—"Liszt is still unrecognised as one of the greatest composers who ever lived."

"Liszt will be venerated, not for an age, but for all time."

"Let us judge Liszt by those works which bear the clear imprint of his genius."

Perfect in Execution.

Van Dieren in "Daily Telegraph," May 9, 1931 :—"Liszt wrote some wholly admirable works"—"as perfect in execution as those of any master." "If every composer were judged by 'his weakest productions instead of by the sublime passages of his best, how much of the world's greatest music will stand the test?' Liszt never was more pedestrian than Bach sometimes is."

"The originality of Liszt consists in his giving himself, at the piano, what others construct with pen and paper."—Wagner.

Envoy.

The author would point out that many hearers may fail to detect the trivialities of a really *great* master, or discern the great moments of a *little* one—and it is possible that the latter may, on occasion, be superior to the former.

Music, like literature, is many-sided, and a master may be great in *one* sphere only—as with Chopin; or in *many* aspects, as with Beethoven and Liszt; or even *universally* great—as was Mozart.

Let us then try to see Liszt's work in its proper perspective by

(1) Getting to really know Liszt in his many aspects.

(2) Estimating his works according to their *class* and the *motive* which inspired them. The simplest Nocturne may be as perfect in its way as the magnificent virtuoso "Don Giovanni" Fantasia.

(3) Put inspiration first—pedestrianism has no place.

Wagner visited London in 1877, and at a banquet given in his honour he declared: "It is now twenty-two years ago since I came to this country unacknowledged as a composer and attacked on all sides by a hostile press."*

Let us compare that with Van Dieren's statement in 1931:

"We are at present on the crest of a wave of Wagner adoration."

It is not too much to say that just as the musical world came at last to see the unparalleled greatness of Wagner in *his own sphere*—so will the many-sided genius of Liszt eventually receive the equally due recognition.

Some Noted Pupils of Liszt.

Amy Fay, Sofie Menter, Adele aus der Hohe, Vera Timanoff, D'Albert, Albeniz, Alkan, W. Bache, Borodin, Brassin, Bülow, R. Burmeister, Friedheim,

---

* Praeger's "Wagner as I Knew Him," 1885 (Longmans).

Joseffy, Klindworth, Lambert, Lamond, G. Liebling, Wm. Mason, McDowell, Raff, Reisenauer, Rosenthal, Saint-Saëns, X. Scharwenka, Sgambati, Sherwood, Siloti, Stavenhagen, Tausig, Weingartner, Zichy. (For a full list see Huneker, p. 353.) Francis Cooke's "Great Pianists on Piano Playing" (Presser).

CHAPTER XXXI.

Liszt's boyhood. His antics. Philharmonic concert. Visit to Ireland. The Thalberg rivalry. The Countess and the Princess. Grieg and Liszt. Liszt in Bayreuth. Game of whist. A musician's narrative. Liszt as diplomat. Without parallel. Lamond's testimony. A gentleman and a Christian.

MEMORABILIA.

I. LISZT'S BOYHOOD (1821-3).

Carl Czerny, in his memories, says:

"Busy and overloaded with work during the daytime and not wishing to accept anything for the lessons which I gave to this genial child, I devoted several hours to him every evening. Never have I had a pupil more industrious in work, more obedient, more talented."

Czerny gave him Clementi's "Gradus" and Sonatas—"the best schooling for the pianist," he says, "when he knows how to practise them."

II. LISZT'S "ANTICS."

Carl Reinecke recounts how that when a boy, Liszt visited Hamburg and gave a recital unassisted, except for the artists taking part in Hummel's Septet.

This recital was given at the Hotel "Alte Stadt, London." He says: "I well remember Liszt's tall, graceful figure." Liszt's execution and poetic feeling draw "the hearer to boundless admiration. But when the fancy took him to dazzle his admiring audience a little, he would let himself be led into all sorts of fantastical tricks, over which I had to shake even my boyish head."

"Many years passed away, and in 1848 Ernst and Reinecke were induced to go to Weimar to pay a visit to Liszt, during which Liszt played the Study in E (Op. 10) that Chopin had dedicated to him. Sadly he exclaimed: "I would give four years of my life to have written those four pages." Reinecke continues: "After I had heard Liszt play that study no other player could ever play it to my satisfaction. It was at such moments, *tête-à-tête*, that Liszt played most beautifully; often in the face of a great audience a demon seized him, and as I have already said, he descended to eccentricities."*

Liszt himself in writing on Berlioz said: "Eccentricity will always be a sublime and enviable fault in every musical genius," and elsewhere: "Genius is the agency by which the supernatural is revealed to man."

What would poor old Carl Reinecke, whom I met in Leipzig, and who represented the staid Leipzig traditions and the antipathy of the Mendelssohn-Brahms school, have said to the "antics" of another

---

* "Musical Record," June, 1896.

great pianist, Pachmann? After all, it was nothing more than desire for sociability; and Liszt was the first to introduce the *salon* element of mingling with his audience between the solos at his recitals.

It was about this time (1848) that Liszt retired from recital-giving to devote himself to composition and conducting.

III. Philharmonic Concert, London, May 11, 1840.

This concert, conducted by Henry Bishop, the song-composer, was the occasion of Liszt's fifth appearance in London, when he played Weber's "Concertstück." The enthusiasm was such that strangers out of the audience crowded round the piano and insisted on shaking hands with him.

One old gentleman pressed forward "and taking hold of Liszt's hand, pressed a bank note into it, exclaiming 'It was worth more.'"

Many years afterwards, a friend in Miss Ramann's presence said to Liszt, "How very wanting in tact; did you not refuse the money?" "By no means," he replied simply, "I thanked him cordially. I should have hurt the old gentleman's feelings if I had proudly refused his gift." (Hueffer, "Half a Century of Music.")

IV. A Visit to Ireland.

The above incident was during Liszt's fourth visit to London, where he arrived on May 6, 1840, and during the next year he crossed the channel on similar missions some four times.

On December 9, he sailed for Dublin, and gave concerts there in Cork and in Belfast.

In Belfast he appeared at the Music Hall (now a Mission Hall) opposite the Presbyterian Church in May Street.

The Belfast "News Letter" of January 8, 1841, in its preliminary "puff," says: "This pianist is equalled only by Thalberg in point of execution, and we feel confident that all who have the slightest taste for harmonic excellence will patronise the concert of this admirable and all but unrivalled performer." The report stated that "Monsieur Liszt played his arrangement of Overture to 'William Tell,' Finale to 'Lucia,' Chromatic Galop."

The vocalists were the inimitable buffo, John Parry, whose special feature was "Wanted a Governess," Miss Steel and Miss Bassano. Flautist, Mr. Richards.

The "Northern Whig," in its report of January 14, 1841, says: "Owing to the unfavourable state of the weather last night's concert was rather thinly attended. His brilliancy of execution, his vast power over the instrument—the viewless spirit of his lovely sounds surpassed anything we ever heard."

Apparently the aim was not to present a highbrow programme. Unfortunately the whole tour seems not to have been well managed, and shortly afterwards Liszt, in speaking to Sterndale Bennett

21

(on February 22, 1842), was bitter against England, i.e., from an artistic point of view. (Sterndale Bennett, Biography, p. 127.)

The following unfortunate incident related from Kohl's Journal of 1842 refers to this visit during a time of political agitation. (See News Letter, July 30, 1935.)

"I was told at Belfast that the great musician Liszt had the misfortune to be taken for O'Connell in the neighbourhood of that city, and was very near undergoing something extremely disagreeable that was intended for the agitator—they merely wished to duck him in a neighbouring pond, and then to advise him to return to his carriage and be off to the South of Ireland."

V. The Thalberg Rivalry.

"Liszt may gesticulate and knock the glasses over, but at least he has something to say."—Constant Lambert.

Thalberg may be said to have been the antithesis of Liszt in some aspects.

Of quiet, unobtrusive bearing and "not a little resembling the late Prince Consort"—Thalberg "never disturbed that impression by any excess of gesture." His "well-balanced *diminuendos* and crescendos—carried up to a sweeping *fortissimo*—

were achievements that no subsequent pianist can be said to have rivalled." (A. J. HIPKINS.)

As in Paris in 1835 when the critics were divided in their praise or censure of Thalberg and Liszt—Fétis, for instance, stating that Liszt's "passionate temperament" led him "into all sorts of exaggerations." So in London. In London the two did not meet, but the "Athenæum" "praised Liszt's genius up to the skies," while the "Musical World" opined that his "manner of beating his instrument (to pieces one every moment expected) placed Thalberg far before him."

It is reported that Liszt originally proposed that both artists should play a duet in public, as was then the fashion, but Thalberg retorted, "Je n'aime pas d'être accompagné" ("I do not like to be accompanied"), a sally which greatly amused the Parisians.

VI. THE COUNTESS AND THE PRINCESS.

Liszt was introduced to the *littérateure*, Countess D'Agoult ("Daniel Stern") through the medium of Berlioz. She has been described as "a beautiful woman with masses of fair hair," but in disposition as "six feet of snow on twenty of lava." She was half French, half Jew by descent. As his senior, and as a noted *littérateur*, she apparently imposed herself upon him, and afterwards—as the mother of Cosima—she became the mother-in-law of Wagner;

of a jealous disposition, she insisted on accompanying him in the tour of 1841, when, through mismanagement, coupled with her tactlessness, the tour came to a premature end (see Chapter VI). His daughter Cosima, who became the wife of Wagner in 1870, has been described as "the cleverest woman of the century, a judge and a critic," but not an artist.

On the other hand, the Polish Princess Wittgenstein, who in later times became his secretary, sacrificed her country, her social position and her property, to look after Liszt, his mother and his children. She was not musical, nor outwardly attractive, she was devoted to the Church, and wrote boldly and copiously on Church matters—only to incur the displeasure and Index Purgatorius of her Church, the Church which at first sanctioning her marriage to her hero, followed it up with an interdict at the last moment owing to political pressure (see Chapter XI). In each case Liszt was the victim. ("Liszt and the Princess," William Wallace.)

VII. Grieg and Liszt.

Liszt's generosity and ever-readiness to help his brother artists is typified in his relations with Grieg. Unprompted, Liszt, after perusing Grieg's violin Sonata, Op. 8, wrote to him, on December 27, 1868, from Rome, encouraging him to follow natural inclinations, and inviting him to visit him at Weimar.

This unsolicited letter induced the Norwegian Government to make a financial grant, whereby Grieg, a young man of twenty-five, was enabled to visit Liszt at Rome. Arrived with the MS. of another violin sonata, says Grieg, "what does Liszt do? He plays the whole thing, root and branch, violin and piano, nay, more, for he played fuller, more broadly. The violin got its due right in the middle of the piano part. He was literally over the whole piano at once, without missing a note, and how he did play." Later on Grieg met Liszt in Leipzig, when the virtuoso played Grieg's piano concerto—cadenza and all, from the MS. at sight. Grieg writes: "Not content with playing, he at the same time converses and makes comments, addressing a bright remark now to me, now to another of the assembled guests, nodding significantly to the right or left, particularly when something pleases him" ("Life of Grieg"—Finck.)

VIII. Liszt in Bayreuth.

Sir Robert Stewart, writing from Dublin on September 29, 1884, says:

"I saw Franz (Liszt), the adorable Abbé, and had a long talk with him in Bayreuth. Next week they telegraphed a report from Brussels, that he was suddenly struck with blindness, and that one of the Grand Dukes had endowed him with £300 (English) per annum. As *I* had seen him walking about the Siegfried-strasse in the sunlight, and deciphering a German newspaper, and doing it without spectacles, and as I knew Grand Dukes in Germany are so very *serene*, and so very plodding, that months would, in all probability, elapse ere a pension of money like that would be arranged; as all this occurred to me, I wrote to the London 'Times' discrediting the report, and giving my reasons for doing so. All musical Europe had received the first sad intelligence with dismay, for dear old Franz is beloved like *notre père à tous*. Well, the next day after my letter it turned out that the blind story was all nonsense—Dieu merci—and I have got no end of credit for publicly denying it, I had told Liszt that I had stood beside him when a boy (in 1841) and saw him tearing the thumb out of his glove (!) and heard him execute one of his *then* wonderful piano transcriptions, Rossini's Overture to 'William Tell.' How well I remember his fair hair, which he was wont to toss back, out of his eyes, like a mane." ("Life of Sir Robt. Stewart.")

IX. A Game of Whist.

In 1859, Arthur Sullivan (1842-1900)* when a student at Leipzig, describes in a letter his meeting with Liszt. He says: "In the evening, when nearly everyone was gone, Liszt, David, Bronsart and I had a quiet game of whist together, and I walked home

* Wyndham's "Sullivan" (Kegan Paul, 1926).

with him in the evening." . . . "Liszt is a very amiable man, despite his eccentricities, which are many! What a wonderful player he is! Such power, such delicacy and lightness!"

X. "A Musician's Narrative."

In this, Sir Alexander Mackenzie's autobiography, he describes how Liszt came in 1861 to Sondershausen to hear his "Mazeppa." He was still slim, upright and tall, with thin lips, ascetic, colourless face, and thick mane (already quite grey). "Quite unlike the genial, kind-hearted old man I was privileged to know so well in after time, he looked grim, stern and melancholy. Not long afterwards he left for Rome, only to be disappointed in his marriage project, and thus it was in the most troubled period of a phenomenally brilliant life that I saw him first in '61. Liszt aged rapidly.

"Twenty years later when meeting Liszt in Italy, time had changed the slim, erect figure to that of a bent, round-shouldered, stoutish old man." The final occasion was on Liszt's visit to London in 1886—"an exciting fortnight such as musical London has rarely witnessed"; when "the visit provided the last happy weeks and the final blaze of triumph in a uniquely successful life." "Death came barely three months after he had left us with the words, 'I am coming here next year.'"

Liszt retired at the height of his fame as a virtuoso at the age of thirty-eight ("in '47 he appeared on the platform for the last time for money) to devote himself solely to his art and the service of others."

XI. Liszt as a Diplomat.

Liszt, on one occasion, when asked what profession he would have chosen, apart from that of music.

His reply was characteristic of the man. "*I would have been the first diplomat in Europe*," Sir Charles Stanford relates in his "Pages from an Unwritten Diary" (p. 150).

Liszt was announced to give two recitals in a small German town. "At the first concert there was only a handful of people present."

Liszt thereupon pointed out that the room was large and cold, "and if they would do him the pleasure to come round to his hotel in half an hour," he would arrange for their reception and play them his programme. "They came, and he provided them also with a champagne supper—at the next concert crowds were turned away at the doors, but there was no champagne."

XII. Without Parallel.

We remember that Liszt "at the height of his renown" abandoned his virtuosic career "in order to devote himself to what he considered to be the best interests of his art. The unselfishness and the true humility of his life for the rest of his days are *without parallel*."—Sacheverell Sittwell, p. 330.

The closing scenes in Liszt's life are described in Chapter XXVI. It only remains to add the following testimony.

XIII.

The veteran virtuoso, Lamond (see Chapter X) has said:—

'Both as man and artist he has been for me a shining example. To-day, when I look back over a long life, I thank my Creator that I had the privilege of knowing that great artist, that wonderful and unique personality, Franz Liszt, and that it has been granted to me, through my life, to follow out his teachings.

"May the fiery spirit of Franz Liszt continue to live for all time for the good and glory of art!" ("Daily Telegraph," September 15, 1934.)

XIV. Liszt (1811-86). A Gentleman and a Christian.

An Englishman, Burnand (related to Burnand of "Punch" fame), who when young was a pupil of Liszt, and afterwards wrote under the name of Strelezki,* avers:

* "Personal Recollections of Chats with Liszt." Anonymous, but assigned to "*Strelezki*" (— Burnand), (Donajowski).

"I truly believe that there never was a human being more revered and loved by those who knew him than Franz Liszt was. He had faults, but who has not?"

"*A perfect gentleman* and a *kind-hearted Christian.*"

Requiescat in pace.

SELECT BIBLIOGRAPHY. BIOGRAPHIES IN ENGLISH.

RAMANN, L. "Franz Liszt, Artist and Man." 2 vols. (Allen), 1882. This is a diffuse translation of Vol. I only of the German work.

In German.

RAMANN, L. "Franz Liszt als Künstler und Mensch." Vol. I, 1811-40; Vol. II, 1840-47; Vol. III, 1848-66 (Breitkopf).

KAPP, JULIUS. "Franz Liszt," 300 pp., 20th edition, 1924; new edition, 1931. Fairly full biography. List of principal works only.

REUSS. "Franz Liszt" (Reissner, Dresden), 1898.

GÖLLERICH. "Franz Liszt (Recollections)," 1908 (Berlin, Marquardt). Biography (250 pp.), with useful catalogue of works of 50 pp.

RAABE. "Franz Liszt," 2 vols. (Cotta Ed., 1931). Biography and Catalogue. ("The first biography in which modern scientific methods are employed," Calvocoressi.)

HERVEY, A. "Franz Liszt" (170 pp.), 1911 (Lane). A short biography with description of the symphonic works. No index.

CHANTAVOINE. "Liszt" (Librarie Alcan, Paris), 1913. An able sketch of the life and work of Liszt.

CORDER. "Franz Liszt" (170 pp.), 1925 (Kegan Paul). With catalogue of works. No publishers given.

HUNEKER, JAMES. "Franz Liszt" (456 pp.), 1911 (Chapman and Hall). Chapters of 20 and 28 pages on the piano works. No catalogue of works. Chief sections, "Liszt's Pupils and Lisztiana," "Liszt Mirrored by his Contemporaries."

MACKENZIE, SIR ALEX. "Liszt," 1913 (Murdoch). Sympathetic and helpful sketch by one who knew him.

NOHL. "Life of Liszt." Sympathetic sketch, trans. 1884 (Chicago).

DE BEAUFORT. "The Abbé Liszt" (309 pp.), 1886 (Ward and Downey). A readable biographical sketch.

JANKA WOHL. "François Liszt" (246 pp.), (Ward and Downey), 1887. Personal recollections of a compatriot.

SILOTI. "My Memories of Liszt." Trans. from the Russian.

("STRELEZKI.") "Personal Recollections of Liszt" (Donajowski), 1898 (23 pp.). Interesting chats with Liszt (1869-86).

DE POURTALES. "Franz Liszt, the Man of Love." Trans. from the French, "La vie de Liszt" (Thornton Butterworth), 1927. With a new title. Sympathetic and poetic biography (291 pp.).

SITWELL, SACHEVERELL. "Liszt" (418 pp.), 1934 (Faber and Faber, 15s.). Excellent full-length biography. Fairly full catalogue of works, but no publishers given.

POHL. "Franz Liszt," Leipzig, 1883. Studies and recollections.

In French.

SAINT-SAËNS. "Souvenirs et Portraits" (Paris, 1900).

CALVOCORESSI. "Franz Liszt" (120 pp.), (Laurens, Paris), 1926. Able critical sketch. Short bibliography.

BORY, R. "Une retraite Romantique en Suisse" (Geneva, 1923).

BOUTAREL. "L'œuvre symphonique de F. Liszt" (Paris, 1886).

"LA REVUE MUSICALE." Liszt Number, May, 1928.

REFERENCES.

GROVE'S Dictionary, Vol. VI.

DANNREUTHER. "Oxford History of Music" (Romantic Period).

HABETS. "Borodin and Liszt" (Digby and Long"), trans. 1895.

HAWEIS, REV. H. R. "My Musical Life," 1888 (609-72 pp.).

MACKENZIE, SIR ALEX. "A Musician's Narrative" (Cassell), 1927, Chap. XIV.

GLASENAPP. "Life of Wagner," trans. Ellis. Work at Weimar.

WAGNER. "Prose Works," trans. Ellis. Vol. III has Wagner's Essay on Liszt's Symphonic Poems.

WAGNER. "My Life," 2 vols., 1911 (Constable). Relations with Liszt.

SHEDLOCK. "The Wagner-Liszt Correspondence," Mus. Assoc. Lecture, 1887-8.

MASON, WM. "Memories of a Musical Life," 1901.

FAY, AMY. "Music Study in Germany" (Macmillan), 1885.

MAY, FL. "The Girlhood of Clara Wieck," 1912 (Arnold), Chap. XV.

WALKER, BETTINA. "My Musical Experiences," 1890 (Bentley), Chap. IV.

KUHE. "Musical Recollections," 1896 (Bentley).

MACARTHUR. "Anton Rubinstein," 1889.

HUEFFER. "Half a Century of Music in England" (Chapman and Hall).

KELLY-UPTON. "Remenyi, Musician and Man," 1906 (McClough, Chicago), Chap. VIII, Liszt and Brahms.

GILMAN. "Edward Macdowell" (Lane).

KARASOWSKI. "Life of Chopin" (trans.), 2 vols. (Reeves).

GREGOROVIUS. "Roman Journal," trans., 1911.

ANTCLIFFE, HERBERT. "Art, Religion and Clothes," 1926 (The Hague). "The real Liszt."

JOHNSTONE, ARTHUR. "Musical Criticisms," 1905 (Manchester, University Press).

FINCK "Success in Music," 1910 (Murray), Chap. XVI.

FINCK. "Songs and Song Writers" (Murray). Songs of Liszt.

KOBBÉ. "How to Appreciate Music" (Sisley), 1907, Chap. VII.

BERINGER. "Fifty Years' Experience," 1907 (Bosworth).

WEINGARTNER. "Post-Beethoven Symphonists" (Reeves). The symphonic works of Liszt.

WEITZMANN. "Hist. of Pf. Playing," 1880 (1897 trans.).

WESTERBY, HERBERT. "Hist. of Pf. Music," 1924 (Kegan Paul). Pt. III, Chap. XV; Pt. IV, Chap. III.

BIE, OSCAR. "Hist. of the Pf.," 1899, trans. (Dent), Chap. IX.

DICKINSON. "Growth and Development of Music," 1921 (Reeves), Chap. XXXV.

HULL, DR. EAGLEFIELD. "Music, Classical, Romantic, Modern" (Dent), Chap. IX.

LISZT. "Collected Writings" (in German), 1880-1883 (Leipzig). Also in 4 vols., 1910.

"Correspondence." See Pt. II, Chap. XXVI.

SEIGNITZ. "Franz Liszt's Kirchen Musik" (Beyer).

ARTICLES ON LISZT IN PERIODICALS.

FROM THE PERIODICAL INDEX OF 1888.

"The Academy," No. 24, page 136, J. S. Shedlock.

"The Academy," No. 30, page 95, J. S. Shedlock.

"The Nation," No. 37, page 295, Finck.

"Temple Bar," No. 78, page 55 (Reminiscences).

"Century," No. 10, page 655, "A Summer with Liszt," by A. M. Bagby.

"Scribner," No. 10, page 700, "Liszt and Bülow."

"Galaxy," No. 18, page 389, "Liszt and the Music of the Future."

INDEX OF 1892-6.

"Century," No. 23, page 517, "Liszt," by Saint-Saëns.

"Quarterly," No. 167, 65 pages, "Liszt-Wagner Correspondence."

"Nation," No. 56, page 308, "Liszt and Paderewski."

"All the Year," No. 63, page 113, "Reminiscences of Liszt."

"Music," No. 3, page 304, "Dante Symphony."

INDEX OF 1897-1902.

"Music" (Chicago), No. 12, page 383, "Liszt as Conductor."

INDEX OF 1902-7.

"Music" (Chicago), No. 21, page 213, "Personality of," W. S. B. Matthews.

"Music" (Chicago), No. 22, page 53, "Programme Pieces."

INDEX OF:

1916. "Musical News," Oct. 14 and 21, "Paganini of the Piano," Finck.

1920. "Musical Standard," Sept. 11, "Liszt's Significance," D. C. Parker.

1920. "Chesterian" (Feb.), "The Glory of Liszt," Aubry.

1919, Dec. "Chesterian," "An Unpublished Letter of Liszt."

1922. "Oxford Hungarian Revue" (Nov.), "Liszt the Magyar."

1926. "Chesterian" (April-May), "The Blind Singer."

1927. "British Musician" (pp. 112, 194), "Gipsy in Music," E. M. Grew.

"MUSICAL OPINION."

1922. Jan., "The Années de Pélerinage," Eric Blom.

1924. Dec., "Franz Liszt," by Cecil Austin.

1927. Sept., "Liszt's French Son-in-law," A. de Ternan.

1927. Dec., "Liszt and Berlioz," Francesco Berger.

1930. Aug., "Franz Liszt," Percy Godfrey.

1933. Dec., "The New David Club Discusses Liszt," Gerald Abraham.

Articles in "The Musical Quarterly," New York.

1917. July, "Liszt as Lieder Composer," Edwin Hughes.

1918. Jan., "Liszt's 'Huldigungs March,'" O. G. Sonneck.

1920. July, "Baron de Tremont's Souvenirs of Beethoven and Contemporaries," Prodhomme.

1921. Oct., "Two Liszt Letters to Mosonyi," Béla Bartók.

1923. Oct., "Seroff's Relation to Wagner and Liszt," Reisemann.

From "The Etude," Philadelphia, U.S.A.

Selected Articles on Franz Liszt.

"Bülow as Liszt's Pupil" (Finck), March, 1896, p. 58.

"Liszt and Tausig" (Finck), Dec., 1896, p. 369.

"Reminiscences" (Rohlfs), April, 1900, p. 131.

"As Composer and Artist" (Law), Nov., 1907, p. 710.

"Influence in Music" (Editorial), Sept., 1907, p. 609.

"Liszt versus Chopin" (Editorial), April, 1907, p. 229.

"As Pianoforte Writer" (Niecks), Oct., 1905, p. 400.

"Rhapsody," Biography (Davidson), April, 1908, p. 222.

"Study with Liszt" (Sherwood), May, 1908, p. 285.

"Personality" (Beranger), June, 1908, p. 362.

"Childhood and Youth," Sept., 1908, p. 598.

"Recollections" (Olbersleben), June, 1909, p. 371.

"Piano Transcriptions," Jan., 1910, p. 21.

"On Contemporaries" (Niecks), Jan., 1910, p. 24.

"Teaching Pieces" (Perry), April, 1910, p. 227.

"The Symphonic Poems" (Saint-Saëns), Sept., 1910, p. 577.

"Lessons with Liszt" (Sauer), Nov., 1910, p. 721.

"Liszt Centenary" (Breithaupt), Sept., 1911, p. 587.

"As I Knew Him" (Rosenthal), Dec., 1911, p. 817.

"A Russian View" (Borodin), July, 1913, p. 477.

"Memories of Liszt" (Zichy), Oct., 1913, p. 771.

"Schubert-Liszt's 'Hark, the Lark'" (Stojowsky), Feb., 1914, p. 106.

"Original Compositions" (Kroeger), March, 1914, p. 176.

"How Liszt Arranged Meeting of Chopin and Sand," Feb., 1915, p. 135.

"Last Word in Pianoforte Playing" (Lachmund), Nov., 1915, p. 785.

"Liszt's Piano Arrangements" (Hughes), March, 1916, p. 172.

"As the Paganini of the Piano" (Finck), Aug., 1916, p. 553.

"Liszt and Paganini Compared" (Finck), Sept., 1916, p. 635.

"Tribute to Hungarian Gypsy's Art," Jan., 1917, p. 20.

"High Lights in Life of Liszt" (Pierce), Jan., 1918, p. 23.

"Secret of Success" (Pirani), July, 1919, p. 417.

"Memoirs of Liszt and Rubinstein," July, 1920. p. 447.

"Memoirs of Liszt and Rubinstein," Aug., 1920. p. 523.

"A Personal Recollection of Liszt" (Johns), April, 1926, p. 265.

"How the Young Liszt Taught" (Reed), March, 1929, p. 179.

"The Majesty of Liszt" (Editorial), Oct., 1930, p. 687.

"The Liszt Rhapsodies" (Frampton), Oct., 1930, p. 701.

"A Visit to Ed. Schütt" (Francis Cooke), Nov., 1931, p. 769.

"Is Culture Progressing in Musical Art?" (Rosenthal), Nov., 1931, p. 777.

"From Liszt to Einstein" (Friedheim), Jan., 1932, p. 19.

"A Lesson from Liszt in 1832" (I. Philipp, Sept., 1932, p. 614.

"When Liszt Renounced the World" (Pirani), Aug., 1934, p. 451.

"Liszt as Lieder Composer" (Edwin Hughes), July, 1917. "The Musical Quarterly," New York.

ARTICLES IN ENGLISH MUSICAL JOURNALS.

"MONTHLY MUSICAL RECORD."

Jan., March, 1872. "Incidents of Liszt's Youth," communicated by C. F. Pohl.

July, 1873. "Liszt's 'Tasso.'"

Oct., 1875. "Liszt in Leipzig."

Mar., 1880. "Liszt Concert in Rome."

Oct., 1881. "Franz Liszt, Artist and Man," by Ramann.

March, 1882. "Liszt's Graner Mass," by J. S. Shedlock.

April, 1886. "Franz Liszt."

May, 1886. "Dr. Liszt in London."

Sept., 1886. "Death of Liszt at Bayreuth."

Sept., 1891. "Consolations," by F. Niecks.

June, 1894. "Letters of F. Liszt."

June, 1896. "Recollections of Liszt," by Carl Reinecke.

April, 1897. "Liszt on Music and Musicians."

April, 1902. "Liszt in Russia," Mrs. Newmarch.

June, 1902. "Liszt in England," Constance Bache.

Nov., 1905. "Franz Liszt," Herbert Antcliffe.

April, 1908. "News from Liszt" (reprinted from the "Musical World," August 6, 1853).

Jan., 1909. "Liszt and Brahms," Herbert Antcliffe.

Oct., 1909. "Liszt and his Biographers," Niecks.

Oct., 1911. "Franz Liszt—the Centenary of his Birth."

July, 1916. I, "Literature, Franz Liszt," by Prof. Niecks.

Aug. and Sept., 1916. II, "The Man."

Oct., 1916. III, "The Pianist."

Nov. and Dec., 1916. IV and IVa, "The Composer."

March, April and May, 1926. "New Documents on Liszt," Dr. Friedrich Schnapp.

Sept., 1927. "Liszt, 'Years of Pilgrimage,'" A. E. Hull.

Jan., 1929. "Hugo Wolff on the Death of Liszt."

April, 1930. "Retrospects " (Franz Liszt), Francesco Berger.

May, 1930. "Cosima Wagner," Rose K. Farebrother.

Oct., 1932. "New Lights on Liszt" (Raabe Biography, by Calvocoressi.

May, 1933. "Liszt and his Countess," Fr. Schnapp.

March, 1934. "Liszt's Influence on the Russian Nationalists," Gerald Abraham.

ARTICLES ON LISZT.

"MUSICAL TIMES."

Obituary Article, Sept., 1886.

"Franz Liszt," by Ernest Newman, Oct., Nov., Dec., 1911.

"Liszt and the Organ," by Harvey Grace, August, 1917.

"Liszt and the Pianist," by Camille Saint-Saëns, Sept., 1921.

"Reflections on Liszt," by Erik Brewerton, Jan., 1926.

"A Study by Franz Liszt," by Alex. Brent-Smith, May, June, 1929.

"Reminiscences of Felix Weingartner," March and July, 1933.

"Musical Opinion."

"The New David Club Discusses Liszt," by Gerald Abraham, Dec., 1933.

WRITINGS BY LISZT—IN ENGLISH.

"The Gipsy in Music" (trans. by E. Evans), 2 vols. (15s.), (Reeves).

"Life of Chopin" (trans. by Broadhouse), (Reeves).

See also Part II, Chap. XXVI.

THE NATIONAL LISZT MUSEUM AT BUDAPEST.

This is housed in the Palace of the Liszt Conservatory of Music, which was founded in 1875. It contains a collection of relics connected with the life of Liszt, including portraits, busts, costumes, and the sword of honour which was bestowed on him in 1840 with this dedication:

"To the great artist, Ferencz Liszt, in appreciation of his artistic merits and fervent patriotism. Dedicated by his compatriots who honour him." The Salle Liszt contains a collection of laurel, silver and gold wreaths, a gold conductor's baton given by the Princess Wittgenstein, a desk in silver, adorned with a medallion of the master, and small silver busts of Beethoven, Schubert and Chopin. Various instruments used by Liszt and manuscripts add to the interest. Dr. J. Francis Cooke, writing in "The Etude" (Oct., 1930), says: "The school is located in one of the very finest buildings of its kind in the world. In fact, it is a veritable palace. The library contains one hundred thousand works, including most of the books and instruments owned by Franz Liszt. In the Museum are pianos which belonged to Beethoven."

GRAMOPHONE RECORDS.

The following Liszt records are available: Concertos in E flat and A, "Pathetic" Concerto (two pianos), "Les Preludes," Spanish Rhapsody, Hungarian Fantasia, Sonata, Hungarian Rhapsodies, Nos. 1-4, 6, 8-12, and 14, Fantasia and Fugue on B.A.C.H. (organ), "Funerailles," "Storm" March, Paganini-Etude, "Campanella," Study in D flat, "Au bord d'un Source," "Gnomes' Dance," "Feux Follets," "Waldesrauschen," "La Leggierezza," "Consolation," No. 3, "Liebesträume," Nos. 2 and

3, "Mephisto Valse," No. 3, Polonaise in E, "Petrarca," Sonnet in E, "Valse Impromptu," "Valse Oubliée," "Spinning Chorus," "Flying Dutchman," and "Liebestod" (Wagner-Liszt), "Hark, Hark, the Lark," and "The Erl King" (Schubert-Liszt), "Cujus Animam" (Rossini-Liszt), "Weinen und Klagen," the "Lorlei," Tarentella and Venice and Naples Tarentelle.

COMMEMORATION OF THE 50TH ANNIVERSARY OF LISZT'S DEATH.

This was celebrated by a series of broadcast performances of Liszt's works at the B.B.C., in London, commencing on Monday, December 30. Bernard van Dieren in an article on "The Originality of Liszt," says that Liszt "catches the ear of the untutored as often as he holds the attention of the sophisticated," and that with regard to his Transcriptions and Paraphrases "Beethoven wrote numerous variations on operatic airs, and those of Liszt are only more coherent and more brilliant." Liszt "generously supplied the prestige of his name to the Romantic movement in music, which to the world in general signified revolution against the classical idiom and against all accepted faith." On the other hand "he refrained from public defence of his productions, although in word and deed he was always ready to champion the activities of his contemporaries."—"Radio Times," December 27, 1935.

B.B.C. LISZT COMMEMORATION RECITALS.

Under the Direction of Bernard van Dieren. Dec. 30, 1935.

Nos. 1, 2, 3, The 12 Trancendental Etudes, Egon Petri. No. 4, Three Paganini Etudes, Nos. 1, 2 and 4 and Gounod "Faust" Waltz Fantasia, Egon Petri. No. 5, Donizetti "Lucia and Parisina" Fantasia and Mendelssohn "Wedding March" Fantasia, Egon Petri. No. 6, "Cantique d'Amour and "Mephisto Waltz No. 2," Frank Mannheimer. No. 7, "Consolations," 1 to 6 and Rhapsody No. 12, Frank Mannheimer. No. 8, Two Ballades, Frank Mannheimer. No. 9, La Lugubre Gondola" and Two Legends, Frank Mannheimer. No. 10, Schubert's Transcription "Praise of Tears," "Wandering," "Dance in the Village Inn."

INDEX OF LISZT'S PRINCIPAL WORKS.

Of the numerous transcriptions of songs in collections representative numbers are given. Full lists of these, together with details of Liszt's oratorios, melodramas, chorales, masses, choruses with orchestra, etc., Psalms, songs with piano and orchestra, and 4 hand piano arrangements and works for violin, 'cello, etc., can be found in the 53 page catalogue in Göllerich's work. A smaller catalogue is to be found in Corder's Liszt—but without publishers' names.

For CHORAL AND ORGAN works see Part II, Chapter 25 in this work; ORCHESTRAL works in Chapters 23, 24 and 29. A few (*given in italics*) are also included in this Index. For any Album piece not mentioned here refer to the Collective Title.